Pride of Place

Pride of Place

The Role of the Bishops in the Development of Catechesis in the United States

by
Mary Charles Bryce, OSB

The Catholic University of America Press
Washington, D.C.

Library of Congress Cataloging in Publication Data

Bryce, Mary Charles.
 Pride of place.

 Bibliography: p.
 Includes index.
 1. Catholic Church — Education — United States —
History. 2. Catholic Church — United States — Bishops —
History. 3. Christian education — United States —
History. 4. Catechetics — Catholic Church — History.
5. United States — Church history. I. Title.
BX932.B79 1984 207 84-17065
ISBN 0-8132-0595-6

This book is dedicated to the faculty and students of the Department of Religion and Religious Education, The Catholic University of America, Washington, D.C. Individually and corporately they served as both an inspiration and a challenge to the writer during her tenure at Catholic University from 1964 to 1982. It is with loving appreciation that she dedicates this work to them.

Contents

Preface

A book like *Pride of Place* comes only after years of study, research, and prayer. Thanks to its gifted author, Sister Mary Charles Bryce, the Church in the United States now has a history of the role of U.S. bishops in the development of catechesis. This book is the first of its kind and the only one of its kind, and it is a superb and magnificent "first and only." Without reading it, one simply cannot consider oneself a true student of catechesis. At once thorough and concise, *Pride of Place* is a well-documented and informative history of catechesis providing a lucid and provocative revelation of the struggle of the Church in the United States to pass on to generations the fullness of our faith. Sister Mary Charles has so much to say to us about what we do not know or have lost the memory of. Moreover, she writes with such an inviting and graceful style that the reader eagerly reaches for more of what she has to offer.

Beyond this general strength of the volume, however, it must be noted that the author accomplishes two specific tasks. First, she not only contributes a factual history of U.S. bishops and catechetics (a notable feat in itself), but she also narrates the development of ideas about the meaning and purpose of catechesis and places the evolution of these ideas within the life of each bishop and the times in which he lived. Second, she forcefully documents the priority that the U.S. bishops have given to catechesis from the beginnings of the U.S. Church down to the present day and chronicles their efforts to remain true to the Church's basic teachings while facing the reality of the cultural diversity and religious pluralism within the country.

In addressing catechetical experts at the Fifth Session of the International Council for Catechesis (April 1983), Pope John Paul II said: "On you, in fact, depends in great measure the efficacy of the Christian message, which is destined to bear fruit in the daily life of the baptized." In this significant contribution to catechetical ministry in the United States, Sister Mary Charles Bryce has done her share in promoting the

"efficacy of the Christian message." Anyone who ventures into the world
of catechetics as we move toward the Third Millennium will need to consult this work. Like catechesis in the life of the Church, this volume
deserves "pride of place" in every catechist's library.

The Most Reverend James P. Lyke, O.F.M., Ph.D.
Titular Bishop of Fornos Maggiore
Auxiliary to the Bishop of Cleveland

August 21, 1983
St. Pius X

Acknowledgments

A study such as this, though the work of a single author, could not come into existence without the cooperation and assistance of others. The writer acknowledges the initial and perduring inspiration and direction that Gerard S. Sloyan gave her during graduate studies. She acknowledges also the support and encouragement of Dr. Carl J. Peter, the Dean of the School of Religious Studies, The Catholic University of America, of Dr. Berard L. Marthaler, then chairman of the Religion and Religious Education Department of that university, and of Kathleen and Edgar Merkle. In addition she benefited from the faithful and tireless commitment of Kathy McMahon, Agnes Hetherington, Laura Way, and Carole Smoley as they typed the intermediate and final drafts. Not only acknowledgments but a debt of gratitude is owed to all nine.

In a distinctive way two other groups merit special commendations. First are the women who have stood in the background but whose loving and communal support have made this book possible, the Sisters of Benedict, Red Plains Priory, Oklahoma City, who form the community of which the writer is a member. Second are the bishops of the United States, who continue to encourage the serious inquiry and research that Catholic University fosters and yields. The bishops deserve credit and acknowledgment for making possible this and other studies sponsored and published by the University.

Abbreviations

AAB   Archives, Archdiocese of Baltimore

AAS   *Acta Apostolicae Sedis*

ACHS   Archives, American Catholic Historical Society, Philadelphia, St. Charles Seminary, Overbrook

ADC   Archives, Diocese of Charleston

APF   Archives, Propaganda Fide, Vatican

ASMS   Archives, St. Mary's Seminary, Baltimore

ASS   *Acta sanctae Sedis*

CT   *Catechesi Tradendae* (Pope John Paul II)

GCD   *General Catechetical Directory*

Mansi   J. D. Mansi, ed., *Sacrorum Conciliorum Nova et Amplissima Collectio*

NCE   *New Catholic Encyclopedia*

SLF   *Sharing the Light of Faith*

UND MC   University of Notre Dame—Microfilm

Introduction

The U.S. Church Viewed through Different Lenses

During the Second Vatican Council, in their decree on the bishops' pastoral office, the conciliar fathers addressed themselves, as it were, to the matter of catechesis. The exhorted each other and their successors "to present Christian doctrine in a manner adapted to the needs of the times . . . to use the various means at hand for making Christian doctrine known; namely, . . . preaching and catechetical instruction which always hold pride of place."[1]

It is that phrase, "pride of place," from the council document *Christus Dominus* that provides the title for this book. It is clear that the prelates in the council called for upholding a long-standing episcopal tradition of catechizing and fostering good catechesis. It appears, too, that the council participants were affirming the advances made in catechetical theory and practice during the previous several decades.

Pope John Paul II echoed the spirit of Vatican II when, in his apostolic exhortation *Catechesi Tradendae* (1979), he emphasized and sanctioned the important role of catechesis: "The Church has always considered catechesis one of her primary tasks. . . . The more the Church, whether on the local or universal level, gives catechesis priority over other works and undertakings the result of which would be more spectacular, the more she finds in catechesis a strengthening of her internal life as a community of believers and of her external activity as a missionary Church" (1, 15).[2] Furthermore, the pope pointed out a legacy and tradition inherited from earliest times when he stressed the "striking

I

fact" that "some of the most impressive bishops and pastors, especially in the third and fourth centuries, considered it an important part of their episcopal ministry to delivery catechetical instructions and write treatises" (12).

Does history sustain and support that heritage? From the present perspective even a superficial glance at past centuries seems to validate the tradition as one acknowledges the works of nineteenth-century Félix A. P. Dupanloup, bishop of Orleans, eighteenth-century Richard Challoner of London, George Hay of Edinburgh, and James Butler of Cashel;[3] eighth-century missionary bishops Boniface of Mainz and Pirmin of Reichenau;[4] and such giants of the Church as fourth-century Gregory of Nyssa, Cyril of Jerusalem, Ambrose of Milan, Augustine of Hippo, John Chrysostom of Constantinople, Theodore of Mopsuestia, and second-century Ignatius of Antioch.[5] The Church in each nation and in each era carries its own particularizing characteristics which assist one in identifying the uniqueness of ecclesial communities in different places.

The question arises: is that tradition verified and discernible in the U.S. Church? The present study endeavors to respond to that inquiry. It offers an examination of the catechizing activities of certain U.S. bishops, especially those who, according to the demands of their eras, actually catechized, wrote manuals, or commissioned the writing of manuals with the hope of better forming and informing the faithful whom they served. According to George Delcuve, "studying the catechisms of an epoch or a country means studying the catechesis, of which they are both its product and its makers. A catechism, especially if widely used, is a mirror — more or less faithful no doubt — of the catechesis prevalent at that time. It is also a privileged witness . . . [to] religious history itself."[6]

To understand who we are as the U.S. Church requires that we look not only at the multiple ethnic and national groups along with the potpourri of their cultural practices, origins, and customs, but also at the catechesis they experienced and the catechisms they used. This is an area of ecclesiastical history and an apostolate which few historians or episcopal biographers have explored. The majority of histories of the Church and biographies of its leaders relate to the public life of the institution and its interfacing with the issues, conflicts, and attitudes of the respective eras under scrutiny.

Looking through the diaries, correspondence, and archives of the bishops, one discovers an unexplored dimension of church history, one, as it were, from the internal forum. This dimension was the concern of many U.S. bishops for the catechesial formation of the faithful entrusted to them. For some prelates it became a major element in their episcopates.

They responded to the recognized need by writing catechisms and by catechizing in person. During the nineteenth and early twentieth centuries at least eighteen bishops wrote or commissioned the writing of catechisms or religion manuals for their dioceses. Some also began diocesan newspapers that included sections on basic doctrinal and moral questions through which the faithful could inform themselves on specific matters. These U.S. bishops were, in fact, carrying on a tradition that spanned many centuries.

In this context one might logically call into question the relationship of Catholic schools in this country to the ministry of catechizing. Certainly the parochial and private schools carried and continued to carry a large responsibility in this field. Two points must be made here: first, careful and thorough histories of Catholic schools are available. That of Harold A. Buetow, *Of Singular Benefit*,[7] is an excellent study of formal education in the elementary and secondary schools under Catholic auspices. There are a number of others which treat the ideals and history of Catholic education in the United States.[8] The role of catechesis and Christian formation is considered the bedrock of these institutions, but no in-depth study concentrates on catechesis in a particular way—an understandable fact given the whole prospectus of such histories.

The second point is that catechesis as such is not confined to the structured setting of a formal classroom program, though it has a central and significant role to play there. Of its nature catechesis is an ecclesial ministry which may, and indeed does, take place in classrooms; but its setting is also the marketplace, the home, the playground, the business office, the restaurant, the sanctuary, along with places of formal inquiry and learning. In short, catechesis takes place wherever people are. Jesus taught and answered questions at the lakeside, on the mountaintop, in the plains, on the roadside, at marriage celebrations, at the dinner table—as well as in more formal, organized settings, for example, in the temple (Mark 12:27–33; Luke 2:45–47). Catechesis is a people word, a people ministry, and occurs by design or by chance where people are. The present work may be classified as a "new" look at the history of the Church in this country—a study made from a particular perspective, a view through different lenses.

"Catechesis" Reexamined

"Catechesis." What is the sense of this awkward, archaic term overloaded with consonants? Isn't there a modern word that captures and imparts its meaning and glides more comfortably across the tongue? No, not exactly. But the question calls for a response that will disclose the fullness and richness of the concept as well as of the term itself. Because of frequent and consistent use in Christian literature, catechesis is sometimes considered indigenous to Christianity. In fact, it is a rarely used, late Greek term, the senses of which were either that of informing or of recounting something to someone.[9] Etymologically the word (*katechein*) means to resound, to communicate orally, to hand down to, to deliver a message from above, sometimes used as "to echo." Two illustrations may exemplify its earliest use. One is that of a dramatic poet in a descriptive address from a stage—a level spatially above the listeners; the second, that of a physician informing and explaining the nature or treatment of a particular disease to someone who was not a doctor.[10]

The term occurs in the New Testament: Luke 1:4; Acts 18:25, 21:21; Rom. 2:18; Gal. 6:6. Each use is in the verb form, and each bears one of two interpretations: (1) to relate something, to narrate or describe a situation or (2) to receive and/or pass on the news of something, to inform or instruct. Luke opens his Gospel account using a form of catechesis to verify the reliability of the accounts he had already heard (Luke 1:4). In Acts 21:21, James tells (catechizes) Paul about a rumor concerning him and his teaching among the Jews in the diaspora. In neither instance is there reference to imparting doctrinal information as such. Paul, on the other hand, uses the term exclusively in the sense of giving instruction concerning Jesus and the truths he taught.

As a noun, *catechesis* describes in doctrine and practice the Church's formative and informative message of Christian reality. Although it connotes a formal educational concept to many contemporary Christians, its use in early Christian times was not confined to instruction alone. It included all activity which resounded God's revelation: verbal instruction as well as the unfolding communication in the Scriptures; the formative influence of the Church's worship and sacramental celebration along with the daily witness of Christian living. Without so stating it, the early Christians seemed to know that the truth proclaimed by Jesus Christ could never be totally captured in verbal formulations.[11] The impression is that one could justifiably observe the interrelationship of *lex orandi* and *lex credendi* to *lex catechizandi*.

Another dimension of catechesis in the early centuries of Christianity is that it was essentially an adult enterprise. Catechesis was for those believers seeking admission into the Christian community as well as for those already baptized. Peter's First Letter is considered a catechesis reminding his baptized readers of what it means to be Christian and how, ideally speaking, the transparency of their lives testified to their commitment. Fourth-century bishops already referred to—Ambrose, Augustine, Cyril, Chrysostom, and Theodore, among others—testify to the fact that catechesis was directed to "grown-up" Christians. Under close scrutiny one discovers that the purpose, the objective, of catechesis was/ is faith, increased faith, growth in faith, "maturity of faith," as current scholars describe it.[12] It is distinct from the Scripture's use of *kerygma*, evangelization, which originally had to do with announcing, heralding the Gospel truth to those to whom it was unknown. Although there is a quality of "good news" (*kerygma*) in catechesis, catechesis as such is a follow-up to evangelizing, a lifelong follow-up for those who, having accepted Christianity, seek to comprehend that reality in its fullness. In the sense that all Christians strive continuously to know and to understand more fully the meaning of their being Christian, catechesis addresses believing Christians of every age — young, middle-aged, and elderly.

Many of these earlier understandings of catechesis have been rediscovered in the present century and are so identified in modern Christian literature.[13] The emphasis on "rediscovery" is important because during the intervening centuries the original concept and objective of catechesis sometimes became obscured. This was especially the case in the post-Reformation era of which the present study is a part. Catechizing has varied in mode and manner, in emphasis, approach, and effectiveness during the two thousand years of the Church's history. But in fact it has been constant. Church leaders have consistently recognized catechesis as a pastoral endeavor integral to the Church's life.[14] Sometimes preoccupied with administrative matters or with conflicts that dominated their time, attention, and energies, bishops have not always been able to accord it "pride of place." Nevertheless, records indicate that many Church leaders have endeavored to emphasize its importance from time to time. At times this was done by delegating their charge to others and at other times by becoming directly involved in the catechesial enterprise itself.

Before proceeding it is imperative that the reader be informed of the scope of the present study. The earliest history of the Catholic Church in this country is associated with Spanish and French missionaries and settlers dating from the fifteenth through the seventeenth centuries.[15] Significant as their contributions were and important as they are to the overall history of the Church in this country, the present study, while acknowledging them, begins with the post-Revolutionary and national period, the first century of the young republic's independent existence, from the time of John Carroll, this country's first Roman Catholic bishop, through the deliberations of the Third Plenary Council of Baltimore (1884) and its results pertinent to catechesis down to the recent publication of the National Catechetical Directory, *Sharing the Light of Faith* (1979).[16] It is in light of the beginning years of a recognized "church" that one can come to discern the distinguishing features of catechesis in a Catholic body marked by diversities of national origin, linguistic and cultural differences, and lingering allegiances to respective homelands. As one surveys the nearly two-hundred-year history of the Church's life in this country, one discovers that the principles of adaptation and respect for diverse circumstances have been in many cases hallmarks of catechesis in the U.S. Church.

The Catechism

The catechism has been so identified with religious instruction that until quite recently it was almost synonymous with catechesis. In fact, it is a comparatively recent tool introduced into extensive use during the upheaval of the sixteenth-century Reformation. In other words, for fifteen centuries the Church catechized without it. The once-popular catechism owes its origin to Martin Luther, who decided that a small question-and-answer handbook would be an effective instrument for instructing his followers in basic Christian doctrine. His manuals became widely known and soon came to be recognized by leaders in the Roman Catholic Church as influential vehicles for disseminating reform teachings. It was viewed as a practice deserving of emulation in order to stem the tide of the Protestant Reformation.

Peter Canisius (1521–1597), a Dutch Jesuit, produced the first major catechism — actually a compendium of theology — for Catholics. His work, *Summa Doctrinae Christianae* (1555), received a surprisingly welcome reception, and he proceeded to write two others for smaller children. All three of his volumes, written first in Latin, were translated into German and subsequently into other languages.[17] The Council of Trent (1545–1563) ordered the writing of a catechism which, in its eventual appearance (1566), was directed toward the clergy for their assistance in catechizing and preaching.[18] Toward the end of the sixteenth century the Italian Jesuit Robert Bellarmine (1542–1621) wrote a catechism at the request of Pope Clement VIII.[19] From then on the question-and-answer handbooks became the accepted way of catechizing. Edmund Auger, SJ (1530–1591), wrote a manual for the French Church,[20] while Jerome Ripalda, SJ (1535–1618), and Gaspar Astete, SJ (1537–1601), each wrote catechisms for Catholics in Spain.[21] Lawrence Vaux (1519–1585), Henry Turberville (1609–1678), and Richard Challoner (1691–1781) composed manuals for English-speaking Catholics. James Butler (1742–1791), archbishop of Cashel, composed one for the people of Ireland. In its conception, according to Roderick MacEachen, the catechism was "intended to be a defensive expedient against heresy."[22]

And this apologetic, defensive tone remained a hallmark of catechisms well into the twentieth century.

The movement toward universal schooling and making education available for all children, whether from rich or poor families, those residing in both rural and urban areas, provided a specific focus for catechisms, and soon catechesis came to be considered a ministry specifically directed toward children. Thus by the beginning of the seventeenth century and down to the mid-twentieth century, catechesis was identified with (1) the catechism, (2) children, and (3) classrooms. It was a far cry from the more comprehensive concept and practice of catechesis in the early centuries of the Church.[23]

Catechesis in an Immigrant Church

When the sixteenth-, seventeenth-, and even eighteenth-century newcomers arrived in the present United States they brought with them more than the clothes on their back, the anticipated basic necessities, and whatever treasured mementos they could pack in hand-carried luggage. Many of them also brought their prayer books and children's textbooks, especially catechisms.[24] Library holdings today count numbers of these well-worn, dog-eared catechisms among their rare books and special collections.[25] There is ample evidence that these catechisms were used by the immigrants. However, there were those missionaries who responded to the particularities of their new surroundings and wrote catechisms adapted to the language and culture of the people they served. A prime illustration of this is Andrew White, SJ (1579–1656), who, with two other Jesuits, landed on St. Clement Island in southern Maryland in 1634 to serve as a missionary in the area. White wrote a catechism in the native tongue of the Piscataway Indians who lived there.[26]

The status of the Church in this country when John Carroll returned to it after twenty-six years of study and teaching in Europe was that of a harassed and discriminated against minority. Clifton Olmstead observed that there were "not more that 25,000 Roman Catholics in the colonies" by the opening of the Revolution.[27] At this writing the Catholic population is nearly 55,000,000.[28] While numbers alone are not an accurate indicator of the strength or the faith of the Church, they serve to illustrate a kind of physical growth. The present study traces one aspect of that growth and development through the catechizing ministry of bishops of the U.S. Church from its small beginnings down to the most recent publication, the National Catechetical Directory, *Sharing the Light of Faith*. The concentration is principally on the printed works though it is not always limited to them.

1

John Carroll and Early Bishops

It seems characteristic of people to portray their heroes as larger than life-size. Unhampered by the weaknesses that affect most mortals, those idols excel in virtue, courage, leadership, and steadfastness. George Washington never told a lie. Socrates, great teacher that he was, projects the image of the most virtuous of men. Thomas Aquinas comes across as all but impeccable. In a particular way the Church's first bishop in this country, John Carroll, shares that same kind of heroic status. Not only was he the first native Roman Catholic to accept episcopal leadership in this country but he became for a long time the model by which many United States bishops measured their own episcopal stature and manner of pastoral care. Carroll himself manifested no awareness of the esteem in which he was held. Certainly he knew his limitations of character and personality. Nevertheless, as one studies his biographies, reads his correspondence, and examines his relationships with relatives, friends, and ecclesiastical and state authorities, one recognizes the large moral and religious stature of this nation's first Catholic prelate. For a long time his shadow extended effectively across the lives of the people and clergy in the U.S.

THE MAN AND HIS TIMES

Born in 1735 of a distinguished Catholic family,[1] the fourth of seven children, John Carroll grew up in the pre-Revolutionary period in Upper Marlboro, Maryland, not far from what would later become the nation's capital city.

9

With his cousin Charles, young John, at the age of thirteen, sailed off to St. Omer's, the English Jesuit school in French Flanders. Five years later, in 1753, he entered the novitiate of the Society of Jesus and in 1755 became a Jesuit scholastic. After finishing his scholasticate he taught philosophy at Liège, subsequently made his profession of vows in 1771, and taught at the Jesuit college in Bruges, Belgium. No documentary evidence discloses the date of his ordination, but Peter Guilday concludes from available evidence that he was ordained in 1769.[2]

The next few years were filled with teaching, traveling, and a series of unexpected events that affected his life. Late in 1771 Carroll left Bruges to tour Europe as the tutor and companion to eighteen-year-old Charles Philippe Stourton, son of an English lord.[3] When he returned he received news of the dissolution of the Society of Jesus. Shortly afterward he was arrested when Austrian officials invaded the Jesuit college in Bruges. Released sometime later, he served as chaplain at Wardour Castle until the spring of 1774 when he came back to the United States to live with his mother at Rock Creek, Maryland. There he found his country on the verge of revolution. Though his studies had taken him to Europe for twenty-six years, he never forgot that he was an American by birth, affection, and apostolate. He seems to have resumed his life as naturally as though he had never left his native land.

In 1774 the Continental Congress asked Carroll to accompany his cousin Charles, Samuel Chase, and Benjamin Franklin to Canada. The purpose of the trip was to endeavor to win the northern neighbor's support in the colonies' revolt against the mother country. The mission falied, but it provided the grounds for a new and lasting friendship for Carroll. The former Jesuit accompanied the ailing Franklin on the return trip to Philadelphia. The two came to admire each other. Franklin was particularly impressed. "I could hardly have got so far but for Mr. Carroll's friendly assistance and tender care of me," he later observed.[4]

With Rock Creek as his base, Carroll became a sort of itinerant missionary for the area, traveling as much as sixty miles at a time to reach the members of his widely scattered congregation. In 1784, partly through the recommendation of Benjamin Franklin, Carroll was named the juridical head, prefect apostolic, of the Catholic missions in the territory of the United States.[5] Five years after that, Pope Pius VI sent the papal bull commissioning Carroll the bishop of Baltimore. The corpus of the bull included the information that Carroll was the popular choice of the clergy.

> Whereas by special grant, and for this time only, we have
> allowed the priests exercising the care of souls in the United
> States of America, to elect a person to be appointed Bishop by

us, and almost all their votes have been given to our beloved
son, John Carroll, priest . . . we . . . do therefore by pleni-
tude of our authority, declare, create, appoint and constitute
the said John Carroll, Bishop of and Pastor of the said Church
of Baltimore [November 6, 1789].[6]

Following Bishop John Carroll's consecration (August 15, 1790) in
Lulworth Chapel in Dorset, England, he came back to Baltimore where
his genius for administration began to surface. He was keenly aware that
the unique conditions of the United States in relationship with the
Church would bring their own tensions and difficulties, but he was confident that the two could live and grow compatibly, supporting and complementing each other. One thing that fostered that belief was Carroll's
conviction of the principle of religious freedom. He considered freedom
one of the primary elements of the young nation's strengths. That people
of different religious beliefs should live together amicably was an innovative and remarkable asset to the country and explains his opposition to
discrimination based on religious differences. He held that those who
had fought side by side in the Revolutionary War had earned the right to
religious liberty. "Freedom and independence acquired by the united efforts, and cemented with the mingled blood of Protestants and Catholic
fellow-citizens, should be equally enjoyed by all."[7]

Carroll furthered congenial relations with the government and its
chief executives; visited George Washington at Mr. Vernon; later enjoyed warm relations with Thomas Jefferson; and, despite his opposition
to the War of 1812, defended James Madison "for his religious principles
and his endeavors to preserve peace."[8]

The first bishop knew what being an American meant. It was no
static concept but a continuous discovery and achievement. He knew the
ideals, values, and contradictions of a country whose bloodstream had
plurality and complexity as its major ingredients. Almost innately, he
sensed when to expect and to demand the utmost. He also knew when not
to ask the limit, to delay until the *kairos*, the proper moment, when to
"bring forth the new and the old" (Matt. 13:52).

In Carroll one discovers a gifted administrator and a personable
pastor. In him the two roles were complementary. He kept his finger on
the management pulse of his vast diocese and at the same time retained a
warm, approachable posture that endeared him to those he served. His
correspondence reveals his sensitivity to different personalities. It discloses, too, his appreciation of human nature in general and his generosity toward individual foibles and differences. A sense of humor
equipped him to see the ridiculous in circumstances and in people, especially his best friends. Furthermore, he could laugh at himself. The

characteristic most distinctive about him, though, was his tireless and constant ministry to and care for others.

Carroll could be firm on occasion. The threats of schisms and separate churches, the spirit of independence in certain laity, the rebellion of individual clergymen provoked forthright and stern responses. Painful though he found it, he did not hesitate to reprimand and to suspend priests who arbitrarily bypassed his authority and sought to establish independent congregations. "Carroll's firm and undeviating insistence upon episcopal authority in spiritual matters and his forthright representations to the Holy See"[9] are a matter of public record. Throughout, Carroll strove to be patient and compassionate. His saving feature in those incidents was his personal agony over them and a kind of dismay at the recalcitrant characteristics he encountered in the people involved.[10] He described his efforts on behalf of one cleric, William Elling, in a letter to Caesar Brancadoro, secretary of the (Sacred) Congregation de Propaganda Fide.

> I gladly received him in spite of his record for shiftlessness; I treated him most generously until he went over to the unholy faction, a victim, apparently, of their promises. I did not, however, abandon all efforts to save him from such a disastrous step. I wrote him showing my good will, but he did not reply. Then I met him in Philadelphia and spoke most kindly with him; at first he gave me reason for hope, but before long the unhappy subjection into which he has allowed himself to fall made all efforts useless.[11]

JOHN CARROLL AND CATECHESIS

One of Carroll's major concerns was that of the Christian formation and education of the young. It is a kind of melody that courses like a theme song in and out of his writings, correspondence, and sermons. He believed that solid religious instruction would sustain Christians for life. "I have considered the virtuous and Christian instruction of youth as a principal object of pastoral solicitude," he wrote in his pastoral letter of 1792.[12] That concern is clearly demonstrated in the synod of 1791, the pastoral letter just cited, and his approval of specific catechisms.

When Carroll issued the invitation convoking the synod, he stated its sevenfold purpose: (1) preserving episcopal succession in the Baltimore See; (2) the matter of a coadjutor or a division of the diocese; (3) uniformity of discipline in the U.S. Church; (4) strengthening the bonds of unity with the Vatican; (5) regulations for administering the sacraments; (6) clerical life and discipline; (7) cautions and protections for the faithful and clergy against the religious indifference and worldliness prevalent in the post-Revolutionary era in the young republic.[13]

The synod opened on November 7 and ended on November 10. Twenty-two priests participated in the sessions, but at the heart of the assembly was the leader and formulator of the twenty-four statutes that emerged from it. "In every line you see the Bishop," according to Simon Bruté years later. "In all you see how extensively he had studied and the spirit of faith, charity and zeal in that first assembly has served as a happy model for its successors."[14]

Peter Guilday described it as the *Magna Carta* of all ecclesiastical legislation in the U.S. Church. "Carroll's statutes not only inspired subsequent conciliar decrees but were the norm of practically all legislative enactments of the seven Baltimore Councils from 1829 to 1849."[15] The fathers of the First Provincial Council considered the statutes of that synod so important that they mandated their inclusion in the printing of those enacted at their first provincial assembly in 1829.[16]

Four direct references to catechesis stand out in the statutes: candidates for the sacrament of confirmation must be properly instructed (#4); no one who is ignorant of the fundamental doctrines of the Church should be permitted to marry (#15); catechetical instructions are to be given following the celebration of vespers (#16); after Sunday Mass the children and those needing instruction are to be questioned and instructed (#18).[17]

Carroll's pastoral letter is of equal significance for its focus on education. Notable, however, is that in his concentration on Catholic education at all levels his underlying concern was for religious formation and religious education of Catholic youth. He stated unequivocally that the Christian instruction of youth was a principal object of his pastoral ministry.[18] Characteristic of his era, catechesis for Carroll concentrated on children and youth. Two other aspects stand out in that pastoral letter. The first is the responsibility of parents as primary catechists and the second, the importance of instilling Christian morals as integral to catechesis.

"Who can contribute so much to this [religious formation] . . . as parents themselves?" he asked. "Parents should be unwearied in their endeavors" in catechizing. In events and struggles in later life their sons and daughters will recall gratefully "the religious instruction received in their early age."[19] Christian morals, too, were upheld as integral to that formation. They were set in the broad perspective of the nation's well-being. "Our country depends on the morals of its citizens," he insisted.[20] "Habits of obedience, dread of . . . fraud and duplicity . . ., respectful behavior to their fathers and mothers" were all part of youths' catechesis, according to Carroll's pastoral letter.

Carroll did not neglect the clergy in this all-important ministry. He praised the Sulpicians in particular and addressed the clergy in general. Theirs was the duty "to teach, to admonish, to reprove . . . to instruct . . . children and servants in the doctrines and exercises of religion . . . to watch perpetually over the morals of all and to prevent the contagion of error or evil example."[21] Furthermore, he urged the adult faithful to look to their pastors for guidance and understanding in their growth in faith. Those pastors "will instruct you how to walk in the observance of all Christian duties."[22]

In light of his recognizing catechesis as central to a growing faith, it is essential to examine the small manual that bears his name.

GENESIS AND SOURCES OF THE "CARROLL CATECHISM"

One of the first clarifications is that in all likelihood John Carroll did not write the so-called "Carroll Catechism." Not only is there no indication in available sources that Carroll actually wrote the manual that bore his name through generations of admiring users, there is little evidence that his very full and busy life afforded him the time to compile such a work. This does not in any way minimize the significance of the small handbook identified with him as author. By comparison, one might call attention to the *Catechism of Pius X* (1906),[23] which that pontiff did not write. The work is neither lessened nor enhanced in quality or value by authorship alone.

Nevertheless, there is a certain legitimacy in crediting Carroll with the manual which first appeared in 1785 and went through numerous printings. He sanctioned it; his name appeared on its title page witnessing to his approbation.

In fact, convincing evidence points to Carroll's close friend, Robert J. Molyneux (1738–1808), as the author.[24] In Molyneux's 1785 correspondence with Carroll the Philadelphia priest referred four times to catechisms evidently in various stages of composition.[25] None of those books bore a by-line identifying Molyneux as the author, but blind authorship was not uncommon at that time. Neither is it today. Many episcopal works have been ghost-written by a person or a group of persons commissioned by a bishop or bishops. Those commissioning the works ordinarily have initiated the idea/concept and served as the final censors/editors of the work(s) that bear their names. The Roman Catechism of the Council of Trent carries no by-line identifying its three Dominican authors. Nor did the widely circulated catechism enjoined by the Third Plenary Council of Baltimore in 1885 acknowledge John

Lancaster Spalding and Januarius de Concilio as its writers-compilers. Even in our own day the documents published under the aegis of the national bishops' conference credit no individual authors.

What is perhaps more significant is to discover that the small, forty-page manual bearing Carroll's name is a direct descendant of the sixteenth- and seventeenth-century catechisms which claim Laurence Vaux (1519–1584), Henry Turberville (1609–1678), Richard Challoner (1691–1781), and the Douai tradition as their originators. Vaux compiled the first catechism for English-speaking Catholics in 1562. He titled it *A Catechisme of Christian Doctrine necessarie for Children and ignorante people . . .*[26] and credited Peter Canisius as inspiration and partial source for his work.[27] The second in the lineage of English catechisms was written by a Douai priest, Henry Turberville. Because of his identification with the region, Turberville's work, *Abridgement of Christian Doctrine,*[28] came to be called the "Doway Catechism" in much the same way as the "Baltimore catechism" was called for the city wherein it was conceived.

Challoner's work, carrying the same title as Turberville's, was published by St. Omer's, Carroll's alma mater, in 1772. It carries a high degree of authenticity in its own makeup because Challoner was a practicing catechist. He lived what he taught. Even after he was bishop he mingled with his flock in the places where they lived and worked. "He taught his people tirelessly," J.D. Crichton wrote, "not as a bishop from the height of a throne but in the humblest of circumstances." Furthermore, catechizing had the widest connotation for him. "He sought to provide for the entire religious needs of the people and he seems to sum up in his work all the great tradition that had gone before him. Scripture, doctrine, history, spiritual reading, meditation, liturgy (in however narrow a sense) and catechism, all were the subjects of his many books."[29]

It is the Challoner catechism which seems to be the link between the English catechism tradition and the newly formed Maryland diocese, its bishop, and "his catechism." It is most likely that both Molyneux and Carroll were familiar with Challoner's work, and it follows logically that it would be the model and/or source for a catechism for English-speaking Catholics in this country.

A further clue substantiating a reliance on Challoner's catechism is the opening question, "Who made you?" Challoner's manual popularized that opening in contrast to Bellarmine's short catechism which began, "Are you a Christian?" Turberville's first question was, "Child, what religion are you?" The "Carroll Catechism," like Challoner's, began with, "Who made you?" and follows with, "Why did he make you?" which is Challoner's second question too. The two manuals are not identical word-for-word throughout but the relationship is close. It must be noted here that all the manuals cited above are in the so-called Canisius-Bellarmine tradition, treating the creed, commandments, and sacraments (in that sequence) and including a section on prayer. However, Challoner adopted more of Canisius's style and appeal than that of Bellarmine.[30]

Carroll and the Fénelon Catechism

Another catechism which bears Carroll's "expressed approbation" is a 169-page volume, *Catechism on Foundations of the Christian Faith*, published in 1811.[31] In itself the book witnesses to Carroll's breadth of catechesial vision. It is unique in several ways. In questions and answers the work concentrates on one theme, "a summary of proofs of Christianity . . . for all . . . who are desirous of obtaining a thorough knowledge of the foundations of Christianity!" (Introduction). The last fifty-three pages are excerpts from letters and conversations of the esteemed French Sulpician bishop of Cambrai, Francois de Salignac de La Mothe-Fénelon (1651–1715).[32] Furthermore, it is one of the rare catechisms addressed to adults. Although the title page explicitly states that it is a catechism "for the use of both the young and the old," the very style and corpus of the manual direct it to mature readers. One wonders how many children under twelve would find the following passage engaging:

> Q. What is the fourth proof of the existence of God, which you deduce from yourself?
> A. The fourth proof of the existence of God, which I deduce from myself, is founded upon the wonderful relations which exist between man and the world, and which are of such nature as to render it evident, that the world, was made for man, and man for the world; for, in order to establish these relations, infinite combinations must have been formed, of which none but an infinite mind could be capable.[33]

The manual is explanatory throughout and dialogic in tone with the inquirer frequently posing the questions in the first person. For example, "Show me that all these predictions have been accomplished in the person of Jesus Christ."[34] The dialogic nature of both the catechism itself and the extracts from Fénelon's letters and conversations reveals a reliance on Augustine's fifth-century writings. Lacking some of the unction, warmth, and completeness of the Bishop of Hippo's address to the deacon Deo Gratias, the Fénelon work is expository and apologetic in tone, appealing more to reason than to faith. No treatment of the sacraments or the commandments is included. Fénelon's conversation with Mr. Ramsay, "given by Ramsay himself,"[35] is a discussion of the difference between Deism and Christianity.

Of note, too, is Carroll's approbation of the catechism written by Bishop George Hay of Edinburgh. The U.S. publication of Hay's manual was in 1809 by Bernard Dornin of Baltimore.[36]

While Carroll did not object to the promulgation of catechisms other than that ascribed to him, he did have a concern for orthodoxy and for the union of congregations with local authority. Early in his episcopate he encountered schismatic tendencies and incipient trusteeism in Boston, ambitious German nationalism in Pennsylvania and Maryland, and the possibility of an independent church in Charleston (1815).[37] These disquieting factors could only be dealt with as they surfaced from time to time. In the case of pro-German nationalism which sought independence from Carroll's episcopal authority in both Philadelphia and Baltimore, difficulties perdured even beyond Carroll's time. During his episcopacy one of the priests who endeavored to act independently of Carroll's jurisdiction wrote an unacceptable catechism.

In 1797 Carroll accepted Friedrich Caesarius Reuter, OFM, Conv., a newly arrived priest from Germany, to minister to the German Catholics in Baltimore.[38] Within a year Reuter urged his fellow Germans to erect their own church edifice. Carroll's objections were ignored and the building progressed. However, the parishioners came to realize that alone they could not support a pastor or the edifice. Reuter then returned to Germany, journeyed to Rome, and registered false complaints of anti-Germanic attitudes and actions against Carroll (1798). Rome was at first sympathetic until correspondence from Carroll refuted the Reuter stories. Then point by point Propaganda Fide refuted Reuter's charges against the bishop. They denounced Reuter's catechism, too, which he had written in German soon after his arrival in Baltimore. He presented a copy of it to the Propaganda while he was in Rome. Evidently the man did not realize that the catechism which Rome held in highest esteem was that of Robert Bellarmine.[39] He must have received with some chagrin the Roman official's advice "that it would have been better had he translated into German Cardinal Bellarmine's excellent catechism since the multiplication of such books had often caused difficulties in the Church."[40] Hyacinth Cardinal Gerdil, consultor of the Holy Office, further advised Reuter that it was far easier to write a *cursus universae theologiae* than a small catechism.[41]

An examination of Reuter's *Katechetischer Unterricht* illustrates the reasons for Rome's critique of it. The manual had a dominant moral orientation with pervasive emphasis on laws and regulations. This is not surprising when one discovers that it opens with the Ten Commandments, proceeds to a treatment of the saints, then the sacraments, followed by the creed and finally ceremonies and prayers.

Some of the statements are curious indeed and explain in part the Propaganda's refusal to approve it. Regarding the Trinity Reuter wrote that "all three are the same age, the same height, the same might, perfect and alike in all."[42] "Sins committed on Sundays exceed in gravity."[43]

Q. Was this fruit [the apple in Genesis] of itself bad?
A. Yes, because it brought bad [evil] results.[44]
Q. What is the meaning of the "Communion of Saints"?
A. That the first Christians had all things in common including worldly as well as spiritual goods.[45]

Reuter was not easily deterred. Despite Rome's admonition to him not to return to the United States, the recalcitrant pastor went back to Baltimore and led his congregation into open schism. Four years later, after much travail, the matter was finally settled with a civil court action in May 1805. This appeal to civil law was an innovative and distinctive American procedure. Carroll was vindicated and later acknowledged as the legitimate episcopal authority by the trustees and their erring pastor.

One cannot fail to appreciate the German Catholics' desire to hear homilies in their native tongue, converse with a priest who needed no intermediary as translator, and have a catechism in the language they could read. Carroll recognized and sympathized with their plight. He also endeavored to respond to their needs. "I try as much as I can to promote their welfare no less than that of others," he wrote to Caesar Brancadoro.[46]

> When I come upon priests of that nation who are qualified and in sufficient number they are assigned to them as pastors; and, if I may speak my mind, in general there are none of the laity in this diocese whom I esteem more highly for their piety and good morals than the Germans. Here Christian faith and piety are more indebted to no one than to some priests of that nation . . . they always used the catechism brought here by the first missionaries from Germany and later reprinted. Indeed I believe this was the catechism of Venerable Bellarmine, translated into German. Since I knew that, I recognized that the new text made by Caesarius was a sharp contrast. I saw in him a young man quite unfamiliar with our ways, and altogether a novice in dogmatic theology.[47]

Carroll and Schools

That people in his diocese, old and young alike, would grow in faith was Carroll's great hope, and he made every effort to make that possible. He foresaw that formal education was one means by which that could happen directly and indirectly. He dreamed of and planned for a seminary as well, an institution of higher learning.[48] Later he described what he had long envisioned, "a college on this continent for the education of youth, which might at the same time be a seminary for future clergymen."[49] Carroll had to "sell" the idea to a reluctant clergy. After a time the opposition was overcome, financial and other steps taken, construction begun, and finally the "Academy of George Town, Patowmack River, Maryland," opened in September 1791.[50] Rev. Robert Plunkett was its first president.

The institution endured an initial storm of jealousies and financial and administrative difficulties and, after the first decade, emerged as a permanent and promising institution. In 1805 Georgetown was handed over to the Society of Jesus as Carroll had expected it to be and from that point on developed steadily into a reputable institution of higher learning.

Carroll's zeal for education is further illustrated by his sanction of Elizabeth Seton and her educational projects.

Seton, mother of five children and widowed at the age of twenty-nine, was baptized into the Church in 1805.[51] A strong and intelligent woman with a generous and courageous character, she accepted William DuBourg's invitation to found a school for girls in Baltimore near the newly founded St. Mary's Seminary on Paca Street.[52] Shortly after the opening of the school students filled its rooms. Teachers volunteered, too. Subsequently John Carroll directed her in admitting young women to a sisterhood, provided her with a set of rules, and allowed her to design and wear a religious habit. She pronounced her vows of religion to him, after which he gave her the title "Mother." In 1809 Mother Seton moved to Emmitsburg and adopted permanent rules according to the Sisters of Charity of St. Vincent de Paul. It was during those years that she laid the foundation for the Catholic school system. Her frequent correspondence with Carroll indicates the reverence she had for him and the understanding and cooperation that existed between them.

The Sulpicians Come to the United States

An event seemingly unrelated to the Church in the United States indirectly played an important part in its growth and formation. It took place on July 14, 1789, when Frenchmen stormed and destroyed the Bastille, a state prison in the eastern part of Paris. The incident initiated the French Revolution, a violent and decisive overthrow of the ancien régime and of the Church authority which had been associated with it.

On July 12, 1790, the Constituent Assembly, which had replaced the monarchical political structure in France, enacted new statutes which ultimately marked the end of national unity and induced a civil war. On November 27 of that year the Assembly promulgated a statute requiring priests to take an oath to uphold the new government. The law made the clergy responsible and subservient to the civil authorities alone, thus dissolving ecclesiastical authority at many levels.[53] Although some bishops and curés remained in the new structure, many priests and bishops left the country rather than swear to accept the "Civil Constitution of the Clergy," as it was called. The U.S. Church, whose needs were great, provided a place of safety as well as a fertile missionary field for some of these French clerics who fled from the Revolution's violence and persecution in their homeland.

When John Carroll was in England for his consecration, Jacques André Emery,[54] the French superior general of the Sulpicians, contacted him in his search for a haven for the French Sulpicians. The Sulpicians had an apostolate of preparing seminarians for the priesthood, and they were well known to Carroll. At the time Carroll had neither students for the priesthood nor funds to support a seminary. He was also aware that some former Jesuits had embryonic plans for clerical education. Nevertheless, Carroll responded favorably to Emery's request and one year after his consecration welcomed nine Sulpicians to his diocese.

Four priests and five students of the Society of St. Sulpice arrived on July 10, 1791. Fifty-seven-year-old François Charles Nagot (1734–1816) was superior of the group. Less than three months later (October 3, 1791), they opened St. Mary's Seminary in Baltimore for clerical students.[55] It was a humble beginning and got off to a slow start, but no overview of catechetical history in this country would be complete without attention to the work of these French followers of Jean Jacques Olier.[56]

The apostolate of the Sulpicians was explicitly defined as that of training young men aspiring to the priesthood according to the decrees of the Council of Trent. In the United States, the paucity of vocations, coupled with the missionary demands of an immense diocese with too few priests to minister to the faithful, soon found individual Sulpicians in remote pastoral settings. Benedict Joseph Flaget (1763–1850) was sent to the French settlement at Fort Vincennes, Indiana. Later he became the first bishop of Bardstown, Kentucky. Gabriel Richard (1767–1832), who had arrived in this country in June 1792, served the missionary territory in Illinois for six years before being transferred to Detroit, which became the heart of his missionary work until his death.[57] Ambrose Maréchal (1764–1828) served the Catholic communities on Maryland's Eastern Shore and subsequently taught theology and philosophy at St. Mary's Seminary and Georgetown College respectively. In 1817 he became the third archbishop of Baltimore.[58] William DuBourg (1766–1833) went to Havana, then to Louisiana,[59] and John Baptist David went to Bardstown.[60] Meanwhile a skeletal faculty maintained the seminary and preparatory school.

The Sulpicians brought with them a theory and practice of catechizing which had become integral to their curriculum in preparing young men for pastoral ministry. Probably the best description of the Sulpician method comes from the pen of Félix Dupanloup (1802–1878) in his work *The Ministry of Catechising.*[61] Chronologically Dupanloup belongs to a later, nineteenth-century period, but there was no decided progression in catechesial practice between the Carroll episcopacy and Dupanloup's delineation of catechizing as a ministry in his 1868 work.

Dupanloup wrote out of his long experience with and knowledge of the *méthode de S. Sulpice.* One could argue, justifiably, that the method is more a matter of citing practical principles than of structuring a methodology. Such fine distinctions apparently offered no obstacle for the nineteenth-century catechist.

It becomes clear, in reading his work, that Dupanloup implemented those principles into practicing realities. Catechizing, according to him, is the *"l'oeuvre par excellence"* and "the highest part of ministry."[62] Catechesis is not "simply instruction, it is education; it is not only to teach Christianity to children; it is to educate the children in Christianity . . . Introduction provides the mind with the knowledge of certain things; education lifts up the whole soul. Instruction addresses itself directly only to the understanding; education forms at the same time the understanding, the heart, the character and the conscience."[63]

Sounding like an echo of the synod of 1977 rather than its anticipation, Dupanloup insisted that catechesis "is the work of the parish itself."[64] Although his focus was primarily on children and youth, his vision of the work of catechizing was not confined to the catechist or to the curate. Catechesis as he saw it was the "real cradle of the parish, a great parochial work."[65]

Prayer, too, was an essential goal as well as a means of catechizing for the Sulpicians. Dupanloup wrote, "Till you have brought your children to pray as they should, you have done nothing."[66] He was in the best tradition when he advocated prayer as a goal. Not only is this found in the New Testament (1 Thess. 5:17) and in patristic writings (e.g., the *Didache*), it is stated as an objective in the *General Catechetical Directory* (1971) (#22, 25, 79), the United States Directory, *Sharing the Light of Faith* (1979) (#84, 140–145), and the synodal statements of 1977.[67]

Sulpician theory falls short, however, when compared section by section with these contemporary writings. For example, it was almost totally child-centered and did not adequately emphasize the liturgical life of the Church. Nevertheless, the Sulpician approach was innovative in its philosophy, theory, and practice in the context of the prolonged Counter-Reformation era. It had some qualities that are timeless and deserving of careful study in any era—a sense of respect for the catechized, a stress on conviction and dedication which provides an understanding of the ideal that the transplanted Sulpicians held before them when they came to the United States. They maintained that catechesis included instruction but was more than that. It was both an introduction into and a continuous deepening of Christian faith. The primacy of charity on the part of the catechist was essential.[68] In view of that, it is no surprise that certain Sulpicians assumed leadership roles in catechizing and wrote or authorized catechisms for their respective missions and dioceses.

On August 6, 1811, Benedict Joseph Flaget, a Sulpician and Bardstown's first bishop, wrote to Carroll that "a little catechism for confirmation is to be printed in a very short time, meanwhile I prepare young and full grown people for their first communion . . . when all the young people above fourteen have made their first communion then I will proceed to the administration of the sacrament of confirmation."[69] The catechism appeared in 1811 "by the authority of Bishop F. by N. Wickliffe, Bardston, Ky."[70] No author is credited with writing this work, but in light of circumstances and subsequent writings it is highly likely that Flaget's colleague, John Baptist David, contributed to it. David had joined Flaget in Bardstown in June 1811.

Baltimore Becomes an Archdiocese

Interlinked with the influx of the Sulpicians to this country is that of the division of the large Baltimore diocese into four distinct suffragan sees, thus setting Baltimore up as a metropolitan see with John Carroll as archbishop. The subdivision of the large, original diocese was inevitable; Carroll himself had asked for it.[71] When it came about, it accentuated a varied plurality within the American Church, each new diocese carrying its own unique characteristics dictated by geography, diversities of national origins, and remoteness from the mother see. The new sees, Bardstown, Boston, New York, and Philadelphia, generated their own particular vitalities. Each, in turn, responded to the unique catechetical needs of the Church in their areas.

Two of the new bishops authorized or sanctioned catechisms soon after assuming responsibility for their respective dioceses. Mention has already been made of Flaget's manual for Bardstown. Jean Lefebvre de Cheverus (1768–1836), Boston's first bishop, approved the republication of the remarkable seventeenth-century catechism written by Claude Fleury.[72]

The publication, *Short Historical Catechism* (1813), emerged as a project of the Boston clergy which easily won the bishop's approbation.

In fact Cheverus revised it for final publication. Fleury's manual first appeared in Paris in 1683. It was a concrete protest against, as well as an alternative to, the skeletal doctrinal catechisms which were becoming more and more common throughout the Catholic world. Fleury maintained that Christian doctrine could best be comprehended in its scriptural-historical context and that isolated dogmatic statements needed a setting in which they could make sense to the inquiring Christian. Cheverus, like most of the French clergy, knew and appreciated Fleury's *Catéchisme Historique*, and it was only natural that he wanted it used in the American Church. Unfortunately, most of the U. S. editions deleted the introduction, a long clarifying rationale for the work itself and an essential part of the manual.[73]

Cheverus was indefatigable in his zeal and endeavors to assist people in their growth in faith. At one time, "he worked laboriously over a six-page catechism for the ones who were preparing for their first communion."[74] The setting was an Indian village on an island in the Penobscot River. Cheverus, who was just beginning to understand the language of the native Americans he was serving there, soon knew each of the individual members of the tribe by name. The thirty-year-old French exile had been in this country just two years. His natural linguistic ability was challenged but not conquered by the tongue of his *chers sauvages*, as he referred to his red-skinned friends.

Though he was an intellectual possessing an array of talents along with personal integrity, Cheverus had little taste for writing. At one time, in fact, he expressed a dislike for the "scribomania" which he considered symptomatic of the period.[75] Nevertheless, his boundless missionary zeal and pastoral concern kept him from sitting idly by when needs arose. Four writings claim his authorship: the revision of Fleury's catechism; a manual of devotions, hymns, and prayers; a translation of the New Testament; and published correspondence countering harsh and false accusations against the Church.

The first has already been described. The second, entitled *Anthems, Hymns etc., usually sung at the Catholick Church in Boston,*[76] was a seventy-two-page manual with forty-seven pages dedicated to hymns. Cheverus had observed the participation of the faithful at liturgical celebrations and concluded that the "age-old custom of chanting the hymns of the Church . . . had been of great benefit not only to the solemnity of the service but to the preservation of the Faith."[77] In 1800 he published a revised version with the title *Roman Catholic Manual*, a collection of hymns, prayers, and devotions for the people he served. Three years later he produced a third edition (287 pages) in which he added the Sunday and feast day collects, prayers for confession, etc.[78]

According to Francois A. Matignon, Cheverus's good friend and former mentor, "a very excellent edition of the French New Testament of Sacy [was] done here under my care and that of Mr. Cheverus."[79] That work appeared in two editions.

Cheverus's third extant writing was in response to charges that the Roman Catholic Church was guilty of "bigoted tolerance," persecution, gross idolatry, and granting permission to sin through indulgences. The original charges came in 1804 in a letter written by a Bostonian traveling in Europe. The writer cited his reactions to Catholicism as he saw it on the Continent. When he returned to the United States, he gave his letter to the *Monthly Anthology and Boston Review*, which published it in 1807.[80] The article appeared over the signature of "An American Traveler," who later identified himself as John Lowell. Cheverus wrote a cool reply that appeared in the April issue.

> I am a Roman Catholick, and in points of doctrine, perfectly agree with my brethren in Italy and elsewhere but neither they nor I hold such a doctrine concerning indulgences and persecution, as you attribute to us in your letter.
>
> Where did you read, sir, from whom did you ever hear, that indulgences are permissions to commit offences: Not, I am sure in any writers, not from any member of our church. Had you asked even the ignorant beggars you met with at Loretto and in other places, whether indulgences authorized them to get drunk, steal, etc., they would have looked at you with astonishment, and perhaps mistaken a christian for an infidel.
>
> We ourselves publish indulgences in our church in Boston; and if indulgences are permissions to commit offences, let our church be pulled down, and every Roman Catholick be banished from this hospitable land. But, I dare say, sir, you do us the justice to believe, that instead of encouraging crimes, we do our best to prevent them, and with the blessing of God, not unsuccessfully. If I am not misinformed, the American Traveler's respectable name is inscribed among the benefactors of our church in this town; I acknowledge it with pleasure and gratitude, and feel happy in assuring you that you have not contributed to the establishment of a school of corruption and idolatry.
>
> Your venerable forefathers fled not from a popish, but from a protestant persecution. They landed here, and were at full liberty to show what was the spirit of their sect. Was it toleration? Many other virtues, they possessed, no doubt; but to this they were utter strangers.[81]

Taking his cue from his antagonist, Cheverus signed his response "A Roman Catholick."

What is significant about the published works of Cheverus is their pastoral character and tone. He wrote in response to grass roots needs or questions. It was the growth in and preservation of the faith-life of the people which were his main concerns. Insofar as that relates to the purpose of catechesis, it is justifiable to cite the four published works referred to above as "catechesial" in nature and purpose.

CARROLL'S CATECHISM CASTS A LONG SHADOW

In terms of catechesis the gentle figure of John Carroll pervaded the first three decades of the Church's institutional life in this country. Nor was his influence confined to his physical presence. Seventeen years after his death the first diocesan Synod of Philadelphia (1832) sanctioned the use of the "Carroll Catechism" written more than forty years before that assembly convened.[82] Seven years later (1839) the initial synod of the diocese of St. Louis decreed that the same manual be used in that region.[83] Boston's second bishop, Benedict J. Fenwick, issued a revised version of that identical catechism in 1843 to supplant the editions "which of late years had been published without authority."[84] When the first plenary council assembled in Baltimore (1852), the three-bishop catechism committee suggested that the 1793 "Carroll Catechism," with some minor revisions, be submitted to the Holy See for approval and adoption.[85] Similar commendations abound, testifying to the esteem accorded the reputedly ideal forty-page question-answer handbook attributed to the venerated archbishop of Baltimore, John Carroll.[86]

On might justifiably observe that John Carroll himself personified Christian catechesis. Perhaps a nonsectarian Boston newspaper expressed it best. Following Carroll's three-week stay in the spring of 1791 in that "hub of the universe" city, which at the time was far from a "Catholic metropolis," *The Boston Herald of Freedom* published an appreciation of the Baltimore prelate.

> As a preacher, his talents were admired; as a companion, his society was sought; as a man, he was esteemed, revered, and honoured. The narrow prejudices entertained by the ignorant or the illiterate vanished from the radiance of his candour, and shrunk from the test of his piety. Under his auspices, even the prejudiced view with more favorable eye, a religion which he so truly adorned . . . Boston would congratulate the hour of this Gentleman's return, and will remember with gratitude and pleasure, his visit to the state.[87]

In an overall retrospective view one cannot fail to note that the early bishops, the contemporaries of John Carroll, were strong, far-sighted individuals in their own right. Flaget and Cheverus, the two briefly studied here, exemplify that. The characteristic that they, Carroll, and the others seem to have in common is a profound pastoral sense. Administrative and financial matters were demanding in the pioneer years of the Church in this young country, but it was their overriding concern for the faith-life of both clergy and faithful that took precedence. Management details were seen in light of their necessity and service for pastoral concerns. Growth in and maturity of faith, a comprehensive understanding of Catholic Christianity, were paramount.

2

Catechesis in the Expansion and Americanization of the U.S. Church

An 1841 catechism published in New York included the following questions:

Q. What is the meaning of the word Roman Catholic?
A. It means a Catholic in communion with the see of Rome.

Q. Do you adopt that name?
A. We glory in our communion with the see of Rome, but call ourselves American Catholics.[1]

These questions and those that followed isolated a sensitive issue which the nineteenth-century Catholic minority in this country encountered as the Church expanded. The issue was one of hostility on the part of their non-Roman Catholic neighbors who possessed an exaggerated fear of papal authority. Tensions mounted gradually as Catholic immigrants increased the nation's population. Concomitantly the fear of many non-Catholic citizens grew as they projected the Church in the image of "essentially a foreign power [Rome] which, if allowed to expand without limitation, would bring to an end the American way of life."[2] These were fears inherited from the sixteenth-century Reformation mentality and nurtured through generations. They became magnified in this country which, ironically enough, fought two wars (1776 and 1812) to establish itself as a free and independent nation, wars in which Catholics and non-Catholics fought side by side against a common enemy.

The hostility affected both the Catholics who were its targets and those who harbored its antipathies. Non-Catholics tended to interpret (or misinterpret) most of Catholic life and worship with suspicion and ill-founded prejudices. Catholics, especially Catholic leaders, faced a twofold difficulty: (1) educating Rome to the uniqueness of this democratic republic, which officially decreed a separation of church and state without being hostile to religion as such; (2) confronting anti-Catholic hostility at home while endeavoring to make friends with their neighbor church bodies and at the same time cogently defending Catholicism as a value to the pluralistic life in the United States.[3]

Under the circumstances Catholics became more defensive and their approach to their own commitment and convictions was increasingly apologetic. This was clearly and undeniably evident in catechesis, especially in catechisms.

So close were all to the situation that it seemed impossible for them to perceive the contradiction in discrimination of any kind in a young nation dedicated to egalitarianism for all its citizens. Ideally Americanization could not imply erasing all differences, obscuring identities, melting down everyone and every ideal into a single, blurred mass. "Catholics do not cease to be Catholics when they become Americans."[4] Neither do others cease to be Presbyterians, or Episcopalians, etc. They usually forgo their citizenship in the mother country, but they are free to retain their religious affiliation. Joseph Fichter relates the two in terms of ideals. "There is an interesting similarity here between world-wide Catholicism and culture-wide Americanism. The Catholic Church embraces people of all nationalities who are Catholics despite their national or ethnic differences. The United States embraces people of all religions who are Americans despite their religious differences."[5]

Fichter wrote in 1960. Between the first decades of the nineteenth century and his writing in the last half of the twentieth there was much adjusting and growth, along with many experiences. Some of those were cruel and bitter. Meanwhile the Church lived through internal as well as external conflicts related to adjusting and expanding in a new societal structure.

The Church in the 1820s

John Carroll died in 1815. "At the time of his death," according to Peter Guilday, "not only had the American Church been moulded into the hierarchical order of government common to all the rest of the world but the problems which seemed almost insurmountable in 1790 had been solved and the foundations laid deep and strong for all future construction."[6]

In the first five years after his death the disappearance of concord and unity in the U.S. Church occurred. Two major internal issues were central to that disappearance. One was the nationalist rivalry between French and Irish clergy; the other was the problem of "trusteeism" which racked the U.S. Church intermittently for nearly 100 years, from 1785 until the 1880s.

The Church in America owed an immeasurable debt to the French clergy who fled the revolutionary situation in their own country after 1790. However, the priests from France were not followed by a proportionate number of Catholic lay people from that country. It was Ireland that produced the greatest increase in the U.S. Catholic population during the nineteenth century. Its Gaelic sons and daughters soon became articulately critical of hearing sermons in "broken" English and of being "ruled" by French priests and bishops.[7]

Sometimes the two issues, nationalism and trusteeism, were interrelated. Trusteeism was particularly unique to the American scene because of its "democratic" connotation. Europe and Rome were uneasy with the concept of "democracy" because for them it smacked of Protestant administrative practices and influence. The word also implied, for some, a defiance of canon law. According to Church law and existing practice, the appointing and dismissing of pastors was the sole responsibility of local bishops. Certain lay trustees in the U.S. Church attempted to usurp the rights of the bishop to name their own pastors and to legislate their own parishes. The first incidence of this occurred in Philadelphia in 1787 during John Carroll's superiorship when a group of German-born Catholics proceeded to incorporate themselves legally and started "the first American Catholic parish on a nationalist basis at Holy Trinity Church."[8] The move was precipitated by their dissatisfaction with the way English-speaking clergy at St. Mary's Church ministered to and managed the parish. That Philadelphia situation was incipient evidence of a "virus" among U.S. Catholics, a "virus that was to be with them until well into the present century."[9] The contagion spread rather rapidly, and soon Baltimore, Charleston, and other cities were infected with it. The previous chapter touched briefly on its effects in Baltimore and the upheaval it caused through Friedrich Reuter.

As John Carroll had been prominent in the Church's life earlier, another John was destined to dominate ecclesiastical as well as ecclesial life for the next twenty-odd years. He was John England (1786–1842), the first bishop of Charleston. The times and circumstances were extremely different from an earlier period and so were the personality, style, temperament, and philosophy of England in sharp contrast to those of Baltimore's first bishop. Both envisioned similar ideals but by nature chose different approaches to realize them.

John England, the fifth Irish-born prelate[10] named to a see in the United States, was born and educated in Cork. As an apprentice he explored the legal profession for two years and then turned to the clerical life, entering St. Patrick's College at Carlow. He was ordained at the age of twenty-two on October 11, 1808. He successively lectured at the cathedral, served as convent chaplain, city prison chaplain, school inspector, philosophy teacher, president of St. Mary's College, and, for three years, parish priest at Bandon (1817–1820). He was at Bandon when he was notified that he was to be bishop of the American see of Charleston (South Carolina), a diocese carved out of the metropolitan area of Baltimore. It comprised 140,000 square miles, included about 5,000 Catholics, and covered the three states of Georgia, North Carolina, and South Carolina. England was consecrated in St. Finbar's Church, Cork, on September 21, 1820, and arrived in his new home on December 30 of that year.

The young bishop brought a freshness to the Catholic scene on the western shores of the Atlantic. He quickly recognized the multidenominational population of his vast diocese and accepted it with equanimity and grace. He assessed the state of trusteeism and worked effectively to ameliorate it. History has accorded him a place in this country as an erudite and remarkable intellectual, a foremost apologist, and an astute political genius.[11] He once accepted an invitation to address the Congress of the United States (January 8, 1826), the first Catholic prelate to do so, and that address displayed his thorough mastery of the ideals and principles of the United States government and the high regard he had for true religious pluralism in this nation.[12]

John England's Innovative Episcopacy

Shortly after receiving word of his appointment to Charleston, England wrote from Ireland to the "Principal Roman Catholic Clergymen at Charleston."[13] It was the first gesture of a decisive man who knew that the helm of the ship was in his hands, that he would guide it henceforth, and who wanted to inform others of that fact.

Less than six months later and ten days after he had stepped ashore in Charleston, he wrote his first pastoral letter to the entire diocese, on January 15, 1821. In a way it was a confirmation of his earlier epistle but was lengthier and more comprehensive in its three themes: (1) the fall of Adam and humanity's need for redemption; (2) spiritual authority in the Old and New Testaments; (3) the responsibility of all to both church and state, rendering to Caesar and to God their respective prerogatives. England's pastoral was the first such inaugural message delivered by a U.S. bishop to his diocese. His message was that of a loving leader; it was clear and strong but not arrogant. He addressed the issue of trusteeism without singling out the trustees in a specific manner, including them, instead, in the context of the total Catholic community's responsibility.

> We have been selected, appointed, consecrated, and sent to govern your church. We are placed in the midst of you, unworthy as we are, yet vested with apostolic power, having, through the Holy See, received that power from Jesus Christ himself.
>
> . . . We are placed over you as a father to teach you the doctrines of truth, to guide you in the way of salvation, to feed you with the bread of life, and to spend ourselves for your eternal welfare — as we must render an account for your souls at his great tribunal. . . . In proportion as the dignity of our order is great, so is our responsibility awful and with you, beloved children, in a great measure it rests to lighten this burden.[14]

The third innovative action and, undoubtedly, the most outstanding that Charleston's first bishop took was to draw up a constitution for the diocese in the Cathedral Church of St. Finbar, signed by the clergy and many "well-disposed laymen." It was a move toward a gentle defusing of the explosive tension of trusteeism in the diocese — and it worked.

The document had an extensive preface which distinguished between the two systems of government, the one of divine institution, the other of human regulation. The dependence of the latter on the former was stated, with an insistence that it may not in any way interfere with the former. The constitution included seven sections following this preface: (I) doctrine; (II) government; (III) property; (IV) church membership; (V) district churches; (VI) the convention; (VII) amendment of the constitution.

The constitution reaffirmed the complete separation of church and state, acknowledging also that the pope had no "power or right . . . to interfere in . . . the concerns of civil polity . . . of the United States of America." It added further that Catholics were not expected to believe the pope alone was infallible.

> We are not required by our Faith to believe that the Pope is infallible; nor do we believe that he is impeccable, for it is not a consequence of his being vested with great authority that he should be exempt from the frailties of human nature, but we do not believe that his authority would be diminished, nor the institutions of our blessed Savior destroyed, even if the Pope were to be guilty of criminal actions.[15]

Present-day readers may be astonished at that statement. However, the pope's infallibility was not specifically defined until Vatican Council I in 1869–70.

Probably the most novel of all England's "innovations" was the call for representative conventions found in Section VI of the constitution.[16]

These were to be held annually in the three general areas of the diocese, South Carolina, North Carolina, and Georgia. Each convention was comprised of the bishop, the house of lay delegates, and the house of the clergy. Each year all the clergy of the diocese were to convene at an appropriate place and time. Joining them in genuine felicity was the house of lay delegates chosen by the Catholic lay people whom they represented. The convention had no authority over "spiritual matters" and appointment of pastors. It did have control over temporal matters, appointed its own officers, and in general managed the money matters of the diocese. All proposals and motions had to be approved by both houses and by the bishop. The bishop could veto appropriations or other "temporal" bills but he could not rule alone in the area of temporalities. At face value the constitution claimed that the houses were solely advisory and that Rome could countermand any decision made by the convention. Fifteen conventions were held at Charleston for the South Carolina District, from 1823 to 1838, eight in Georgia during that same span of time, and two in North Carolina.

The convention brings into clear focus England's ideal: "the Church in the south was constructed along the lines of a constitutional democratic-republic."[17] All practicing Catholics had a right and share in electing delegates for the annual convention. Lay people had *no* right to interfere in purely "spiritual" matters. The bishop alone was to make clerical assignment, but grievance procedures and what we might call today "due process" was allowed for complaints. England included a clause indicating his willingness to look into parishioners' complaints.

Leon LeBuffe assessed England's genius in handling the troubling problems he had inherited in this way: "He harnessed the energies and interest of his people, rid himself of most financial worries and buried the trustee issue. Throughout the 1820's and the 1830's trusteeism ripped apart the fabric of the Catholic Church in Philadelphia and New York, while peace reigned in Charleston, where the problem had been the worst in an earlier period."[18]

Viewed from another perspective, it was England's way of helping everyone realize that all were members of and essential to the Church's life. It was a defining of roles in a unity of action. England insisted that community counsel was imperative and that a structure had to be made whereby corporate members could address issues of mutual concern. At the heart of his conviction was his image of the Church as a body of believers united in the same faith. The bishop himself observed that the convention "has prevented discord, it has banished jealousy, it has secured peace, it has produced efforts of cooperation, and established mutual confidence and affections between our several churches, as well as between the bishop and the churches and by confirming the rights of all, it has insured the support of all."[19]

JOHN ENGLAND AND CATECHESIS

In visiting people in his vast diocese England learned numerous things about the state of Catholicity in that three-state region. Among others things, he discovered that many Catholics were poorly instructed and unknowledgeable about Catholicism. Their ignorance along with their neighbors' prejudices took its toll in terms of their fidelity. In his 1832 pamphlet, "The Early History of the Diocese of Charleston," England described some of his discoveries.

> The writer of this sketch has frequently discovered and introduced to each other as Catholics, persons who had during several years been residing in the same vicinity without the slightest suspicion on the part of either, that the other was of the same religion as himself. In many instances these persons intermarried with those of other religions, without even intimating what was their own, and at this day it is believed not to be an exaggerated estimate to state that in this diocess [sic] the descendants of Catholics who, by reason of the want of a ministry, now belong to other denominations, are four times as numerous as the actual number of those who belong to the church.[20]

To raise the level of understanding and knowledge among Catholics England took four distinct steps: (1) he established book societies; (2) he compiled a catechism; (3) he published a missal in English; and (4) he began publishing a Catholic newspaper, *The United States Catholic Miscellany*, this country's first Catholic weekly.

Before examining each of these projects, it is a matter of justice and honesty to call attention to a factor that undoubtedly influenced and perhaps directed England in his early years as bishop. The writer refers to information that has gone unrecorded by his biographers up to this time. Early in 1820 the Congregation de Propaganda Fide had in hand a twenty-nine-page document from G. M. Mazzetti, O. Carm., a consultor for the Congregation of Rites. Mazzetti had evidently been sent to this country for a firsthand assessment and report on the "case of Father R. Browne," a priest in the Carolinas who had become involved in arbitrarily setting his own course. Mazzetti's "expert opinion,"[21] as the Propaganda archives labeled it, contained fourteen points covering the state of religion in the United States, the evils and difficulties of the Church there, and the means needed to correct or overcome them.

The first recommendation was to establish a new diocese to comprise Virginia and the Carolinas. Other steps included opening a seminary (England did that on January 8, 1822), the teaching of catechism, restrictions on trusteeism, a paternal letter (England wrote one from Ireland shortly after his nomination and a more "official" one less than a month after his arrival in Charleston), administration of church temporalities (no doubt his constitution qualified as a fulfillment of that), rules to be given to trustees (covered in the constitution and continuously tended to in the conventions).[22] On August 12, 1820, England received the apostolic briefs appointing him bishop of the new see of the Carolinas and Georgia. England's subsequent decisions are too closely related and immediately made to be independent of Mazzetti's recommendations.

Book Societies

One of the earliest things England did "to meet and remove the ignorance among Catholics as to the doctrines of their religion and their duties"[23] was to organize a "Book Society." He hoped to establish a branch of the society in each parish and thus encourage parishioners to read Catholic literature and discuss their readings. He refused to be discouraged by the indifference with which this endeavor was met. It appeared to be difficult, actually next to impossible, to create a taste for Catholic reading. Nevertheless, there were some who became members of the society. Even a few readers were an improvement over the previous situation. Undismayed, England did not forgo the project and in December 1822 obtained an act incorporating it.

England's Catechism

John England had been in his new diocese less than three months when he began compiling a catechism. According to his diary, on March 2, 1821, he noted that "on this and subsequent days I was principally occupied in writing a Pastoral Letter on the observance of Lent . . . [and] an English Catechism."[24] Later he made the following entry:[25] "On the last week of Lent was published a Catechism which I had much labor in compiling from various others and adding several parts which I considered necessary to be explicitly dwelt upon under the peculiar circumstances of my Diocess [sic]."

The catechism, a copy of which is in the Propaganda Fide archives, Rome,[27] contains thirty-two chapters in addition to four introductory pages of prayers and a five-page Latin section, "The Manner of Serving a Priest at Mass," at the end.

The opening questions are: "Who made the world?" "Who is God?" "Why is God called Creator?" "How many Gods are there?" "Could there be more Gods than one?" "Where is God?" Each question is followed by its answer. The popular catechism of James Butler, bishop of Cashel, opens with "Who made the world?" "Who is God?" "How many Gods are there?" "Where is God?" "Where is heaven?"[28] It is evident from this and a further examination of the text that England relied on the Butler manual, which enjoyed wide popularity in Ireland. However, it is also clear even from this brief examination that he did not limit himself exclusively to that source.

Certain questions and answers stand out as directly related to the circumstances of the United States. For example:

> Q. Am I to consider those persons who are opposed to the true religion, as my neighbors?
> A. Yes, undoubtedly; to punish for voluntary error is the prerogative of God, to show mercy and kindness to his fellow mortals, is the duty of man. *Luke X, 37.* [Lesson XVII, p. 35]

> Q. Am I obliged to love my enemies?
> A. Most certainly. *Love your enemies,* says Christ, *do good to them that hate you, bless them that curse you, and pray for them that persecute and calumniate you.* Luke 6. Matt. 5. [Lesson XXI, p. 45]

> Q. From whom are we to learn the doctrines of Christ?
> A. From the Bishops who have succeeded to the Apostles as the first Christians learned from the Apostles.

> Q. Cannot these Bishops teach us erroneous doctrines instead of truth?
> A. No; we will infallibly receive the doctrine of Christ, from the great body of Bishops, with the Pope at their head. [Lesson XIII, p. 27]

How the catechism was received is difficult to determine. It had its critics from within the Church and from without. Both Jean B. David, coadjutor bishop of Bardstown, and Bishop Henry Conwell of Philadelphia wrote Archbishop Maréchal of Baltimore negative criticisms of it. England sent a copy of his catechism to the Propaganda office in Rome, and no recorded critique of it exists in their files.[29] Nor does the copy in the Propaganda archives bear any editorial markings.

Records indicate that it was carefully read by certain Protestant clergymen. One of them, Rev. Richard Fuller of Beaufort, South Carolina, had his critique of it published in a local newspaper, *The Courier,* in 1838. In his lengthy assessment Fuller cited in full the two questions from Lesson XIII quoted above. England's response exceeded the length of Fuller's letter.[30] The free publicity given to the catechism in that exchange could certainly not have hurt the small manual's dissemination and sales.

An advertisement for the catechism appeared in the *U.S. Catholic Miscellany* six times in 1822. It read: *"The Catechism of the Roman Catholic Faith* published by the Right Reverend Dr. England, price 18¾ cents; and printed copies of Altar Cards, elegantly executed, at 50 cents each may be had at the office of the Catholic Miscellany in this city."[31]

In 1873, thirty-one years after England's death, a revised edition of the catechism was published. It was faithful to the original with but a few exceptions. For example, on page 29 the following three questions appear:

> Q. Is the Pope infallible without the Bishops?
> A. Yes; when he teaches "Ex-Cathedra."
>
> Q. What means Ex-Cathedra?
> A. It means when the Pope as head of the Church defines any doctrine pertaining to faith or morals.
>
> Q. How can we be certain of that?
> A. Because Christ promised that the *Gates of Hell* (that is error) *should never prevail against that Church* which he founded upon St. Peter; *Matt.* xvi.; because Christ said to Peter: *"I had prayed for thee, that thy faith fail not, and thou being once converted confirm thy brethren."* *Luke* xxiii. Because Christ *promised to his Apostles the Spirit of Truth, John* xv., *who should teach them all truth. John* xvi. That also in their teachings he would himself *remain with them always to the consummation of the world. Matt.* xxviii.[32]

The English Missal

In some ways the most creative action taken by England was his publication of the English missal. After all, catechisms at that time were the accepted means for imparting doctrinal truths. Book clubs, too, were not as revolutionary as they seem when one considers their prevalence for other subject areas. Even the first Catholic weekly newspaper had its forerunners. But a missal in the vernacular was almost unknown in the U.S. Catholic world. The fact that it was *not* among Mazzetti's recommendations illustrates the inventiveness and seriousness with which England addressed the problem of catechizing his diocese. On his own, England was fully capable of perceiving the needs of the people and responding to them. The missal, too, roused the greatest stir among the bishop's peers.

In the preface to this work, England stated the purpose of his translation of the Roman Missal.

The object of the present publication is to instruct the members of the Roman Catholic Church on the nature of the most solemn act of their religion. The Council of Trent lays a solemn injunction upon pastors frequently to explain to the people the nature of the Holy Sacrifice of the Mass. To discharge his duty of obeying those distinct directions of Christ and His Church, in the best manner he could, was the intention of the editor of this work.[33]

The preface was followed by a lengthy section, "Explanation of the Mass," which included a summary of the rubrics, a detailed account of the Holy Sacrifice, its various ceremonies, prayers, vestments, language. England endeavored to make it a thorough yet clear account of the eucharistic liturgy. He pointed out that "the Mass is not a common prayer, but an *act of sacrifice* in which by the ministry of the priest, God does acts beneficial to people. The benefit to the people is derived not merely from the words said, but from the acts done."[34] The bishop justified the use of the Latin language, explained the rites, and proceeded to illustrate that all cultures and nations share a common and unifying experience in the celebration of the Lord's Supper. Catholic doctrine, he insisted, is not merely the doctrine of an isolated people, but of many peoples who share the same faith and meet at the same table.[35]

England's fellow bishops, both his metropolitan, Maréchal, in Baltimore and those in other sees, criticized him for publishing the missal which first appeared in New York in 1822.[36] At the outset Maréchal had refused to approve the project, maintaining that such approval should come from Rome. After all, England had published it at a time when translations of the missal into the vernacular were forbidden. What neither Rome nor his ecclesiastical peers seemed to realize was that he "had merely reprinted the Missal in use for many years in England and Ireland."[37] It was not an arbitrarily free translation but one already well known and approved. Ireland's Dr. Patrick Curtis, archbishop of Armagh, verified that to both Maréchal and Ercole Cardinal Consalvi, secretary of state under Pope Pius VII.[38] The preface and explanatory sections which enhanced the volume were England's own valuable and personal contributions.

England had written to Maréchal endeavoring to allay any fears the archbishop of Baltimore might have harbored about the content or the orthodoxy of the missal. Following a gentle reminder of his, England's, futile efforts to consult with his fellow bishops in council, he explained that

not having that opportunity I was thrown to act altogether upon my own judgment. Of course I can make *No Changes* in the liturgy — except having Archbishop Carroll's excellent form of prayer for the President . . . prefixed to the book, instead of the prayer for the king which is in the English edition, and on omitting several special Masses of particular feasts in

Ireland and England which are quite useless here I cannot
meddle with the Missal.[39]

In the whole missal affair the Charleston prelate felt keenly the
jealous, secret, and not-so-secret opposition of his peers, and he wrote to
Cardinal Fontana in the Sacred Congregation that if it would ease things
he would willingly resign his see.[40] That offer was not accepted.

In fact, the missal enjoyed wide sales and popularity. A second edition
was published in 1843, twenty-one years after the first edition and one year
after England's death.[41] A third edition (described by some as the "first
revised edition") came out in 1861. That volume offered some brief additions, but "the fine explanation of the Mass was entirely omitted."[42]

The U.S. Catholic Miscellany

"Bishop England was a born journalist," according to Peter
Guilday.[43] He had entered this country with five years of successful editorial experience with the *Cork Mercantile Chronicle* in his native land.
He knew the power and potential of the press, which stood him in good
stead when he was faced with a largely uninformed and outnumbered
Catholic population in his new diocese. Armed with such a background,
England considered that one means of countering that ignorance and
providing bases and explanations of Catholic doctrine was through a
regularly published newspaper. Other church groups had their own
presses and through them kept their people informed. Such publications
also served to nurture existing anti-Catholic prejudices.

England, aware of the value of a regular periodical, intended to use
it to the Church's best advantage. His ideal was "to establish a purely
Catholic journal"[44] devoted to teaching Catholic doctrine and to por-
traying Catholic history in its true light. Anti-Catholic articles appeared
in the secular journals as well as in the denominational ones. Catholics
knew themselves voiceless and at the mercy of a hostile public. The
bishop perceived that a weekly newspaper could contribute to Catholics'
increased faith and confidence and even pride in their commitment.
According to Guilday:

> Bishop England found the Catholic body in the United
> States without any means of defense. He taught both clergy
> and people in the pages of the *Miscellany* the inestimable privi-
> leges of their Catholic Faith and of their American citizenship.
> He inspired them to protect and defend both the one and the
> other with a fearless advocacy of the truth and with a courage
> that never faltered before any danger or opposition. The
> *Miscellany* would alone be a noble monument to his wide-
> spread fame as an orator, a divine, a patriot and a scholar.[45]

The *Miscellany* published its first issue on June 5, 1822. It was the beginning of a healthy tradition of Catholic newspapers in the United States. England's weekly exerted an enormous influence on Catholic thought in the early nineteenth century. It was not smooth sailing, however; the periodical ran into financial difficulties and publication was suspended after the December 25, 1822, issue. One year later, January 7, 1824, it resumed its regular appearance, but unfortunately it was forced to suspend publication again on December 20, 1824, because of subscribers' failure to pay for their subscriptions. On July 22, 1826, the *Miscellany* resumed publication again, and this time it appeared regularly until Civil War days. By then it had earned the reputation of being the leading Catholic weekly in the country.

The catechesial worth of the Catholic press, with special focus on weekly newspaper and journals, for the formation and maintenance of Catholic thought, life, and growth deserves its own study. The record of the *U.S. Catholic Miscellany* as the earliest weekly supplies a model and supports the thesis that such periodicals have a clear catechesial value to the Church.

In face of the evidence there can be little doubt about John England's pastoral concern for the people whom he served. He made every effort to provide them with assistance in comprehending Christian doctrine and values and in discovering intellectually, experientially, and affectively what it meant to be a Catholic Christian. He was a master of the pen and an artist in oral expression and exchange. His diary (*Diurnal*) records numerous one-to-one conversations and catechizing events with people in cities as well as outlying districts. He was not remote from the people. Leafing through his diary randomly will illustrate that:

> 1821 — *January 22.* Heard Confessions, celebrated the holy Mass, and gave Communion to seven persons, also gave an exhortation . . .
> *February 1.* Celebrated the holy Mass, preached and heard confessions. Catechised the children . . . In the evening instructed and heard confessions.
> *February 2.* . . . In the evening instructed and heard confessions.
> *February 4.* . . . I then conversed with some persons who sought explanations . . . I then instructed and baptized Mr. Lewis R. Beamon, who requested Baptism in consequence of the sermon this day.
> *March 2nd.* Preached my second lecture on the nature and necessity of Religion, etc. On this and subsequent days I was principally occupied in writing a Pastoral Letter on the observance of Lent, etc., an English Catechism, etc., and in giving private instructions to a number of uninformed persons.

> *May 26.* Celebrated Mass . . . Afterwards . . . gave instruction to several who wished for Confirmation, and had a long conversation on some points of faith with a respectable man who had been in early life a Roman Catholic, but had serious doubts on some points, upon which he became satisfied and went to Confession. Heard Confessions and preached in the evening.
>
> *July 19.* Celebrated Mass in my rooms, gave a short instruction and heard confessions of the family, and preached again at night . . . to preach near Salisbury.[46]

Subsequent pages through 1823 carry numerous diary entries similar and almost identical to these.[47]

England was an intellectual with a quick and penetrating mind. One writer called him "Our American Bossuet."[48] He perceived the whole of a situation with alacrity and turned immediately to possible solutions or means of improving things. For this reason he was sometimes considered overbearing and autocratic. However, he could be and was humble. He was far more concerned with truth and justice than with his own self-importance. Nowhere does this stand out better than in his response to those who criticized him. When he found himself in error, he admitted it and corrected himself.

Jean B. David, coadjutor bishop of Bardstown, had found a "theological inaccuracy" in England's definition of faith in the constitution. England acknowledged the mistake publicly in the *Miscellany*. He amended the sentence "Faith is the sincere disposition to believe all that God has taught" to read: "Faith is the belief upon the authority of God, of all those matters which he hath revealed to us, even though they should be above or beyond the comprehension of our reason."[49] Under criticism for the orthodoxy of some of his statements in the "Explanation . . ." in his missal, England had written that "he was under the impression that its doctrine was perfectly correct, but if in anything he had deviated from the form of sound words held by the Holy Roman Catholic and Apostolic Church, he was anxious immediately to correct it."[50]

One may justifiably assume that David's correction of England's inadequate description of faith was *not* an unalloyed zeal for accuracy. In David's eyes, as in those of his French clerical compatriots, England was one of the "offensive" and "aggressive" Irish bishops and clergy. It appears that the animosity, far from being mutual, was more on the side of the French than on that of the Irish. Nevertheless, David and England had some ideals and practices in common. In the history of the catechetical apostolate of the U.S. Church, David, like England, had an effective role to play.

JOHN BAPTIST DAVID AND CATECHESIS

John Baptist David (1761–1841), a "rotund, good-natured Breton whose learning was equalled by his piety," according to Charles Herbermann,[51] was a Sulpician who came to the United States in the French exodus of 1791. He was a close friend and confidant of Benedict Joseph Flaget, the bishop of Bardstown, and the last thirty-one years of his life (1810–1841) were spent in close collaboration with Flaget in Kentucky's heartland. They made a good team, complementing each other's assets and gifts. Flaget adapted to the pioneer culture and circumstances of the missionary setting. David, essentially the professor and prayerful intellectual, maintained a stance of the old world, transplanted but not transformed.

Both men were deeply concerned about the deplorable ignorance of the rising generation and the need for native clergy. The obvious solutions to these problems were schools and a seminary. The seminary came first. An adequate but makeshift structure opened in 1811.[52] David administered it and taught there. His days were filled with teaching catechism, hearing confessions, giving instruction and celebrating Mass, as well as supervising the work and studies of the seminarians. Meanwhile the applicants to the seminary increased and the demands for more space were responded to by the Thomas Howards, a generous Catholic family who gave property and a larger edifice.[53]

Schools for others, especially girls who had no educational opportunities offered to them, raised other questions and problems. Staffing such institutions was the primary question. The image of Mother Seton's institution was clear in their minds, especially so for David, who had been involved as superior in the spiritual and temporal matters of the Emmitsburg foundation for a short time before he went to Bardstown in 1811.

In 1812 David began directing two young women who wished to dedicate their lives to God. Others joined them, and with six members in June 1813 they officially started their community under the title, the Sisters of Charity.[54] Sometime later the community moved to Nazareth, Kentucky; hence the sisters today are called the "Sisters of Charity of Nazareth." David is considered the founder of this community which grew and spread, undertaking the staffing of schools and hospitals.

David was named Flaget's coadjutor and consecrated August 15, 1819. A tireless worker, his zeal was almost unlimited. A Sulpician to the end, his primary love was the seminary; but related to it was his pastoral dedication in other areas. He wrote and published a number of articles, a Catholic hymn book, and two catechisms. The latter were used in Kentucky and surrounding areas for over 100 years.[55] Both appeared in a single volume in 1825, the first for "Younger Children and Persons of Inferior Capacity" and the second for children preparing for their first communion. Later the two were published independently of each other, but in the first edition the combined catechisms numbered 182 pages, including a final page of fifteen "Errata" and twelve introductory pages, set apart by Roman numerals, making a total of 194 pages.

This *Catechism of the Diocess* [sic] *of Bardstown*[56] was specifically designated as "the only one taught in our Diocess [sic]" (p. iv). That statement was contained in the three-page explanatory letter signed by "Benedict Joseph" under the date November 9, 1825, and bearing the diocesan seal. Of significance is the fact that David's name does not appear in the 1825 manual though he is identified as its author in subsequent editions and in 1826[57] correspondence about the catechism.

The catechism of Robert Bellarmine is the principal model for David's work. The initial questions are identical to those of the Italian Jesuit's manual, but David's is not an exact replica of that sixteenth-century book. David prefaced his catechism with six pages of prayers and hymns to be used before catechism class. Then the "First Catechism" of fifteen short lessons follows. On page 18 the "Second Catechism" begins. In four sections, it occupies the major part of the volume. The sections are entitled: (I) An Introduction to Christian Doctrine and the Mysteries of Faith (including the creed), pp. 17–39; (II) Of Grace and Means of Grace (includes sacraments), pp. 40–77; (III) On the Commandments, pp. 78–104; (IV) The Principal Feasts and Solemnities of the Year, pp. 105–154. These are followed by a twenty-two-page section (pp. 155–177) of prayers for special occasions and the "Table of Contents." It becomes clear that the aspirants for first communion were not seven-year-olds as they are today.

No doubt the spiritual intensity of David's personality had much to do with the manual's early success, but its use went beyond his lifetime. It was revised in 1853 by a Kentucky priest, Charles Boeswalt.[58] After the definition of the Immaculate Conception in 1854 it was reedited. Raymond J. O'Brien writing in 1934 testified to the continuous use of David's catechism at that date.[59]

AMBROSE MARÉCHAL

John England and Ambrose Maréchal (1764–1828) had more things in common than either of them realized or could have realized under the circumstances of their own times. Both were highly gifted with intellectual prowess, were well-read, were excellent conversationalists, and had different but winning personalities. They both foresaw a strong, native clergy as essential to the Church's life and growth in this country. Individually they recognized also the potential that the U.S. held for the Church. Both were pastorally sensitive and zealous. Because each was defensive about his respective nationality, allegiance, commitments, and points of view, they remained in a stalemated relationship from the time of England's appointment to Charleston until the archbishop died on January 29, 1828.

Maréchal, Baltimore's third archbishop, was a French Sulpician who had fled twice from France. With Gabriel Richard and Francis Ciquard, fellow members of the Society of St. Sulpice, he arrived in the United States for the first time after having been compelled by the events of the French Revolution to flee from his native land on the very day of his ordination, March 25, 1791. After a circuitous and lengthy odyssey, the trio arrived in Baltimore and Maréchal officiated at the eucharistic celebration for the first time, on June 24, 1792.

John Carroll assigned Maréchal to the missions in southern and eastern Maryland where he served for seven years. In 1797 he began a two-year teaching stint as a theology professor at St. Mary's Seminary in Baltimore. Then he taught philosophy at Georgetown College in Washington, 1801–1802. Recalled to France by the superior general of the Sulpicians, Jacques André Emery, Maréchal returned to Paris in 1803 and was immediately sent to teach at the diocesan seminary of Saint Flour. Subsequently he taught in the seminaries of Lyons, Aix, and Marseilles. When the Sulpicians were again expelled from France (1812), Maréchal came back to the United States and to the theology faculty at St. Mary's Seminary. For a brief time he served as president of St. Mary's College. Throughout Maréchal held firmly to Sulpician ideals and principles. His objective in working with the seminarians was ultimately to assist in building up the Church as a whole. Thus he felt that his teaching and directing in the seminary was a key component in contributing to the Church's vitality.

So essential did he consider his educational apostolate that when recommended to the see of New York, Maréchal declined, despite the fact that the Americans bishops of 1814 nominated him unanimously.[60] Sometime later he also declined the nomination for the see of Philadelphia. In so doing he was acting in the best Sulpician tradition, for members of the Society of St. Sulpice promised, on entering the society, to avoid ecclesiastical dignities. They did not make positive vows to refuse the episcopacy, but they did pledge themselves to shun elevation to ecclesiastical positions, specifically bishoprics.[61] History records the members' reluctance and even distaste for these positions, yet circumstances and higher obedience influenced certain ones to respond affirmatively. Bishops Flaget and David were two such exceptions. Ultimately Maréchal, too, was persuaded.

In 1817 Archbishop Leonard Neale, in failing health, asked Rome for a coadjutor to assist him in the archdiocese of Baltimore. He proposed Maréchal. On July 4, 1817, the bull designating him as coadjutor, with right of succession, was signed in Rome. It reached the bishop-elect on November 10 of that year. Neale had died on June 13, 1817, so Maréchal was immediately consecrated and took charge of the archdiocese without delay.

The pastoral ideas he had practiced, fostered, and promulgated served him well. These were in the best Sulpician tradition and included catechesis, which, according to Félix Dupanloup, "is our great duty."[62] Catechesis both by specific instruction and by emulation of dedicated Christians, especially the clergy, was considered integral to the pastoral ideal of Jean Jacques Olier,[63] founder of the society. In light of that it comes as no surprise that Ambrose Maréchal, like Flaget and David before him, sanctioned a catechism which carried his expressed approval. It appeared about 1826.

The sixty-three-page volume entitled *A Short Catechism for Use of the Catholics in the United States of America*, "with the approbation of Most Rev. Ambrose Maréchal," was published in Baltimore.[64]

The copy available to this writer[65] is a very small (2¾" x 4¼"), tightly packed volume with seven chapters in between "Daily Exercises" — prayers for many occasions — and a selection of hymns at the end. Chapter by chapter it is identical to the "Carroll Catechism." Thus Maréchal knew himself to be in an acceptable tradition when he reedited the popular work of this country's first Catholic bishop.

A TALE OF TWO CATECHISMS

In the spring or early summer of 1821 a thirty-four-page catechism of Christian doctrine appeared in Philadelphia. The title page read:

The Most Rev. Dr. James Butler's Catechism
Revised and Corrected by the Rev. William Hogan
Pastor of St. Mary's Church
Philadelphia
1821[66]

Six years later (1827) another catechism was published in the same city. Its full descriptive title read:

A Catechism of Christian Doctrine
Wherein the Principles of the Roman Catholic Religion
are Briefly Explained
With Morning and Evening prayers
by the Right Reverend
Doctor Henry Conwell
Bishop of Philadelphia[67]

Together the two brief volumes number less than one hundred pages. Combined or separate, they admit one to the turbulent and unfortunate events of Philadelphia's early history as a diocese. That history is closely associated with the two authors of the respective catechisms, William Hogan and Henry Conwell.

Hogan was the first to appear in Philadelphia, having arrived in the summer of 1820. He was a thirty-two-year-old Irish priest from Limerick who followed his cousin George Hogan to the United States. George was ordained in Baltimore by Archbishop Maréchal on March 21, 1820. When Maréchal did not encourage William to locate in the same diocese as George, William moved to Philadelphia where Louis deBarth was serving as administrator of the diocese until a new bishop would arrive. DeBarth accepted Hogan conditionally. He soon realized that even conditional acceptance was an error as Hogan assumed an imperialistic stance almost immediately.

Hogan had been leaning toward an autocratic, self-defined type of Christianity for some time. Unbeknownst to many, he had been under censure in Limerick and had come to the U.S. without his bishop's exeat.[68] When he reached Philadelphia, where trusteeism had developed in the long absence of episcopal authority, he ingratiated himself with the lay trustees, filling the role of clerical leader among them. He obviously possessed certain qualities of personal magnetism which contributed to his acceptance and success in their company.

Very quickly he became identified with the trustees of St. Mary's Church. After Bishop Conwell was installed Hogan belittled the new prelate, ridiculing him for his simplicity and slight hesitation of speech.[69] At a public meeting sometime later he insisted that St. Mary's Church was the property of the laity and only they could determine matters regarding its use. Furthermore, according to Hogan, the clergy were subject to the laity for their election and support as pastors.

Meanwhile Hogan edited a thirty-four-page catechism to affirm his own leadership position and to satisfy his "loyal" trustees. The work also emanated from a zeal to catechize children, with whom he had a good rapport. Justifying his publication, Hogan explained: "I have examined with some degree of attention the various Catholic Catechisms published in this country for the instruction of youth and observing the prolixity of the answers on some, and the extreme conciseness of others have judged it best to republish the Catechism of Rev. Dr. Butler for their instruction. William Hogan."[70]

Like John England, Hogan based his catechism on the manual most familiar to him from his youthful days in Ireland, the work of Dr. James Butler, bishop of Cashel. Unlike England, he "revised and corrected" the manual. Hogan would have been more accurate had he described his volume as an abridgment of Butler's. The 1807 Butler edition, available at the time, counted 410 questions and answers in its thirty-nine chapters. Hogan reduced that content to thirty chapters with 392 questions and answers. His critics justifiably faulted him for deleting the chapters on confession and indulgences. They questioned his orthodoxy, too, in his statement regarding perfect contrition.[71] A comparison with the "Butler General" (1807) indicates the difference between the two on that question:

> Butler: Lesson XV — p. 29
>
> Q. Will perfect contrition reconcile us to God?
> A. It will; and it is the only means we have to regain God's friendship, when we cannot go to confession.
>
> Hogan: Lesson XII — p. 14
>
> Q. Will perfect contrition reconcile us to God without confession?
> A. Yes; and it is the only means we have to recover God's friendship.

In a letter to Maréchal dated June 15, 1821, Conwell rejected the Hogan catechism, forbidding the faithful to purchase or possess copies of it.[72]

Hogan was repeatedly admonished, agreed to amend, and subsequently reversed himself. At one point John England intervened, hoping that he could better control the strong-willed clergyman.[73] Hogan agreed to join the Charleston diocese but shortly thereafter changed his mind. Meanwhile he continued to exert great influence on a widening number of St. Mary's parishioners and their friends. Finally Pope Pius VII intervened and suspended him on August 24, 1822.[74] Hogan contested the authenticity of the document presented to him but eventually accepted the suspension and moved out of the area.[75] When he left, Philadelphia was in a state of turmoil with a bishop who was not Hogan's equal in wit, eloquence, or cunning but superior to him in fidelity, loyalty, and guilelessness.

Henry Conwell arrived in Philadelphia on December 2, 1820, about four months after Hogan had "moved in." A gentle and zealous man from County Derry, Ireland, he was unprepared for the intrigue, open rebellion, scandal, and schismatic events awaiting him. Born in 1745, Conwell was seventy-five years old, a parish priest loved and supported

by both his parishioners and the clergy of the diocese which he left. He
came to a situation foreign by virtue of geography, culture, and excessive
strife. His advanced age is often blamed for his inability to handle the turbulent diocesan situation which he inherited. In fact, he was a man of no
small abilities. Among the clergy in his native country he was recognized as
a classical Latinist and a Greek scholar who spoke French fluently and
Spanish and Italian with little difficulty. He had a solid knowledge of
moral and dogmatic theology and persistently studied canon law on his
own.[76] Unfortunately he was not a fluent orator in his native language,
and it was this that Hogan targeted on their first encounter.

On Sunday, December 3, 1820, the diocese celebrated Mass at St.
Mary's with the new bishop. William Hogan was homilist for the occasion. He used the opportunity to attack Father deBarth, who was seated
in the sanctuary, severely and viciously. He derided him for his poor
management of the diocese. One week later in the same setting he turned
on the new bishop, insulting him, ridiculing his hesitancy of speech, and
challenging his authority in parish affairs. Conwell was stunned. Two
days later (December 12) at a gathering of the clergy of the diocese Conwell publicly withdrew Hogan's faculties. That incident served as a kind
of declaration of war between the two. In the long run the people of the
diocese were both the subjects and victims of that conflict.

Conwell assumed a mildly strong stance with regard to pastoral duties
and diocesan practices. He was a man of prayer, accustomed to serving the
faithful in their ordinary lives and needs. But Hogan and his enthusiastic
followers were ever an obstacle and annoyance, making difficulties and
complications a way of life for the prelate. Even after Hogan left the
diocese Conwell could not gain full control. The conditions of everyday living, the form of national government, the character of the Church in this
new world, especially the trustee problem, all were foreign to what he knew
so well on the other side of the Atlantic. But he did not give up.

Conwell concentrated on spiritual and religious matters, among
them the importance of catechizing the young. In 1827 he published his
catechism to assist in that ministry. It was a fifty-four-page manual including 267 questions and answers and twenty-two pages of prayers and
other information.

There was an originality about his catechism which made it different
from any of the manuals in circulation at the time. This can be perceived
in part from the initial questions and answers:

Q. Who created and placed you in the world?
A. God.

Q. Why did God create you?
A. To know him, love him, and serve him and by these
means to gain everlasting life.

Q. What is necessary to be done for that end?
A. Four things.

Q. Which is the first?
A. It is to believe firmly whatever God has revealed and declared to us by his church, as articles of faith.

Q. What is the second?
A. To keep the commandments of God and of the church.

Q. What is the third?
A. To receive the sacraments with the requisite dispositions.

Q. What is the fourth?
A. To put our whole trust in God, and to have recourse to him frequently by prayer.[77]

The catechism went through two editions within a year of its appearance. There is no explanation for this in the available records, but it may be attributable to the exhaustion of the first edition. The passages criticized in the first edition were unchanged in the second, which leads one to label that appearance of the manual a "second printing" rather than a new edition.

The reception of Conwell's catechism by his peers was considerably less than enthusiastic. England wrote a critique of it in a letter to Maréchal dated February 12, 1827.

I have just now lying before me a publication purporting to be a "catechism of the Christian doctrine, wherein the principles of the Roman Catholic religion are briefly explained, etc. by the Right Rev. Doctor Henry Conwell, Bishop of Philadelphia." On page 29, Lesson IV *of the Eucharist* is the following question "Q. Is there anything else in the Eucharist, besides the body and blood, the soul and divinity of Christ?" To which the answer is "A. Yes the father and the Holy Ghost are present there also." Another question "Q. How comes it that the father and the Holy Ghost are there?" To which the answer is "Because they are indispensable from the divinity of Christ." May I request you to inform me whether those questions and answers are a portion of the doctrine of the Roman Catholic Church. I do not make the inquiry, I trust, in any spirit but that which becomes my place and my order. I do not make it of Doctor Conwell lest it might appear to owe its origin to a feeling which I trust I do not indulge. I have no hesitation in stating that in the catechism are many passages which I consider to be at least injudicious. But so long as the deposit of Faith is preserved, I do not consider it to be my duty to remark upon what under other circumstances, I should not approve. I greatly doubt the orthodoxy of the assertion "the father and the Holy Ghost are present in the Eucharist." Should you think the expression correct or compatible with truth, you will oblige me by stating upon what ground you rest your opinion.[78]

Another specific critique of the manual appears in correspondence held in the Propaganda Fide archives. The criticism is picayune, pointing to an error in the chronological listing of the popes.[79] Pope Boniface VII is cited as succeeding Celestine V on page 40. It should have been "Boniface VIII," an obvious printing error.

Maréchal, too, disapproved of the Conwell manual and expressed that disapproval in a letter to Propaganda Fide dated October 1, 1827. However, he also stated his disapproval of the Flaget (David) and England catechisms in the same correspondence.[80]

One prelate, far removed from the U.S. church, found no objection to the work. This was Bishop William Poynter, vicar apostolic of the London District, whom Fr. Frederick Rese visited and to whom he presented Conwell's catechism. Rese was vicar general of Cincinnati at the time. He reported that Poynter examined the catechism, "approved it but . . . will give his approbation only after Rome asks his opinion."[81] Rese added that he had discovered that Poynter's views were highly respected in Rome and that he was recognized as a great authority there. In a later letter, several months after Poynter's death (November 26, 1827), Rese reiterated Poynter's assessment, adding that the Sacred Congregation will give "the approbation only when your Lordship will be here in person. The Holy Father and the Sacred Congregation have always the greatest esteem and the highest regard for your Lordship, as for a persecuted Bishop, and wish to see you here."[82]

Meanwhile the trustees continued to antagonize Conwell. Rome had been called on three times to intervene and settle disputes. On March 8, 1828, Propaganda Fide notified Conwell that the sovereign pontiff, Leo XII, requested his coming to Rome. The aged bishop reluctantly left Philadelphia on the eleventh of July. His administration of the diocese was virtually over. Though he returned, contrary to the Vatican's orders, he did not resume the government of the diocese. In 1830 Francis Patrick Kenrick was appointed coadjutor and administrator of the diocese. Conwell accepted the situation but it took some time before he completely resigned himself to it. In his declining years, despite a loss of sight and the inconvenience of advanced age, he regained some of his cheerful and gentle disposition. After a brief illness he died on April 22, 1843, at the age of ninety-seven.

Conwell and Hogan, their two catechisms, and the period in which they lived called attention to a critical time in U.S. church history when the incipient Church sought to identify itself with the positive features of a young government without sacrificing its own essential characteristics. Because Philadelphia endured the intensity and continuance of the crisis, it served as a kind of microcosm of conditions that characterized the

Church in the United States in the first half of the nineteenth century. Largely because of the schism, Philadelphia, at the beginning of the fourth decade of the nineteenth century, had no seminary, not enough priests (and some of the ones serving were vagrant or unstable), no college, no academy for girls, only a few schools, and, according to John G. Shea, a "disheartened people."[83] In other words, it lacked the centers where the formal catechesis of the era would normally have been carried on. Both Hogan and Conwell were sensitive to that situation. The tale of their two catechism provides a close-in look at the total and tragic reality.

Chronologically one must refer here to the apostolate of Joseph Rosati (1789–1843), first bishop of St. Louis. A Neapolitan Vincentian who accepted the invitation and challenge to come to the United States to assist Bishop William Louis DuBourg, he learned English and taught theology in Bardstown and then went to Perryville, Missouri (1818), to participate in the establishment of St. Mary's Seminary there. Despite multiple academic and Vincentian community duties he served numerous missions in Missouri. In 1824 he was consecrated coadjutor bishop of Louisiana and placed in charge of the northern part of the Louisiana Territory. Three years later (1827) he was named bishop of St. Louis, retaining responsibility for New Orleans as administrator apostolic. His zeal seemed endless as he continued to serve the faithful in the Mississippi Valley and beyond. At some time during that period he commissioned the writing of a catechism for the Louisiana Territory, *Catéchisme de la Louisiane.*[84]

Episcopal Catechesis among American Indians

In this period two individual missionary bishops stand out for their dedication to American Indians. They are Frederic Baraga (1797–1898), first bishop of Marquette (Michigan), and Francis Norbert Blanchet (1795–1883), first bishop of Oregon City.

At the age of forty-three and having been ordained for seven years, Frederic Baraga responded to a deeply felt call to serve the Indian people in the United States. He volunteered for the diocese of Cincinnati and was accepted.[85] He made arrangements to leave the small parish in Metlika, Slovenia, near the Croatian border, where he was curate, and began the long journey to his new mission in the western hemisphere. After a month-long voyage he reached New York, December 31, 1830. Following a brief introduction to this new land via New York, Philadelphia, and Baltimore, he arrived in Cincinnati on January 18, 1831. At the time the Cincinnati diocese included the state of Ohio and the territories of Michigan and the vast Northwest, an area equivalent to ten dioceses in modern times. Someone assessed it as being greater than that of the whole of France.[86]

Bishop Edward Fenwick, Cincinnati's first bishop, welcomed Baraga warmly. He perceived the sincerity and earnestness of the newcomer and was delighted at his impatience to begin his missionary apostolate with the Indians. Because the intensity of the January weather prevented northward travel into the location Fenwick had selected, Baraga busied himself in pastoral work in the area. In addition he polished up his English and began studying the language of the Ottawa Indians while temporarily residing in the seminary. An eighteen-year-old full-blooded Ottawa seminarian, William Maccatebinessi,[87] son of the chief, was his tutor. Baraga's natural gift for languages was of immense assistance to him. He was proficient in Slovene (his native tongue), German, Latin, French, English, and Italian. That foundation enabled him to acquire a fluidity in the Indian languages more readily than most people did.

As the spring thaws came, the prospects of going to northern Michigan brightened. Soon Baraga and Fenwick were en route to Arbre Croche (Crooked Tree), where the bishop had assigned the new missionary. On the way they stopped in Detroit, where Baraga met the "hero of Michigan," Gabriel Richard, the Sulpician priest who had pioneered the southern Michigan area since 1798. Richard was to be Baraga's immediate superior in that region. The travelers reached their destination on May 28. For two years Baraga would call this small Indian village home.

Baraga's assignment to Arbre Croche lasted twenty-eight months. During that time he mastered the Ottawa tongue, won the friendship and confidence of the tribespeople, and added 481 individuals to the Catholic population. Subsequently he was moved to Grand River (Grand River Rapids) in 1833 and from there to the Chippewas at La Pointe, Madelein Island, in 1835. In 1843 he established L'Anse mission on Keweenaw Bay and proved himself a far-sighted missionary with the erection of a church building, school, and rectory. More important to him was Christianizing the native Red People in these areas and providing means by which their faith could continue to be nurtured and sustained, an apostolate in which he was tireless and unswervingly committed.

In July 1853 Michigan's Upper Peninsula became a vicariate apostolic with Sault Ste. Marie as the central point. In Cincinnati, on November 1, Baraga was consecrated bishop with the title of vicar apostolic for the area. Four years later the vicariate was elevated to the status of a diocese, and Baraga became its bishop. In 1866 he transferred the see from Sault St. Marie to Marquette. In all his assignments Baraga served people of different nationalities and races. It was not uncommon for him to give three homilies on Sunday, one in German, a second in French, and the third in one of the Indian languages. But throughout all his missionary experiences until his death, he considered himself "essentially an Indian missionary."[88]

In a sense he was a "walking catechesis," foreshadowing what the U.S. bishops were to consider ideal catechesis in their 1979 directory, *Sharing the Light of Faith.* He personified the Christian message, portrayed a challenge and response, raised profound inquiries, and provided answers in his personal life. A man of prayer, he provided others with the model of prayer. He lived what he taught, fostered and developed community. His life was one of unstinting service to all who called on him. He also catechized formally and wrote catechisms.

He had deep respect for the natives and desired to communicate with them on their own level and in their own language. Thus he learned to speak the various tribal tongues and even compiled a *Dictionary of the Ojibway Language*[89] (Ojibway is the Chippewa language). Baraga's first work was a collection of prayers and hymns and included a catechism. It was written first in the language of the Ottawas in 1823 under the title *Anamie-Misinaigan.*[90] Later Baraga translated it into the Chippewa tongue. Combining prayers and a catechism should come as no surprise. Both have worthy roles to play in the nurturing and growth of faith. There was precedent for the combination, too, especially in the works of Peter Canisius and others.

Mindful of the inspiration to be gained from knowing more about Jesus Christ, he wrote *Jesus Obimadisiwin, ajonda aking* (The Life of Our Lord Jesus Christ), first in Ottawa and then in Ojibway for the Chippewa.[91]

Publishing was costly and no funds existed in the coffers of the missions for the publication of books. So Baraga turned to Europe, especially to the Leopoldine Society (Leopoldinen-Stiftung), an Austrian missionary society organized in Vienna in 1828 through the influence of Frederick Rese, who later became the first bishop of Detroit. Baraga went to Europe to solicit funding for the apostolate and to find an editor and publishing firm for his books. On December 8, 1836, he wrote to Rese that "the Council of *La Propagande de la Foi* . . . has unanimously granted me the money to print my two Indian books . . . they voted for 3000 copies instead of 2000 of each" as Baraga had requested.[92] The grant was for printing; no financing for the binding was given at that time.

Baraga's chief difficulty with the catechism occurred in Rome. He had gone with several copies of each work to present to the cardinal prefect. Visiting the latter, Baraga learned that a Sulpician priest, a Father Thavenet, was in Rome. Thavenet had been in Canada for some time before going to Rome and was familiar with certain Indian languages. At the cardinal's recommendation, Baraga submitted his works to the Sulpician for his critique. Thavenet listed several errors he had detected and gave the list to Baraga. However, in his report he observed only "one real error." It was an important one, "in the words he [Baraga] used to express the difficult concept of *Transubstantiation*. Speaking of the Transubstantiation, he says that the Body of Jesus Christ is changed into bread and the Blood is changed into wine."[93]

Thavenet then wrote a corrected text in the Indian language. Maksimilijan Jezernik pointed out that the archival copy of the catechism contains this single correction,[94] despite the fact that Thavenet summed up his assessment, "In a word, I can say that the catechism is very badly done, but also that the missionary could not do otherwise than do it badly."[95] He offered no explanation, but one is led to conclude that language difficulties played a large part in his summary statement. The precision one finds in highly developed languages is often very difficult to translate accurately into primal tongues.

Baraga had welcomed the opportunity to have his catechism critiqued, and he assured Thavenet that he would "hasten to make the corrections."[96] His critic was impressed by the missionary's desire for accuracy and observed that he was greatly "edified by the humility of this answer."[97] Another stroke of good fortune befell the Indian advocate. Propaganda Fide decided to pay for the binding of the books and so informed him before he returned to the United States. Baraga considered his journey to Rome successful on several scores: his books were sanctioned (after correcting the catechism), he was able to get them printed and bound, he procured additional financial aid, and he found four priests to take back with him to his missionary lands.

That Baraga was a catechist-bishop is evident in numerous ways. He loved the people who comprised the Church to which he ministered. He enjoyed being with them; he counted no difficulty or hardship too great to overcome in seeking their company, assisting them, communicating or celebrating with them. At one point he wrote a pastoral letter to the Chippewa in their tongue, the first "official document" ever issued in a language of the Red People.[98] Because of his numerous writings in several Indian languages he is sometimes referred to as "the Father of Indian Literature."[99]

Blanchet and Demers in the Pacific Northwest

Two other good friends of the Indian peoples were the first bishop of Oregon City, Francis Norbert Blanchet (1795–1883), and the first bishop of Vancouver Island, Modeste Demers (1809–1871). The two men worked together in the Oregon missions before they were assigned episcopal roles.[100] In 1838 Demers, a pioneer missionary in the area since 1836, wrote a catechism and dictionary in Chinook, a jargon which, while based on the language of the Chinook tribe, combined English and French words and phrases and was the common tongue for red and white people in that far northwest region. In 1867 Blanchet approved and used the catechism in his own apostolic mission. With the help of L. N. St. Onge he made further corrections and published it again in 1871.[101]

The apostolate among the Indians was both rewarding and frustrating, but Blanchet and Demers were untiring and constant in their devotion to the "savage," as the Red People were called. This writer winces each time she reads or hears the term. Even when it is softened, as in "chers sauvages," it is an unfortunate and inappropriate description of people who in many cases had a high sense of morality among themselves and were ingenious in adapting their lives to the land. They had invented tools to use in their mastery of that land and developed complex watering systems long before white people knew there was such a place as the western hemisphere. Charles Carey cautioned against the random use of "savages": "This term is to be taken in its ethnological sense, for they have many admirable traits and show themselves capable of feeling and conduct which might well put their more fortunate white brethren to shame."[102]

ECCLESTON, BALTIMORE'S FIFTH ARCHBISHOP

Through zealous and tireless apostles such as Blanchet and Demers, the Church grew in the far northwest. Meanwhile the eastern seaboard knew its own kind of zeal and growth. Two years after Blanchet's arrival in Orego, Samuel Eccleston (1801–1851) was named the fifth archbishop of Baltimore. Like the first and second archbishops of Baltimore, John Carroll and Leonard Neale, he was a native Marylander. Unlike any of his predecessors, he was a convert. His parents were Episcopalians; but after his father died, his mother married a Catholic man, a Mr. Stenson, and young Samuel was given a Catholic education. While a student at the Sulpicians' St. Mary's College, Baltimore, he became a Catholic and decided to study for the priesthood. After he was ordained on April 24, 1825, he entered the Society of St. Sulpice and went off to France for further study. Upon his return he went to his alma mater, St. Mary's College, where he served successively as professor, vice-president, and president, an office he held for five years. On September 14, 1834, he was consecrated coadjutor to Archbishop James Whitfield in Baltimore—a position he filled for only one month. Whitfield died October 19 of the same year, and Eccleston succeeded him.

In the best tradition of St. Sulpice, Eccleston emphasized catechesis and, like some of his predecessors, issued a catechism. The ninety-six-page manual with twenty-two chapters was copyrighted in his name in 1839.[103] In 1840 he published a thirty-two-page abridgment, and in 1850, one year before Eccleston died, a new printing of the large manual appeared. Though it was not radically innovative, the work differed slightly from catechisms of the period. Preceded by a section of prayers, it opened with a chapter entitled "God and His Perfections":

> "What is God?"
> "Why do you say God is a pure spirit?"
> "Why do you say God is infinitely perfect?"

The next three chapters briefly cover salvation history, after which the fifth chapter introduces the Apostles' Creed which is succeeded by a chapter on the four last things, and one chapter each on the theological and moral virtues, sin, grace, prayer, the Ten Commandments, the precepts of the Church, and the sacraments. Thus the general sequence of creed, commandments, and sacraments popularized by Bellarmine was retained.

THE "CARROLL CATECHISM" FOR BOSTON

Boston's second bishop, like its first, responded to the catechesial needs of that large diocese by publishing a catechism, in 1843,[104] a ninety-six-page manual which, with several modifications, was a revision of the original "Carroll Catechism." Before the catechism appeared, however, Fenwick had already employed the medium of the printed page.

Benedict Joseph Fenwick (1782–1846) was a "thorough-going American," born and reared in Leonardtown, Maryland. "He was practical, willing to see the humorous aspect of a situation, cautious and playfully sarcastic in the presence of such exuberant enthusiasm as that possessed by his good friend John England."[105] An educated and astute individual, Fenwick was a Jesuit, ordained on March 12, 1808. His first assignment was to parish work in New York City. From there he was sent to serve as president of Georgetown College in Washington. After only one year in that post he was sent to Charleston, South Carolina, to arbitrate and bring peace to the warring factions in that area. He remained after England's arrival, working with the new bishop as vicar general. To England's own sorrow, Fenwick was recalled to the presidency of Georgetown, where he remained until named bishop of the see of Boston in 1825.

The Church in Boston was still in a pioneer state when Fenwick assumed office there.[106] Priests were very few in number; there was no seminary and no sacerdotal "candidates" were standing in the wings. Fenwick visited, instructed, and encouraged the Catholics in the far-flung diocese in the face of their minority status and the scarcity of clergy. Two small communities, representing the oldest Catholic stock of New England, held special interest for him. They were the Penobscot and Passamaquoddy Indian tribes who had been faithful to the Church since the Jesuits converted them many years prior to Fenwick's arrival.[107]

In terms of strengthening and nourishing the faith of Boston Catholics in his oversized diocese, Fenwick was ingenious and tireless. Anti-Catholicism was at least as strong there as elsewhere and necessitated extraordinary attention to being faithful and understanding one's faith. Like his friend and colleague in Charleston, Fenwick did not overlook the value of the press. In less than five years after he moved to Boston he published the first issue of *The Jesuit, or Catholic Sentinel,*[108] a paper which, continued (with name changes and brief interruptions) as the *Pilot,* ranks today as the oldest Catholic paper in the United States.

One year later Fenwick launched a second weekly, *The Expostulator, or Young People's Guide.* Intended to explain the Church's doctrine to children, *The Expostulator* was the first Catholic juvenile newspaper published in this country. It was not long-lived—March 31, 1830, to March 23, 1831—but it was a significant and exemplary venture in catechizing.[109]

His 1843 catechism, *A Short Abridgement of the Christian Doctrine; Newly Revised and Augmented* . . ., Fenwick unequivocally prescribed as "the only edition which I approve of, and the circulation of which I authorize, . . . to which I have affixed my signature and the seal of the Diocese of Boston."[110] Although the initial questions and the overall structure relied on the earlier "Carroll Catechism," Fenwick's manual differed from the former and included additions. The question-and-answer section covered fifty-seven pages.[111] Prayers pertinent to the subject matter were interjected from time to time. For example, in chapter 13, "Of Thanksgiving" (after communion), three prayers of thanksgiving were included. Three pages from Richard Challoner's *Catholic Christian Instructed* followed the last lesson. That, in turn, was followed by a section, "Manner of Serving Mass"—in Latin, of course. After that, from pages 89 to 96, were prayers recommended for "before, during and after Mass." Thus the manual appears to have been more than a catechism for small children and certainly not restricted to classroom use.

FRANCIS PATRICK KENRICK

Philadelphia's third bishop, Francis Patrick Kenrick (1796–1863), directed specific attention to catechisms at least three times during his episcopate (1830–1851). It seems that he agreed in principle with Conwell, his predecessor, that catechesis was of major import and required a catechism for its effectiveness, but his approach differed. For one thing, he did not compose a manual for the diocese, acknowledging at one time that "it is a matter of no ordinary difficulty to write a good Catechism."[112] He did, however, work through diocesan synods which he convoked.

On February 29, 1832, Kenrick notified the Philadelphia clergy that the first diocesan synod would meet on May 13 of that year. "We are informing you," he wrote, "of our counsel and plan that we might enjoy your presence and use your advice, zeal and assistance."[113] Open though he was to suggestions and ideas, it is clear that Kenrick dominated that and subsequent synods during his episcopate. The ninth statute addressed the matter of a catechism to be used in the diocese, decreeing the use of the "Carroll Catechism" until another would be approved by the Holy See.[114] However, in 1834 Kenrick did approve a small (thirty-six-page) *Kleiner Katechismus* for German-speaking Catholics in the diocese.[115] The following year a sixty-four-page German catechism bearing his approbation also appeared.[116]

Kenrick was recognized as a leader and influential thinker by his fellow prelates. He appreciated and upheld the insights of Charleston's forward-looking John England. He served as reconciler and consultant to others on a number of occasions. Eccleston, for example, sought his counsel on the catechism proposed by the bishops at the 1837 Provincial Council of Baltimore. Not finding that catechism worthy of commendation, he wrote his critique of it:

> I have hastily marked some of the verbal imperfections of the new Catechism, as they presented themselves to me in the first part. You may find the criticisms morose and unjust, but in a spirit of candor I venture to submit them for consideration. I think it would be well to defer the edition for the Council, and to let the Prelates at their leisure prepare the amendments. It is a matter of no ordinary difficulty to write a good Catechism. The introduction of the present Catechism before its final adoption would be attended with some inconvenience, should amendments take place in a second edition, so that I should prefer leaving my proportion of the cost of this edition without claiming any of the copies.[117]

In Philadelphia's second diocesan synod (1842), ten years after the first one, the question of an appropriate catechism rose again. In the procrastinating malaise of reaching some kind of agreement upon a catechism for use in the United States Church, Kenrick proposed the adoption of the Irish catechism by James Butler for English-speaking Catholics of his diocese. He also proposed the 1836 version of a catechism of Peter Canisius which the diocese of Cincinnati had adopted for German-speaking Catholics.[118] Of special interest is the fact that, although the Butler manual was a popular one in this country, its adoption by the Philadelphia diocese was the first time it was officially accepted by a U.S. diocese.[119]

Kenrick was named archbishop of Baltimore in 1851 and spent the remaining years of his life in that primatial see. He left the diocese of Philadelphia in a healthy state of growth and self-confidence. His Philadelphia experience proved a good preparation for him. He presided over the First Plenary Council of Baltimore (1852) and kept a vigilant and well-informed eye on the life of the Church in his large archdiocese and beyond. Kenrick was a man of courage, keen perception, foresight, and deep faith. He was sensitive to social, political, and religious issues facing the Church in this country and acted accordingly.

After his death in 1863 there was serious consideration given to promoting his cause for canonization. However, a greater move emerged a few years later to foster the cause of his successor in Philadelphia, John Neumann. That cause gained wider and steadier acclaim, and Kenrick's receded.

Kenrick and Neumann shared many ideals. Both were pastoral bishops, gifted intellectually and tireless in their dedication to the apostolate. They differed in origins, personalities, and manners of approaching situations. Kenrick was born and reared in Ireland; Neumann was born and reared in Bohemia.

BLESSED JOHN NEUMANN

John Nepomucene Neumann (1811–1860), Philadelphia's fourth bishop, came to the United States in 1836 after completing his seminary studies in Bohemia. One year later he was ordained for the diocese of New York, where he served in the Buffalo and Rochester areas. Responding to a repeated attraction to religious life, he sought admission to the Redemptorists, and on January 16, 1842, he pronounced vows, thereby becoming the first Redemptorist professed in America.

Neumann's involvement in catechesis was long-lasting and outstanding. While in the seminary, concomitant with his regular course work he began an independent study of the works of Peter Canisius, especially that Jesuit's first major catechesial volume, the *Summa Doctrinae Christianae*. In addition, he studied the Council of Trent and Robert Bellarmine's catechisms along with the works of Augustine and Gregory the Great. He was especially influenced, too, by his professor in pedagogy and catechetics, Dr. Francis Czeschik, who introduced him to the concept of methodology. In these circumstances he developed a special aptitude for presenting the truths of the faith to children in ways that could be understood by them.

This preparation played its role in shaping his pastoral outlook and ministry. One biographer maintained that "by nature he was especially endowed with a talent for explaining in clear, simple language the great truths of faith."[120] He translated that oral talent into writing in his catechisms of 1844, the *Kleiner Katechismus* (16 pages) and a larger one, *Katholischer Katechismus* (147 pages), for German Catholics in Pittsburgh.[121] Neither of these manuals carried a by-line, but they did bear the approbation of Michael O'Connor, first bishop of Pittsburgh. Public credit for the two catechisms came to Neumann only after the First Plenary Council of Baltimore in 1852. The council commissioned the then newly appointed prelate of Philadelphia either to write a catechism for the German-speaking faithful or to choose one already written and submit it for approval to the other German-speaking ordinaries. Neumann submitted his own previously written *Katholischer Katechismus*. His confreres accepted it. Thus his large catechism with his name attached, along with the approbation of the First Plenary Council of Baltimore, appeared in 1853.[122]

Neumann's reputation as a catechist had become established almost immediately after his ordination.[123] On July 4, 1836, he arrived at his first assignment in Rochester, New York, where he found the German community in a sad and neglected state. The next day, in his gentle way, he gathered a group of young German children and began catechizing them. The event served a double purpose. It awakened the children's interest in Christian truths, and it let the community know that there was one among them who appreciated them, spoke their language, and was concerned about them. The pattern was repeated in every missionary parish Neumann served. Circumstances and external characteristics differed, but the parishioners and their children quickly discovered that the young Bohemian Redemptorist adapted himself to them and presented the life and message of Christianity in a winning way.

"No duty awakened livelier interest in Father Neumann," wrote John Berger, Neumann's nephew and one of his biographers, "than the instruction of youth. He knew well how to suit his words and demeanor to the age and capacity of his scholars."[124] Neumann, however, did not limit catechizing to the youth of the Church.

Having a natural talent for writing coupled with a zeal for spreading the Word, Neumann was a prolific writer.[125] He developed a style that reflected his incisive intellect and clarity of understanding. If one judges by his 2,000 hand-written pages of notes, his major interest was theology, for the largest part of those many pages is theological in content. They were so comprehensive, covering fields of moral, dogmatic, and ascetical theology, that his brother priests called them "Neumann's *Summa Theologica.*"[126] He was considered an intellectual by many standards, but Neumann did not lose touch with the general populace and the less learned. His published works were written for them. He is credited with a series of unsigned, informative newspaper articles that appeared in the early 1840s in Baltimore. Max Oertel, editor of the German-Catholic weekly, *Katholische Kirchenzeitung*, in which they appeared attributed them to him.[127] It is safe to presume that, like England and others, Neumann perceived the catechesial significance of newspaper articles and thus cooperated with Oertel when the latter requested his contributions.

Although his best-known works are his catechisms, he also wrote a Bible history and a manual for the clergy. The latter, a sixty-page Latin manuscript entitled *Synopsis Catechismi ad Parochos*, was actually composed before the others but remains unpublished in the Redemptorist archives in Brooklyn. One of Neumann's biographers, Michael J. Curley, described it as "a resume of the great catechism of Peter Canisius."[128]

Biblische Geschichte des Alten und Neuen Testamentes zum Gebrauche der Katholischen, his 108-page Bible history, was published in 1844.[129] Writing that manuscript must have been like returning to an early love: during his second year at the diocesan seminary in Budweis, Sacred Scripture had become his dominant interest. He studied biblical hermeneutics, Greek, philology, and an introduction to an exegesis of the New Testament. Reading "the Scriptures was his daily bread," a fellow student observed in correspondence with Berger.[130] Neumann himself noted that "what appealed to me most were the letters of the apostle St. Paul."[131] He made copious notes, edited, and reedited them. From these notes he wrote his Bible history, begun in Williamsville (near Buffalo) in 1837, working on it late at night after his daytime pastoral activities were finished. The volume was published in Pittsburgh seven years later. Neumann continued to study and write in the area of Scripture, developing a more detailed history, as a lengthy manuscript shows. This work, also in the Redemptorist archives in Brooklyn, was probably written during his second stay in Baltimore (1847–1852). His published volume enjoyed good circulation for a number of years, but it was not translated into English. It seems to have been superseded by the 1869 English *Bible History* of Cleveland's ordinary, Richard Gilmour.[132]

Like Bishop Baraga. Neumann foreshadowed the ideal which the U.S. bishops were later to project in their 1979 directory, *Sharing the Light of Faith.*[133] A man of prayer and service to others, he proclaimed the Christian message in word, deed, and script, constantly participating in the growth and life of the believing community. He did not restrict catechesis to question-answer instructions but expanded it to its fuller concept of all activity which resounds and exemplifies God's loving word, which awakens, nurtures, and contributes to developing the life of faith in Christians. Neumann knew himself as "chief catechist" without any display of authoritarianism. He was one of, with, and for the people with whom he lived, worshiped, and grew in faith. And, indeed, his conviction and way of life were winning and contagious.

The influence of German immigrants manifested itself in catechesis in another way, namely, through the promulgation of the 1847 catechism of Joseph DeHarbe, SJ. DeHarbe's manual, *Katholischer Katechismus oder Lehrbegriff,*[134] became one of the most popular catechisms in Germany. In 1850 John Baptist Purcell (1800–1883), archbishop of Cincinnati, formally introduced the work into his own diocese, and its popularity quickly spread to others. One historian, Anthony Fuerst, observed that in the United States the second half of the nineteenth century may be termed "the era of the DeHarbe catechism."[135] Without having publications and sales records to verify that statement, it is difficult to validate; but DeHarbe's catechism and its derivatives[136] carry U.S. publication dates into the 1930s, thus testifying to their prolonged use in this country.

CATECHESIS AND A CATECHISM ACCORDING TO SPALDING

Martin John Spalding (1810–1872) was a member of a distinguished Kentucky family which had migrated to that southern area from Maryland in 1791.[137] Martin was a bright, enterprising student from his early school days onward. During his seminary years he was influenced by Bishops Flaget and David along with Francis P. Kenrick. Flaget recognized Spalding's potential and sent him to the Urban College in Rome. In 1834 Spalding earned a doctorate in theology, the first American to do so from that college. After his ordination, August 13, 1834, he was appointed pastor of St. Joseph Cathedral, Bardstown, Kentucky.

Spalding's energies and efforts were directed toward the forming and informing of the faithful. Out of firsthand knowledge and understanding of frontier life and mentality, he was well equipped to do so. Among other things, he recognized the importance and power of the press and founded the eight-page weekly, *The Catholic Advocate.*[138] The first issue appeared February 13, 1836. In the *Advocate* Spalding included special columns designed to keep readers doctrinally informed. From time to time he excerpted passages from Bossuet's *Exposition of Catholic Doctrine,* but the more significant contributions were his own editorials. The *Advocate* continued publication despite difficulties and reversals until July 1848, when it merged with Cincinnati's *Catholic Telegraph.*[139]

Meanwhile, life was far from sedentary for Spalding. In 1841 the episcopal see was moved from Bardstown to Louisville. In October 1844 Flaget named Spalding vicar-general of the diocese. Six years later he was appointed coadjutor to Flaget. For all practical purposes, because of Flaget's advanced age and other circumstances, he was the acting bishop of the diocese. Flaget died in 1850, and Spalding became "in name" the prelate he had been in practice for some time.

In 1851 Spalding wrote and/or approved of a thirty-three-page catechism entitled *A Short Catechism for the Use of the Catholic Church in the United States of America.*[140] It was an ambitious title, especially in view of two things: (1) a current desire among some bishops for a uniform catechism—which matter would surface a year after Spalding's publication—and (2) the popularity of the David catechism in Kentucky. As a matter of fact, the Spalding volume made no dent in the sales or usage of the earlier catechism. The experience worked in Spalding's favor, however, when he was appointed to the Catechism Committee at the First Plenary Council of Baltimore in 1852. With minimal alterations and selected incorporations from the "Carroll Catechism," Spalding's manual was promulgated later as that prepared by the order of the First Plenary Council of Baltimore and "Approved by the Most Rev. M. J. Spalding,"[141] who was by that time archbishop of Baltimore. Raymond J. O'Brien observed that "though it became official in some dioceses, and was somewhat popular, it was not universally adopted."[142]

WESTERN NEW YORK'S JOHN TIMON

When John Timon (1797–1867) traveled the 1,600 miles from Texas to Buffalo in 1847 to become Buffalo's first bishop, he brought with him a wealth of missionary experience along with a well-earned title, the "Apostle of Texas." A Vincentian, born in Conewago County, Pennsylvania, of Irish parents and educated at Mt. St. Mary's College, Emmitsburg, and the Vincentian seminary, St. Mary-of-the-Barrens, in Perry County, near St. Louis, he was ordained in 1826. The next decade found him serving as parish priest, traveling missionary, and in administrative positions for his Vincentian community. In 1835 he was named the regional superior and, at the same time, vicar-general of the St. Louis diocese, during which time, according to Bishop Joseph Rosati, he won more converts and returned more lapsed Catholics to the faith than many other priests combined. His subsequent years as prefect-apostolic in the Lone-Star state merited him the title "Apostle of Texas."[143]

For the last twenty years of his life as the bishop of Buffalo, he served and led the Church in western New York. To read his work, *Missions in Western New York,*[144] is to be introduced to Timon's greatness. He appreciated and wrote about those who tilled the ecclesial soil in the area long before he arrived. In his own way and time he acknowledged that the "blood of the martyrs is the seed of the Church," as he related the stories, accomplishments, and martyrdom of Isaac Jogues, John de Brébeuf, and Gabriel Lalemant. "The sons of Loyola never retreated," he wrote.[145] Throughout his work Timon asserted that the many Indian tribes were "wronged before they did wrong,"[146] referring to injustices inflicted by avaricious whites, not the missionaries. In one chapter he extolled the sanctity of the tribespeople and told the story of the now-beatified Catherine Teaghokuita (Kateri Tekakwitha).[147]

Diary-like passages are interspersed throughout his book. Frequent among the activities he mentions are those of "giving instructions," teaching catechism, and catechizing children.[148] These jottings supported in part his perception of the need for a good catechism. His experiences undoubtedly played an important role in his compiling the catechism he published in 1851.

> Having, from long experience in teaching catechism, a deep conviction that answers which contain not a full sense in themselves, but which depend for a meaning upon the question, leave generally but vague impressions on the minds of children; we sought to arrange a catechism which would be free from this objection, and perused many catechisms full of learning, some of them even too profound, but none which, in our judgement, combines in so small a space more information, sweeter simplicity, and holier unction than the catechism of the Venerated Archbishop Carroll.[149]

Timon's manual, *A Short Abridgement of the Christian Doctrine; Newly Revised and Augmented*, is seventy-nine pages in length. He referred to it in his Lenten pastoral of 1852, firmly stating that it was to be the "only English catechism to be taught in the diocese."[150]

The catechism begins with questions and answers identical to Carroll's, but the overall organization departs from that of Baltimore's first bishop. It is divided into three parts. Part 1 includes lessons on doctrine as delineated in the creed, moves to a lesson on prayer, then the commandments, and finally an introductory chapter on the sacraments including a brief treatment of each sacrament. The initial question-answer to chapter 6 is interesting.

> Q. What is a Sacrament?
> A. A Sacrament is an outward sign of inward grace, or a sacred and mysterious sign and ceremony ordained by Christ, by which grace is conveyed to our souls.[151]

Chapter 7, the last chapter in part 1, includes questions and answers on the theological virtues, two precepts of charity, seven corporal works of mercy, seven spiritual works of mercy, eight beatitudes, cardinal virtues, gifts and fruits of the Holy Ghost, and others.

Part 2 contains ten chapters. Beginning on page 40 it offers questions and answers on subjects in the following sequence: the Creation and Fall, the sacrament of penance, indulgences, confirmation, the Eucharist, "a good communion," and the Mass.

The last fourteen pages, forming the third part, present an "Abridgement of History" which reminds one of the catechism of Claude Fleury.[152] While it is not clear whom Timon had in mind as its users, there does seem to be something for everyone in his catechism.

At least one fellow bishop did not find Timon's manual ideal. On September 20, 1852, Martin Spalding wrote what he called a "condensed" critique of it to Francis P. Kenrick, then archbishop of Baltimore. Spalding listed seven objections: (1) Timon's arrangement and organization under the headings of the three theological virtues "is too scientific and scarcely *ad captum populi*"; (2) the historical compendium was "too rhetorical" and complex for children; (3) Timon's definition of the Mass was confusing and erroneous; (4) the Ten Commandments should be juxtapositioned with the precepts of the Church; (5) the definition of absolution should be clearer and more prominent "as many penitents seem ignorant on the subject"; (7) the prayers before and after communion should be deleted "as those can be read in their own prayer books." He also called attention to additional improvements to be found in marginal notes in the catechism itself, which accompanied the letter.[153]

Operative in the background of this critique was the issue before Spalding, along with Timon and Ignatius Reynolds, bishop of Charleston: to produce a uniform catechism for the U.S. Church. The three formed a committee appointed by the First Plenary Council of Baltimore in 1852.

In Spalding's critique one cannot fail to detect the tone of professional competition, if not jealousy. After all, Spalding had also authored and promulgated a catechism for his diocese the year before the council opened.

In 1884 William H. Elder, archbishop of Cincinnati, wrote to Baltimore's Cardinal Gibbons commenting on the state of catechesis at that time. "I used to hear it said that in France a new bishop's first work was to reform his predecessor's catechism, and his second to reform the breviary. I think there is a good deal of human nature in America as well as in France."[154]

The quotation may not accurately describe the situation in the United States in every detail up to the mid-nineteenth century, but it fits to a certain extent. Not every new ordinary busied himself with "reforming" his predecessor's catechism, but zeal for the faith-life and knowledge of the Christian community prompted many bishops to write, approve, or recommend catechisms for their respective dioceses. The decades following John Carroll's episcopacy were marked with "growing pains," administrative problems, problems of extreme and irrational prejudice from without, and national jealousies and continuing trustee problems from within. Concern for the growth in faith amidst such complexities was a constant priority for the growing Church.

Like theme songs in descant, two calls were sounded from time to time during the period. One was for synodal gatherings in which all the bishops could confer with each other, collaborate on their common problems, exchange insights, and extend advice or at least an understanding and perhaps sympathetic ear to unique difficulties. The second was a plea for a single catechism which could be used in all the dioceses. The first call was heeded. In the twenty-year period, 1829–1849, seven provincial episcopal gatherings were held. They acknowledged the validity of both calls, though not all participants heard them in the same way. It took much longer to realize the second.

3

Episcopal Collaboration
on Catechesis

The first recorded call for a "common catechism" in the U.S. Church —
one envisioned as desirable for all dioceses — was registered by Ambrose
Maréchal early in 1827. It was like a faint echo of similar calls made by
Popes Clement VIII in 1598, Benedict XIII in 1725, Benedict XIV in
1742, and Clement XIII in 1761.[1]

In the context of a critique of Henry Conwell's catechisms and a recommendation to improve John England's manual, Maréchal wrote the
bishop of Charleston, observing that what the Church in this country
needed was a single catechism. The implication was that it would solve
"many" if not all catechesial problems. Maréchal repeated his concern in
a letter to Cardinal Cappellari, prefect of the Sacred Congregation de
Propaganda Fide, expressing his fears that a "multiplicity of discordant
catechisms might be introduced," citing specifically the catechisms of
Conwell, England, and Flaget.[2] Interestingly enough, the appeal came
one year after Maréchal's own catechism appeared on the market.
Maréchal's letter was grist for England's mill, providing the latter with a
new opportunity to appeal to the archbishop for a provincial council.
"Upon the subject of a common catechism," the suffragan of
Charleston wrote, "I agree very fully in your views but this and a variety
of others, believe me, will never be settled by us in our separated states.
I shall always be ready when we meet (and) . . . to the best of my
powers do everything I can do for the common benefit, according to the
common decision."[3]

This was by no means England's first appeal for a plenary assembly of the bishops to discuss mutual problems, ideals, and concerns. It was, in fact, one of seven written inquiries, appeals, or urgings, the first of which was sent on March 1, 1821, three months after England arrived in Charleston.[4] The last was written on June 25, 1827, seven months before Maréchal's death.[5] England was not the sole advocate of such a gathering. Benedict Flaget had written to Maréchal from Bardstown in April 1820, expressing his perception of a need for a national synod. In such a meeting, reasoned Flaget, the bishops gathered in repeated sessions "could reach agreement on policies ten times more satisfactorily than they could by writing fifty letters."[6] Conwell too, in correspondence with the archbishop on February 5, 1821, had observed the value of a provincial synod.[7] Maréchal, however, did not respond affirmatively to any request for a meeting of the bishops.

For several reasons, one of which was his own poor health, Maréchal was adamant. In a hand-written communication to England in 1821 the metropolitan of Baltimore stated his case.

> As to holding a Provincial council, I still do not see any sufficient reason to convoke one. It would not be attended by several of my suffragants [sic] who are of my opinion. And truly what would be the matter which would be proposed to its decision? Not certainly mere points of discipline. In 1790 [sic] a Synod was held here and many diocesan regulations were needed. In 1810 others were added by the Bishops who [were] consecrated for the Sees of Philadelphia, Boston, New York and Bardstown. Myself I have published a few ones. The whole of it is comprehended in a pamphlet which Rd. Mr. B. Fenwich [sic] may communicate to you. Some other articles certainly might be added. But each Bishop may do it in his Diocese and frame them to suit exactly the wants of his flock. For my Predecessors and myself have remarked that articles of discipline can with great difficulty be made that suit so immense a territory. A regulation excellent for your Diocese would not answer this of Boston and one used in Kentucky would be impracticable in New York and Philadelphia.. . . .[8]

Even the brief of Pope Pius VII (August 3, 1823)[9] did not change his resolve, though it did induce him to draw up preliminary plans for a council.

It was not until after Maréchal's death in 1828 that his successor, Archbishop James Whitfield, convened the council, during the first year of his episcopacy. It was the first of seven "provincial" councils of Baltimore held in three- to four-year intervals through 1849.

Collaborative organization and legislation were not unknown in the American Church. In fact, two meetings of Church leaders had already been held: the "First National Synod" of 1791, to which Maréchal had referred above, and the meeting of the U.S. hierarchy in 1810 after Baltimore had been made a metropolitan see with Bardstown, Boston, New York, and Philadelphia as suffragan sees. Of the two gatherings the first was by far the more significant.

With twenty-two priests assembled around John Carroll, the First National Synod of 1791 became the "corner stone" of the edifice and "the norm of practically all legislative enactments of the seven Baltimore Councils"[10] which followed it many years later. So important were the twenty-four statutes passed by the synod that the council of 1829 viewed them as the Magna Carta of all future ecclesiastical legislation and insisted on their being incorporated into the records as a part of the council's own enactment.[11]

FIRST PROVINCIAL COUNCIL, 1829

The First Provincial Council opened on October 3, 1829, and after thirteen private, thirteen public, and three solemn sessions and thirty-eight decrees it closed on October 18 of the same year. The thirty-third decree was directed toward the faith-life of the people. It forbade the "promiscuous" use of "unapproved catechisms and prayerbooks" and mandated that a catechism adapted to the needs of American Catholics be prepared and issued with the approbation of the Holy See.[12] Of particular interest, and certainly not surprising considering Rome's affection for "Bellarmine's catechism," is the fact that when the decrees were submitted to Rome for Bellarmine's catechism, Propaganda Fide inserted a clause insisting that the proposed catechism be based on that of Robert Bellarmine.

Decreeing was evidently easier than implementing. No common catechism appeared in the wake of the First Provincial Council. In the succeeding six councils[13] no attention was given to the subject of a single catechism suitable for use throughout the entire United States. In fact, it was in that lacuna that bishops continued to write or to authorize catechisms for their individual dioceses.

This does not mean that the bishops as a corporate body ignored the matter. Following each of the provincial councils they addressed a pastoral letter to the faithful. These letters, according to Peter Guilday, are a "mirror in which the manifold aspects of Catholic thought and affection can be clearly seen" for the periods in which they were written.[14] Catechesial themes weave in and out of them, and three are repeated frequently enough to be outstanding: (1) the important role of parents in the religious formation and instruction of their children; (2) the almost exclusive attention to catechesis of children; (3) instilling Christian morals as the dominant objective and value in catechesis.

In the 1829 "Pastoral to the Laity" the prelates addressed parents directly: "Dearly beloved . . . God has made you the guardians of those children to lead them to his service on earth . . . teach [them] first to seek the kingdom of God and His justice."[15] "Begin with them in their earliest childhood whilst the mind is yet pure and docile and their baptismal innocence uncontaminated." Then, when children are of school age, parents were cautioned to "seek for them teachers who will cultivate the seed which you have sown."[16]

From the time of the first provincial council catechesis was both child-centered and school-centered. The majority of subsequent pastorals presumed a classroom setting for catechesis. The pastoral letter which followed the provincial council of 1833 was explicit in its reminder to parents not only to catechize but "to have their children catechized."[17] The inference was that it was in a school that catechesis took place. Emphasis on the importance of Christian moral teaching in the bishops' letters also showed up most frequently in the context of school and general education.

Addressed to clergy and laity alike, the pastorals' repeated admonitions emphasized the need to provide and promote the best possible catechesis for the faithful. The fact that the "faithful" in this case were almost exclusively interpreted as "children" and that catechesis was heavily school-centered can be fully appreciated only against the backdrop of the times in which they were written. In retrospect, these pastoral letters clearly exhibit the bishops' perduring concern for good catechesis.

PLENARY COUNCILS OF BALTIMORE

First Plenary Council, 1852

The next mention of a uniform catechism as "ideal" for every diocese in the country came up at the First Plenary Council of Baltimore in 1852. By that time there were six metropolitan sees: Baltimore, Oregon, St. Louis, New York, Cincinnati, and New Orleans with their twenty-six suffragan sees.

The council fathers of 1852 represented a very different Church from that of the first and subsequent provincial assemblies. Guilday opined that "few periods in our ecclesiastical history witnessed so marvelous an advance in progress as the three crowded years between the Councils of 1849 and 1852."[18] "Marvelous" or not, they were certainly full.

Because of the famine in Ireland and upheavals in continental Europe immigration swelled enormously. How to absorb this large influx of people, how to acculturate them quickly and effectively without destroying their identity were realities that both the Church and society faced at that time. The large number of Catholic immigrants served to ignite the fires of hostility and induced an upsurge of nativist animosity in the "Know-Nothing" movement which later became the short-lived American Party. Slavery was escalating as a major social question during those years. The fathers of the First Plenary Council knew those tensions. For the most part, however, they addressed only ecclesiastical matters, not social ones.

The council opened on Sunday, May 9, and closed May 20, 1852. Archbishop Francis Patrick Kenrick presided, not only as the host archbishop of the primatial see, Baltimore, but as the apostolic delegate for the council by special appointment of Pius IX issued on August 19, 1851.[19]

At the fifth private congregation of the prelates (May 14) a three-bishop committee was named to settle the "vexed question of a uniform catechism in English."[20] The three committee members were Ignatius A. Reynolds of Charleston, John Timon of Buffalo, and Martin J. Spalding of Louisville. Both Timon and Spalding were experienced in catechizing, writing and/or approving catechisms for their respective dioceses. In that fifth private session the committee prescribed that a single catechism be made available in English for use throughout all dioceses and that its approval by the Holy See be requested.[21] Furthermore, they sought the advice of the ordinary of Philadelphia, John N. Neumann, regarding the best catechism written for German-speaking Catholics.[22]

The final recommendations regarding the proposed catechism cited Bellarmine's catecism as a model.[23] It seems safe to assume that this was a Roman insertion similar to that made in the decrees of the First Provincial Council in 1829. Spalding's letter to Kenrick, September 20, 1852, confirms that assumption. In the context of a critique of Timon's catechism Spalding turned to the projection of the 1852 council's catechism. "The instruction from Rome, I think, recommended Bellarmine's *Dottrina Christiana* as a standard; and if the new Catechism might be deemed advisable, the approval of the Holy See would probably be more speedily attained."[24] The Catechism committee had suggested "that the extensively and favorably known catechism of the Venerated Archbishop Carroll, after having received some few merely verbal and unimportant emendations, be submitted to the judgment of the Holy See, and that when approved a committee be appointed to superintend its publication for general use in this country."[25] This suggestion was marked "Omittendum" in the margin, and it was, in fact, deleted from the final, published decrees.[26] The recommendation of Bellarmine's manual, however, was in that edition of the decrees. Once more Rome's preference for the catechism of its favored son came to the fore.

In the end of Spalding catechism, somewhat revised, was the catechism promulgated as the accepted volume, although it was never "officially approved" by the full assembly of bishops. It carried the title:

A General Catechism of the Christian Doctrine,
prepared by order of the
First Plenary Council of Baltimore,
for the use of
Catholics in the United States of America.
Approved by the
Most Rev. M. J. Spalding, D.D.
Archbishop of Baltimore[27]

The council was not content with recommending a common catechism. In the twelfth and thirteenth decrees it reminded priests of the privilege and duty to institute catechetical classes in their parishes in which they, the clergy, were to instruct the young in the doctrines of faith. That duty was *not* to be delegated to others by the clergy. The last admonition is an interesting one in the context of nearly a century and a half later when the laity forms a large part of the catechetical staff in most parishes.

Second Plenary Council, 1866

After a lapse of fourteen years the Second Plenary Council, meeting in Baltimore in 1866, reiterated the principles and even entire sections of the statements pertaining to catechesis promulgated by the previous council. The matter of uniformity in catechisms came to the fore in the discussion of uniformity in general practices, Title VII, *De Disciplinae Uniformitate Promovenda*. In chapter 2 of that section the conciliar prelates reminded themselves of the recommendation in the First Plenary Council about the importance of a single catechism.[28] A second reference was made in Title XI dealing with the necessary permission to print and publish books, including catechisms.[29]

Raymond J. O'Brien reported some indications of dissatisfaction with the catechism of the earlier council.[30] From a study of the minutes and unpublished manuscripts of the council he discovered that a committee of theologians was appointed to examine the 1865 catechism written by John H. McCaffrey with a view toward adopting it. McCaffrey, a reputable theologian, was the president of Mt. St. Mary Seminary in

Emmitsburg, Maryland. Spalding favored the adoption of the catechism, but John Timon and Augustin Verot, bishop of Savannah, strongly opposed it. Others sided with Timon and Verot, and the recommendation was dropped. Despite the growing concern for uniformity there were "established" catechisms in some parts of the country, especially the David catechism in Kentucky. The McCaffrey manual did not appear superior to them. In the end the statements of the earlier council were repeated.

The catechism was not the only focus for the conciliar leaders in the matter of catechizing. Title V, *De Sacramentis*, included the reminder that children were to be well instructed before receiving their first communion.[31] In section 9, *De Juventute Instituenda, Pieque Erudienda*, the council exhorted pastors to hold catechism classes regularly for all children attending public schools.[32] They were also instructed to build and equip parochial schools in their respective parishes so that children might have the privilege of a full Catholic education. Parents, too, were reminded of their responsibilities both to catechize their children and to see to it that they were educated in Catholic thought and practice.[33]

In the pastoral which appeared in the wake of the Second Plenary Council the bishops alluded to catechesis in two instances. The first reference was in the context of an exhortation to support the Catholic press. They reminded the faithful "that the power of the press is one of the most striking features of modern society; and that it is our duty to avail ourselves of this mode of making known the truths of our Religion, and removing the misapprehensions which so generally prevail in regard to them" (#25).[34]

The second reference to catechizing occurred in the section "Education of Youth" and called for a renewal of "our conviction, that religious teaching and religious training should form part of every system of school education" (#27).[35]

While a certain thrust for uniformity gained ground steadily, individual bishops responded to the needs of their own dioceses as they perceived them. Apparently the catechism of the First Plenary Council was not sufficiently "universal" to satisfy the expectations of all.

THE INTERIM

Between 1866 and 1884, when the full assembly of bishops convened for the third time in Baltimore, new or revised catechisms appeared in New Orleans, New York, Florida, Charleston, Philadelphia, and Leavenworth, each with the approval of, or even compiled by, the bishops of those respective dioceses. The Charleston catechism of John England was revised and promulgated in 1873 and that of Kenrick, in Philadelphia in 1878.

A French catechism for Louisiana, *Catéchisme de la Louisiane*, was first ordered "exclusive of all others" to be used in the diocese of New Orleans in 1846 by Antoine Blanc, first bishop, later archbishop, of that diocese. It was approved again and published by the second archbishop, Jean-Marie Odin, in 1866. In 1875 a revised "and corrected" edition appeared with Odin's posthumous approbation.[36]

Richard Gilmour and Bible History

Attention must be given here to Richard Gilmour (1824–1891), a Scotch-born convert (1842) who became Cleveland's second bishop. His efforts to provide moral and religious formation for Catholic children through textbooks were distinctive. His first work was the *Illustrated Bible History* published by Benziger Brothers in 1862.[37] Gilmour did not compose the volume but translated it from the French, which edition in turn was a version of the German original. "Gilmour's Bible," as it was dubbed, was the only work of its kind in English. It went through numerous printings and editions, the last of which was in 1936. During these years Benziger published the volume in seven languages to accommodate peoples of different national origins in this country and abroad. In 1880 Pope Leo XIII gave a special commendation to Gilmour for his *Bible History*.[38]

Encouraged by the success of the Bible volume Gilmour undertook the project of editing a series of readers for Benziger. The series was titled the *National Catholic Series of Readers*, but like his earlier work they assumed his name and were called "Gilmour's Readers." The first was published in 1874, two years after he was consecrated bishop of Cleveland. These books were the country's earliest classroom readers calculated to impart Catholic moral and religious instruction as well as to teach reading and spelling. By 1877 five readers, a primer, and a speller were published. Gilmour relied on the critiques of experienced teachers for his reediting of the original manuals. For more than forty years the Gilmour readers were the standard readers (sometimes spellers) in Catholic elementary schools in the United Stages.[39]

Augustin Verot, Faithful Rebel

One of the most colorful and articulate of the U.S. Church's nineteenth-century bishops was the French-born Sulpician, Jean-Pierre Augustin Marcellin Verot, better known simply as "Augustin Verot" (1805–1876). Verot's episcopacy spanned this country's civil war, Baltimore's Second Plenary Council (1866), and the First Vatican Council in Rome (1869–70). Verot played a role in each.

He was born in LePuy, France, on May 23, 1805. His formative years and early schooling were routine. On October 15, 1821, he entered the seminary of Issy near Paris which was directed by the priests of the Society of St. Sulpice. Soon after that he was accepted into the society. Sometime later he was assigned to a teaching post at the Sulpician college, St. Mary's in Baltimore. Verot served on the faculty there and at the minor seminary of St. Charles as a professor of mathematics and the natural sciences, chemistry and physics. In 1853 he was released from his academic responsibilities and transferred to pastoral work in nearby Ellicott Mills.

Although he was a successful teacher and dedicated academician whom "few theologians of the land could compete with in point of erudition," according to his biographer, Michael Gannon, Verot found himself "happy and busy" and seemingly exhilarated in his parish ministry. His correspondence reflects his state of being "very much at peace . . . and very happy in good works . . . in parochial life."[40]

The hierarchy began to recognize Verot's qualities, and at one point New York's Bishop John Hughes invited him to become superior of the seminary which he, Hughes, planned to build in Troy, New York. Verot did not accept. Within a year after that invitation Archbishop Francis P. Kenrick (Baltimore) submitted Verot's name to Rome as a candidate for the bishopric of Savannah, Georgia. Though he was not chosen for that see, he was named vicar-apostolic of Florida and consecrated titular bishop of Danaba on April 25, 1858. Three years later, on July 16, 1861, his jurisdiction and pastoral duties increased when he became the third bishop of Savannah while retaining his responsibility for the vicariate of Florida.

Verot participated in the ninth provincial council of Baltimore before departing for Florida on May 22, 1858. That experience helped teach him the scope and context of his new responsibilities. As bishop he quickly became aware of the uniqueness of his vast diocese and sensitive to the peculiar needs of the people he had come to serve. He advocated the amelioration of domestic slavery, especially after the beginning of the Civil War, which position, among others, earned him the title "rebel bishop."

Verot accepted the religious plurality of the people in his diocese, ever hoping for "some reconciliation with Protestants" without neglecting the Catholics whom he served and sought to lead.

In 1869 he published a tightly packed, 108-page catechism.[41] Like its compiler, the manual was unique in several ways. It opened with a selection of brief prayers "that all children must commit to memory." This was followed by eight pages entitled "The Smaller Catechism — for young children and illiterate persons" (pp. 8–15). The next twenty-eight pages, titled simply "Catechism," included eleven chapters of more comprehensive questions and answers. That section, in turn, was followed by "A Short History of Religion" comparable to the seventeenth-century work of Claude Fleury. Beginning on page 56 was a "Short Catechism—for Converts from Protestantism." "A Short Catechism for Converts from Infidelity" succeeds that. The final catechism section began on page 72 with "A Short Catechism for Converts from Judaism" (pp. 72–78). The concluding twenty-nine pages contained a comprehensive selection of prayers and hymns.

Basically the catechism followed the sequential order of treatment characteristic of manuals of the period: creed, commandments, sacraments, with the difference of an intervening section, "Of Prayer," sandwiched between the commandments and sacraments.[42]

In a number of ways Verot was ahead of his time. Like the thrust of the *General Catechetical Directory* (1971) and *Sharing the Light of Faith* (1979), he clearly considered catechesis an enduring element in the faith-life of a Christian and not solely for children. Also, he viewed ecumenism as an important value in Christian living. John Tracy Ellis observed that the ecumenists of the Second Vatican Council would have applauded him if they had heard one of his speeches. Speaking to and about the First Vatican Council, in which he was a participant, he stated: "I confess frankly that this council gave me high hopes of obtaining some reconciliation for the Protestants—high hopes, to be sure, if the exposition of doctrine made by this council were made plain, mild and soothing—as far as the truth will bear—concerning those points which are subjects of controversy between Catholics and Protestants."[43]

In 1873 Verot published a shorter, thirty-two-page catechism, *Short Catechism of the Christian Doctrine on the Basis Adopted by the First Plenary Council of Baltimore for the Use of Catholics.*[44] Neither of his manuals treated papal infallibility specifically, although it is clear that Verot recognized infallibility as residual to the Church. This is evident in his 1869 manual.

> Q. Is there a principle or bond of unity of doctrine in the Catholic Church?
> A. Yes, if any questions arise concerning faith, the decision of the Church, that is to say of the Pope and Bishops in communion with him is final. For Christ has clearly promised to his Church infallibility, that is, the gift of not erring in the faith. He said . . . "I am with you all days even to the consummation of the world."[45]

Louis Mary Fink, Bishop of Leavenworth

Bishops in the plains and on the western edges of the nation's expansion adjusted to the unique demands and pioneer circumstances of the people who comprised the Church in those regions. Louis Mary Fink, OSB (1834–1904) was one such prelate. Characterized as "one of the most active and zealous of the western prelates in encouraging colonization and providing for the wants and necessities of the Catholic settlers,"[46] Fink was a monk and former prior of the monastery of St. Benedict in Atchison, Kansas.

In 1871 he was named coadjutor to John B. Miège, titular bishop and vicar apostolic of Indian Territory. Six years later when Kansas was made a diocese with Leavenworth as its see, Fink was named the first bishop.[47] Confronted with the complexities of a frontier diocese, Fink established mission centers which he called "Christian Forts." Catholic immigrants and westward-bound citizens were encouraged to settle in or near these centers so that they could be mutually supportive while achieving familial, social, and financial stability.

Integral to his conception of developing strong Catholic colonies was his zeal for an informed and faith-full laity. To this end, among other things, he commissioned the writing of catechisms, and he turned to the monks of his home-abbey for that work. The first volume to appear was a thirty-page *Catechism for Beginners*.[48] The title page explained that it was "An Abridgment of the Most Rev. Dr. James Butler's Catechism for Beginners." The "Approbation of Rt. Rev. Louis M. Fink, OSB, Bishop of Leavenworth," also graced the title page.

Other catechisms followed: *St. Benedict's Catechism No. I* (1894), a thirteen-chapter preparation for first communion, and *St. Benedict's Catechism No. II* (1895). The series earned regional support and popularity to the extent that the individual volumes were condensed and published in a single volume in 1915 by Fink's successor, John Ward. The preface to the 1915 manual explained:

> Bishop Fink's Catechisms went out of print ten years ago. Since then the wish has often been expressed that these catechisms be published again. Pastors and teachers asserted, that when they used Bishop Fink's text-books, the children and converts acquired a thorough, practical, and permanent knowledge of their religion. When also the Diocesan School Board expressed a decided preference for these text-books, Rt. Rev. Bishop Ward, D.D., the present incumbent of the See of Leavenworth, gave orders that Bishop Fink's Catechisms be published again, and used in the schools of the Diocese. At the same time His Lordship appointed a Committee to attend to revisions for the new edition. The work of the Committee consisted principally in simplifying words and constructions.[49]

Of particular interest here is the fact that all these manuals were published *after* the promulgation of the catechism of the Third Plenary Council of Baltimore, 1885.

The Call for Uniformity Grows Insistent

The concept of uniformity as essential to unity was not original with the U.S. bishops. Governors and tribal leaders have employed it in various forms from the earliest days of societal living. But it was left to Napoleon Bonaparte to turn to a catechism (among other endeavors) to secure unification of the French Empire early in the nineteenth century. To gain popular support for his position, Napoleon manipulated the Church and clergy as much as possible.

In the Concordat of 1801 the French government, in submission to the emperor, decreed that a single liturgy and a single catechism would be a part of the unification plan already initiated several years earlier. The catechisms of Jacques Bénigne Bossuet and Claude Fleury were cited as models. In 1806 the *Catéchisme à l'usage de toutes les Eglises de l'Empire français* was published.[50] It bore little resemblance to its proclaimed models. Napoleon's influence, however, was clearly discernible in the manual, especially in the treatment of the Fourth Commandment. There, respect and affection due to civil authority was included along with honoring one's father and mother. Furthermore, love, obedience, honor, fidelity "are due in particular to Napoleon I, our Emperor," the catechism stated. Despite the emperor's injunction that the catechism be used universally, submission was merely nominal. The majority of bishops avoided using it on various pretexts. In 1814 Louis XVIII suppressed the "Imperial Catechism" and restored the power of individual bishops to provide catechisms for their respective dioceses.[51]

Napoleon's catechism was like a discordant interlude between the verses of an emerging popular song. The song was "uniformity," the melodic line was "question-answers." It took some time, but the theme "uniform catechism" finally reached a full crescendo at the First Vatican Council.

VATICAN I AND THE "SMALL CATECHISM"

At that council (1869–1870), the first since the Council of Trent more than 300 years before, the overall trend to centralize prevailed. In such a climate it is not surprising that a proposal for a universal catechism should have surfaced, been explored, and been voted on. What may be surprising is that, next to the debates and discussions on the matter of papal infallibility, the catechism question occupied more of the council's time than any other single issue. Of significance, too, is that it was the only pastoral matter which was completely explored and decided on at the council.

The council opened formally on December 8, 1869. The opening was the climax to a five-year preparatory stage initiated by Pope Pius IX's announced intention of convening a council (December 6, 1864). Agenda setting, formation of committees, subcommittees, and meetings ensued. About eight hundred cardinals, patriarchs, archbishops, bishops, abbots, and religious superiors general participated. Thirty-nine of them were from the United States. It was the U.S. Church's first participation in an international gathering of such magnitude.

The proposal for a single catechism for worldwide use is associated with the archbishop of Valladolid, Juan Ignacio Moreno, who, in preconciliar correspondence (1865), suggested and urged the compiling and approval of a catechism suitable for universal use. His suggestion was based on the precedent set by Trent in its catechism for pastors. Just as there is "one faith," he rationalized, "so let there be one way of speaking about faith."[52]

A little more than a month after the formal opening, the schema *De Parvo Catechismo*—the small catechism—was distributed to the large body of participants.[53] Discussion and debate on the schema began on February 10 and lasted, with brief intervals, proposed amendments, and a revised schema, until May 4, 1870. The debate repeatedly touched on four major areas: (1) the existing situation of multiple catechisms; (2) the relationship of uniformity to unity; (3) the responsibility of individual bishops in their local dioceses vis-à-vis their relationship to the Holy See; (4) the feasibility of implementing a common, universal catechism if it were voted in. Throughout the discussions, the accepted assumption was that catechesis and catechisms were distinctly childhood matters. Only rarely was there any allusion to adults.

As the conciliar fathers debated the issues, polarization quickly developed. Proponents of the schema advocating the small catechism formed the majority. They stressed the acute need for a common manual in light of the numerous catechisms circulating at the time. Migration, "ease of travel," as one prelate put it, became a recurrent theme in justifying the cause. Migration was of two kinds. One was a movement induced by the industrial revolution, which attracted many people from rural life to the cities and thickly concentrated urban dwellings. Oftentimes this was accompanied by the deterioration of family and home life, as parents and children alike went to work in factories and industrial centers. Catechesis and religious formation in general declined in such cases. The other movement, more massive, was the intercontinental migration of peoples from Europe to the North American continent, especially to Canada and the United States. One bishop pointed out that there were as many catechisms as there were dioceses and that this multiplicity in itself led to confusion as people moved from place to place.[54]

As a group the Spanish, Latin American, and Italian bishops were the most united and loquacious in favoring the proposal. One of them, Jacinto María Martinez, archbishop of Havana, was colorful and graphic in his advocative rhetoric. With a flourish he questioned, "Quid est catechismus?"

> What is a catechism? A catechism is the milk of the church. . . . There are women of every color, white, black, copper colored, yellow, but their milk is always white to signify innocence. If the catechism is the milk of the Church, no matter who the mother may be the faithful will be nourished. . . . When Pius IX said I propose to you a universal catechism all bishops ought to say: *fiat, fiat* and nothing more.[55]

A French bishop summarily observed: "We are Romans, therefore let our catechism be Roman."[56] Jean Faict, bishop of Bruges, supported this in his recommendation that the words "Roman Catechism" be included on the title page of the proposed manual so that children would know unmistakably that they were Roman Catholics.[57]

The catechism of Robert Bellarmine was extolled as ideal and projected as a model throughout the discourses. Many advocates of the schema upheld it. One Spanish prelate, praising Bellarmine's work, observed that "no other book, except perhaps the Bible and the *Imitation of Christ* had been translated into so many languages."[58] The majority advocates minimized the "exaggeration" that individual rights of local bishops were being threatened. In fact, according to one proponent of the schema, the catechism would subtract nothing from episcopal rights because the bishops themselves would be the very ones to enact it in the council.[59] Another supported that view, citing Cyprian to the effect that bishops were to the pope as the rays are to the sun.[60] One commentator observed that discussion of a uniform catechism seemed to have more to do with the relationship of the bishops to the Holy See than to the improvement of catechesis. Tallying their conciliar orations, one discovers that the proponents of a uniform text relied repeatedly on the argument that since the schema had the pope's endorsement there was adequate reason to support it.

The Minority Positions

Opponents of the schema addressed the matter from more rational and existential perspectives without minimizing their regard for or allegiance to the papacy. The four outstanding spokesmen for the minority position were Joseph Rauscher, cardinal archbishop of Vienna; Félix Dupanloup, bishop of Orleans, France; Augustin David, bishop of

Saint-Brieuc, France; and Lajor Haynald, archbishop of Kalosca, Hungary. In their individual ways they emphasized three main objections: (1) the near impossibility and impracticability of producing and implementing a single, uniform text; (2) the inadequacy of the much-extolled model, the Bellarmine manual; and (3) the threat that the imposition of such a catechism posed to the rights and responsibilities of bishops to select and to edit or write their own catechisms in response to the unique needs of peoples in their dioceses.

Addressing the assembly on the first day of debate, February 10, 1870, Joseph Rauscher (1797–1875) pointed out the fallacy of idealizing a single catechism for the universal Church. Even in a particular nation it would be ineffective when one considered the age variances of different groups expected to use it. A common text could hardly be expected to meet the needs of both children and adults. He then proceeded to illustrate the magnitude of the problem in relation to the educational situation by noting the wide age range of children in schools.[61] Addressing the role of local bishops, he affirmed their competency to decide on the needs and propriety of specific catechisms for their respective flocks. Rauscher supported that position by quoting an apostolic letter written by the reigning pontiff Pius IX to the Austrian bishops on November 5, 1855.[62] In that letter Pius IX commended unquestioningly the prelates' ability and responsibility in sanctioning particular catechisms.

Félix Dupanloup (1802–1878) addressed the council body in one of the longest speeches of the occasion. He was a gifted intellectual who spoke out of a fruitful and protracted experience in catechizing. Not only did he know catechesis from catechizing in a pastoral context but he recognized catechetics as a discipline in its own right with its own theories and principles.[63] His two-volume work, *Méthode Générale de Catéchisme*,[64] was published in 1862, seven years before the council.

In essence, his lengthy address touched on three key issues: (1) the denial of the identity of uniformity and unity; (2) the impracticality of a single catechism for a widely diverse people – diverse in age, understanding, culture, and environmental circumstances; and (3) the infringement of the rights and responsibilities of local bishops. In effect he called for implementing the principle of subsidiarity, although this was neither a term nor a concept in ordinary use at the time.[65]

Dupanloup pointed out the pedagogical weaknesses of the schema when he questioned the emphasis placed on *memorizing*. In a tone of simple inquiry he directed the question toward *understanding*. Is that not where the emphasis should be placed? The question served to inject a modification and an amendment into the schema that was finally voted on.

"What does the Council want?" he queried further. "Unity of doctrine or uniformity in handing on doctrinal truth?" Responding to his own rhetorical inquiry, he stated that unity of doctrine is already present in the creed, commandments, and basic teachings.[66]

Augustin David, bishop of Saint-Brieuc, France (1812–1822), argued that a catechism in common use around the globe was quite simply impractical. The Church had existed for eighteen hundred years without such a manual; why was it suddenly so expedient? Affirming that the faith, indeed, is one, he insisted that unity could not be defined by "uniformity" and that the manner of explaining and teaching Christian truth varies according to the talent, age, and culture of the catechized.[67]

In general, those opposing the schema insisted that age differences, cultural diversity, and national traditions had to be considered. No single catechism could take those multiple factors into account. Uniformity could not be legitimately "canonized" as a primary objective. One bishop, William Clifford, from Clifton, England, further decried the stress on uniformity. He extolled the importance of unity and observed that "if the council wanted to give an example to the world, it would not seek to force or impose unity but would rather encourage it to grow naturally."[68]

There were moderates, prelates whose stated positions favored the schema but who urged certain provisos. Both Gerault de Largalerie, bishop of Belley, France, and Patriarch Ballerini of Alexandria (Latin rite) urged that the approved catechism not be strictly obligatory; that bishops be allowed to issue a second manual more suited to their particular dioceses. However, they insisted that the council's manual should be regarded as the norm for doctrinal presentation.[69]

United States Bishops' Participation

Augustin Verot was the only United States bishop to participate orally in the catechism debate. His address on the catechism question was not, however, his first appearance before the entire assembly. On January 3, 1870, he mounted the ambo in St. Peter's to speak on the schema *De Fide Catholica*. In the context of a section on the harmony between science and faith, he vindicated Galileo and lamented the Church's seeming hostility toward scientific advances. In the same vein he called for social justice for Negroes. They belong to the human family, he insisted, with the same rights and privileges as other people.[70]

The *Chicago Tribune* reported Verot's address as "the most remarkable ever heard in the Eternal City . . ., not only eloquent but a warning and a rebuke . . ., a demand for practical legislation."[71]

Because of his forthrightness and frequent interjections during the council assemblies, his sharp wit, innovative approaches, "barbarous Latin," periodic disregard for protocol, and petite size, he was dubbed *"l'enfant terrible"* by some of his less friendly conciliar peers. In retrospect more than a century later one cannot fail to observe the correctness of Verot's position on many issues.

He addressed the assembly on the catechism issue on February 14, 1870, the second day of hearings on the subject. A proponent of the proposal, Verot argued from the migration perspective, stressing that, because of the rapidity of travel and transportation, the world in effect had become a single city.[72] Thus, he concluded, a "single" catechism was appropriate. He joined the chorus against selecting Bellarmine's catechism as a model, however, and conceded, too, that the proposed catechism should not be made obligatory.

Verot intervened a final time as the catechism debate approached its termination. Sensing the positive outcome of the balloting, he rose and addressed his peers on April 29, 1870. He recommended that a clause be included which would make the favorable outcome only provisory, dependent upon the completion, inspection, and approval of an actual catechism. Verot assured his hearers that he wanted a common catechism with all his heart,[73] but if it was not acceptable to all the bishops it would be useless and ultimately rejected. In fact, he added, the project was more complex than one might think. As evidence of this he referred to the difficulties the U.S. hierarchy had encountered in their efforts of several decades to produce a common catecism. As of that date no catechism acceptable to all the U.S. bishops had been published. Thus he urged an emendation that would include his proviso. It was to no avail: the proposed emendation was not included in the final wording of the schema.

As a whole the U.S. bishops found the sedentary, listening posture strenuous and taxing. James Gibbons (1834–1921), then vicar apostolic of North Carolina, wrote that the experience was a "great trial of physical endurance for many of these men." They often asked each other, "What progress are we making? How long will this series of speeches last?"

Bernard John McQuaid (1823–1909), the first bishop of Rochester, opposed the schema in principle but did not make a public statement against it. His correspondence, however, reflected not only his own attitude but that of others as well. In a letter dated April 25, 1870, addressed to James M. Early, his vicar-general and rector of St. Patrick's Cathedral, he wrote:

> The next point for discussion is to be the old one of the
> Little Catechism. Some are opposed to a uniform little catechism

for one reason, others for another. It is not a question that troubles me much, as the Catechism itself can be reconstructed as often as they find it expedient until they get one that will be satisfactory. The reason alleged for a general one is that uniformity may be obtained. But whilst saying this, they at the same time contradict themselves as each Bishop will still be allowed to have larger ones for his own diocese and according to its peculiar needs. Hence we at once get back to our condition. So long as the faith is taught, the less interference in such matters the better in my judgment. Rumor has it that the infallibility question will follow next.[74]

In the final balloting on the catechism schema McQuaid voted "opposed" (*non placet*). He was one of four U.S. bishops who did so.

On May 4, 1870, the proceedings on the schema came to an end. There were modifications and emendations in the final wording of the proposal as it was presented to the council. Results of the voting were read aloud: 491 — in favor (*placet*); 56 — against (*non placet*); 44 — qualified approval (*placet juxta modum*).[75]

The matter was settled. Implementation, however, was a different matter, and in fact did not come to pass. The council fathers dispersed, and no particular commission was assigned the task. The possibility of implementing the proposal surfaced from time to time in subsequent decades, but it was nearly one hundred years later at the Second Vatican Council that the concept of a "catechetical directory" replaced that of a single catechism for the Church universal.

The contribution of the U.S. bishops to the First Vatican Council was one of keen, pastoral sensitivity to the apostolic missions in a still-young nation. Their situation was unique in comparison with prelates from other parts of the world. They addressed issues out of a multifaceted, pluralistic experience quite unfamiliar to that of any other bishops. When, on the occasion of his initial presentation, Verot pointed out that he came to the council from America,[76] he introduced a "new mentality and a young voice" that could not easily be ignored.[77] The U.S. bishops made little if any impact on conciliar legislation. They did bring to the collegial assembly a particular quality and a fresh dimension which was distinctive and impressive. Their voice would be heard again.

U.S. Bishops at Vatican I	Balloting on the Catechism Proposal
Joseph S. Alemany, San Francisco	*placet* (approved)
Francis N. Blanchet, Oregon City	pl.
John McCloskey, New York	pl.

U.S. Bishops at Vatican I	Balloting on the Catechism Proposal
Claude M. Dubuis, Galveston	pl.
Wm. H. Elder, Cincinnati	pl.
Louis J. M. T. de Goesbriand, Burlington	pl.
Michael Heiss, Milwaukee	pl.
John M. Henni, Milwaukee	pl.
Louis Lootens, Castalola (Idaho/Montana)	pl.
John B. Miège, Messene/Leavenworth	pl.
Eugene O'Connell, Grass Valley (California)	pl.
Wm. O'Hara, Scranton	pl.
Ignatius C. W. Persico, Gratianopolis/Savannah	pl.
Louis A. Rappe, Cleveland	pl.
Stephen M. Ryan, Buffalo	pl.
James M. M. L. St. Palais, Vincennes	pl.
Jeremiah F. Shanahan, Harrisburg	pl.
John J. Williams, Boston	pl.
Boniface Wimmer (Abbot), Latrobe	pl.
Thaddeus Amat, Monterey/ Los Angeles	*placet juxta modum* (approved with reservations)
James Gibbons, Vicar Ap., North Carolina	pl.j.m.
John Hennessy, Dubuque	pl.j.m.
John Loughlin, Brooklyn	pl.j.m.
Augustin Verot, Savannah/Florida	pl.j.m.
John B. Purcell, Cincinnati	*non placet* (opposed)
Michael Domenec, Pittsburgh	n.p.
Bernard J. J. McQuaid, Rochester	n.p.
Richard V. Whelan, Wheeling	n.p.
Martin Spalding, Baltimore	absent
Peter Richard Kenrick, St. Louis	ab.
James Roosevelt Bayley, Newark	ab.
Edward Fitzgerald, Little Rock	ab.
Patrick N. Lynch, Charleston	ab.
Augustus M. Martin, Natchitoches (Alexandria, La.)	ab.
William McCloskey, Louisville	ab.
Francis P. McFarland, Hartford	ab.
John McGill, Richmond	ab.
Ignatius Mrak, Sault St. Marie Marquette	ab.
Tobias Mullen, Erie	ab.

U.S. Bishops at Vatican I	Balloting on the Catechism Proposal
Napoleon J. Perché, New Orleans	ab.
Patrick N. Lynch, Charleston	ab.
John Quinlan, Mobile	ab.[78]

Catechism in the Wake of the Council

When the Atlantic crossing was behind them and the U.S. prelates were back in their respective sees, they continued to respond to the catechesial needs of people as they, the bishops, perceived them.

A sixty-four-page manual appeared in New York in 1872. It carried the approval of John Hughes, late archbishop of New York. Titled *A General Catechism of the Christian Doctrine Prepared by Order of the National Council for the Use of Catholics in the United States of America,*[79] the volume was obviously a reprint of an earlier manual inasmuch as Hughes, first archbishop of New York and a stellar figure in the early history of the Church there, had died in 1864. A catechism identical to the 1872 manual was published in Chicago some years later.[80] It, too, carried the Hughes approbation along with that of P. A. Feehan, D.D., archbishop of Chicago. No date was given on the title page, but it must have been published in or after 1880, the year in which Feehan became Chicago's first archbishop.

The effects of the council were reflected in some of the newer manuals. Bishop Patrick N. Lynch approved a revision of John England's catechism for the diocese of Charleston in 1873. The questions and answers on infallibility differ sharply from the England original.

> Q. Is the Pope infallible without the Bishops?
> A. Yes; when he teaches *Ex Cathedra*.

A question on the meaning of *"Ex Cathedra"* and one on the certainty of "Peter's" irrefutable veracity follows.[81] In 1878 Lynch edited a version of Joseph DeHarbe's catechism. In addition to the introductory section of "Daily Devotions," a thirty-one-page "Short History of Religion" preceded the extensive question-and-answer catechism section.[82]

In the meantime James Roosevelt Bayley (1814–1877), Baltimore's eighth archbishop, approved the catechism series of the Redemptorist Michael Miller in 1875.[83] Four years later (1879) Michael Augustine Corrigan (1839–1902) sanctioned a catechism for his Newark diocese.[84] Corrigan later (1880) became the third archbishop of New York. There were also reprintings and new editions of existing manuals. Fink's catechism was reedited in 1880 and again in 1904. Neumann's catechism was published anew in 1884.

The popular volume of James Gibbons deserves special attention in this pre-Baltimore Three period. His work, *The Faith of Our Fathers*, was first published in 1876 but was reprinted/reedited numerous times. The title page of the 1906 volume indicates that it was the sixty-sixth edition.[85]

The Faith of Our Fathers was designed to enlighten Catholics and to instruct prospective converts, according to John Tracy Ellis. The book "proved to be the most successful work of its kind in the apologetical literature of American Catholicism."[86]

Gibbons wrote the work during his service to the people in North Carolina where he served as vicar apostolic from 1868 to 1872.[87] He also served as bishop of the diocese of Richmond, Virginia, after the death of Bishop John McGill, from 1872 to 1877. It was out of that rich pastoral experience in the heart of the nation's southlands that he wrote what he considered a "simple exposition of the teaching of the Catholic Church."[88]

THE THIRD PLENARY COUNCIL, 1884, AND THE "BALTIMORE CATECHISM": A VEXING MATTER SETTLED

As Augustin Verot had testified in Rome, the complex matter of a uniform catechism had tenaciously and vainly threaded its way through meetings of the U.S. hierarchy for forty-five years. After the seminal statement in the First Provincial Council of Baltimore in 1829, the subject rose again during the plenary councils of 1852 and 1866. No definitive progress was actually made. It was in the third and final plenary council of the nineteenth century (1884) that the deliberations bore fruit. In April 1885 the bishops issued a manual they hoped would be suitable for the widely diversified Catholic population in this country. Its innocent-looking cover and concise question-answer corpus revealed none of the actual deliberations and work that went into compiling, editing, and publishing the small volume.

Preliminary Preparation

On March 19, 1884, James Gibbons, now archbishop of Baltimore, addressed letters to the entire U.S. hierarchy informing them of a forthcoming council and requesting their presence in Baltimore the following November. Among many other detailed preparations, Gibbons notified his colleagues that sufficient requests[89] for a unified catechism impelled him to appoint a committee of bishops to study the question in advance of the pending council. Thus he named Archbishop Joseph S. Alemany of San Francisco as chairman with six bishops serving under him: Louis de Goesbriand of Burlington, Stephen Ryan of Buffalo, Joseph G. Dwenger of Fort Wayne, John L. Spalding of Peoria, John J. Kain of Wheeling, and Francis Janssens of Natchez.[90] In a printed circular sent to each of these prelates, Gibbons instructed the committee to consider and report on three points especially: "1st. On the expediency of adopting a uniform catechism at the Council. 2nd. On naming the catechism which they prefer to be sanctioned. 3rd. Whether the Germans, Slavonians, Italians, Spaniards, French, etc., should have a translation of the catechism to be adopted, or whether another catechism should be approved for them."[91]

The committee met in a special session on November 11, 1884, and requested leave to report at once, eighteen days in advance of their turn on the agenda. When they did so, the matter was referred back to them, but they were given the added support of other bishops and priests with whom to confer and collaborate. None of the examined sources reveals the names of those new members or specific reasons for enlarging the committee.[92] Sebastian G. Messmer, archbishop of Milwaukee, later recalled that at the meeting opinion in favor of a new catechism prevailed over a vigorous sentiment favoring Butler's Catechism, just issued by the Synod of Maynooth (Ireland, 1882).[93] The catechism committee met in special sessions two more times: on November 29—the date originally set for its meeting—and on December 6. In its November 29 session, the committee proposed its statement which, after modification from the floor, was adopted as it finally appeared in decrees 217–219 of the council's *Acta et Decreta*.

The three decrees provided a lengthy rationale for and exhortation to the clergy regarding their responsibilities for catechizing. Specifically, pastors and/or "their assistants" were to "teach catechism" to those preparing to receive first communion. Such preparation was to last for six continuous weeks with a minimum of three sessions each week. Similar instructions applied to those preparing youths for the sacrament of confirmation. Furthermore, the catechism was to be taught in its entirety. It must be pointed out, at this juncture, that the age for first communicants was usually in the early or mid-teens.[94]

With that background, the bishops' catechism committee was called upon:

> 1. To select a catechism and if necessary to emend it, or to start from scratch if they would feel it the necessary and opportune thing to do.
>
> 2. Let them present this work thus finished to the body of Roman Catholic Archbishops who will re-examine the catechism and will provide that it be published. This catechism is

to be published as soon as possible so that all teachers, both religious and lay, may have and possess the book.

Because this new catechism which will be composed in English will be prepared to this end, so that it will not only provide for a means of promoting uniformity by which the above mentioned disadvantages are taken away, but they will be also better adapted to the condition and state of our faithful people, we strongly have in our prayers that the book, having been turned into their idiom, may be used by the faithful of other tongues. Especially since the children born of German, French, or any other nation frequently come to Catholic Churches at a later period, in which churches the Christian doctrine is proclaimed in an English tongue, let us recommend that the youths who understand fully both tongues and who live totally among English-speaking people learn the before-mentioned Catechism in the English tongue.[95]

Popular lore has it that the catechism was compiled in one week's time. The truth of the matter is that a preliminary text, put together in an eight-day period, was distributed to the bishop in the council. The actual circumstances were these.

The committee made its final report during the plenary session held on December 6. Galley proofs of a newly assembled catechism text were distributed to the full assembly of prelates for their perusal and suggestions, but since the council's final session was scheduled for the next day, December 7, those proofs received little attention.[96] With so little time remaining, the committee requested that the bishops take their copies with them, study them, and forward any suggested changes or recommendations as soon as possible to Bishop John L. Spalding. Messmer recollected that the catechism committee had placed the actual making of the trial manual in the hands of Januarius de Concilio, a Jersey City priest, who was theologian to Bishop James O'Connor of Nebraska.[97]

De Concilio had accepted the task of writing the catechism probably during or immediately following the November 29 meeting. One writer, Mark Moesslein, observed that "thinking the matter over, Monsignor de Concilio came to the conclusion that it was not worthwhile taking much pains about the matter of drawing up a catechism, because the Bishops would dump it in the waste basket anyhow."[98] The result was that de Concilio hastily assembled the work in about a week. That hurriedly assembled text was the one submitted to the council fathers on December 6. It was also the basic text from which the final version was derived. At a later time, when the catechism had come under a barrage of criticism, de Concilio minimized his part in the work, but this must have been a change of view from that which he had when the catechism was finished. Within a year after it was published, he esteemed it worthy of translation into Italian for emigrants from his native Italy.[99]

The Catechism Written and Published

From the time of the council's close in early December 1884, until January 25, 1885, John Lancaster Spalding remained in New York City as a guest of the Paulist Fathers. The nearness of de Concilio's parish in Jersey City to the Paulist House in New York made it possible for the two to collaborate regularly during Spalding's winter stay in the East. Thus the work came to rest upon the two men, Spalding and de Concilio, whose names are most frequently linked with the origin of the Baltimore Catechism.

On January 2, 1885, Spalding wrote Gibbons about his progress. "I have examined all the suggestions made in regard to catechism and Mr. Kehoe will in a day or so send you copies of the final amendments of the archbishops. I hope they will send me their observations as soon as possible, that I may get the work off my hands."[100] In the final reference to his work, Spalding reported to Gibbons on February 23 that the archbishops' recommendations were in. "I have received suggestions from all the archbishops concerning catechism and have made such changes as seemed desirable. The corrected proof is now in the hands of Mr. Kehoe, who will send you a copy. He has done all the printing and should have an opportunity to get out an edition before other publishers, or else be paid for the work he has done."[101]

Less than two months later, on April 6, 1885, John Cardinal McClosky gave his imprimatur, and on the same date James Gibbons, as archbishop of Baltimore and apostolic delegate, issued his approval of the manual. On April 11 Spalding was granted a copyright (#8558) on the small, seventy-two-page manual containing thirty-seven chapters with 421 questions and answers. *A Catechism of Christian Doctrine, Prepared and Enjoined by the order of the Third Plenary Council of Baltimore* was the little volume's official title.[102]

A new catechism had appeared. It had been a long forty-five years on the drafting board. But the work was not yet over. In September Spalding published a redaction of the manual. Under the same episcopal approval and imprimatur, *A Catechism of Christian Doctrine, Abridged from the Catechism Prepared and Enjoined by order of the Third Plenary Council of Baltimore* appeared—a smaller volume with an even larger title.[103] This edition was thirty-six pages long, with thirty-three chapters, and 208 questions and answers. The selected questions and answers were identical to the ones in the parent manual, but Spalding had rearranged some of them, placing them in contexts different from their positions in the original manual. He had condensed the subject matter of eight chapters and fitted it into four, which affected the overall number of chapters.[104] The first catechism contained thirty-seven chapters, this one, thirty-three.

The abridged edition, sometimes referred to as "Baltimore Catechism No. 1,"[105] did not gain the popularity of the original volume. Its appearance seemed to testify to the fact that even the author of the Baltimore manual was not entirely satisfied with his first work.

Sources of the Catechism

The full truth of the origin of the Baltimore Catechism, however, is revealed in a textual comparison of the manual with certain of its forerunners. As Gerard S. Sloyan has observed, "though the pen is mightier than the sword, the scissors is mightier than both."[106] Even a superficial perusal of the manual discloses a remarkable similarity to texts in the entire catechism genre. The key to Baltimore's uniqueness lay in its likeness *to* and its difference *from* earlier catechisms, especially those which enjoyed a degree of popularity or widespread use in America at the time.

The present writer made a textual comparison of the Baltimore Catechism with four other manuals on the basis of likeness or contrast of its 421 questions and answers to those in the other catechisms. The manuals selected were: *The Catechism Ordered by the National Synod of Maynooth*, a revised version of the popular catechism by Dr. James Butler (1882);[107] *General Catechism of Christian Doctrine* by Augustin Verot (1869); *A Catechism of Christian Doctrine for General Use* by John M. McCaffrey (1866);[108] and *Catechism of the Diocese of Bardstown* by John Baptist David (1825). The Maynooth-Butler manual was chosen not only for its extensive use in the United States but especially because of the preference given it by Gibbons and a number of bishops at the Third Plenary Council. Gibbons had suggested the use of Butler, and Messmer's correspondence testified to others' favoring Butler as a model.[109]

The writer also selected both Verot's and McCaffrey's catechisms on the basis of their reputed influence on the catechism of the Third Plenary Council. Raymond J. O'Brien indicated that the Baltimore manual was a synthesis of the best in earlier catechisms, "but combined with its original matter is much that was taken from McCaffrey's and Butler's Catechisms."[110] Gibbons had suggested a synthesis of McCaffrey's and Butler's works—the best of both volumes.[111] The special appeal that McCaffrey's catechism had for some was, according to O'Brien, its claim to be in the "Carroll tradition." In addition to this appeal, the writer was persuaded to select McCaffrey because of his association with Spalding. Spalding was a student at Mt. St. Mary's College in Emmitsburg while McCaffrey was president there,[112] and it seemed quite likely that the younger man had firsthand knowledge of the catechism which the college president wrote. Verot's influence is attested to by Sloyan who disclosed that sixty questions in the Verot manual were identical to those in the Baltimore Catechism.[113]

The David Catechism enjoyed widespread use in Kentucky where Spalding was born and reared. The first of nine children, Spalding was born in 1840 in Lebanon, Kentucky, in the diocese of Bardstown. His earliest catechetical instruction came from his mother who had been the first graduate of Loretto Academy in Nazareth, Kentucky, in 1837.[114] David had written his catechism in 1825, and, according to O'Brien, the manual became "such a part of Catholic life in Kentucky that it held its place against the new catechisms" and was still in use during the early 1930s. There can be little doubt that Spalding's mother and his brothers and sisters used David's catechism. Further evidence lay in the manual itself.

The writer discovered that David's catechism was the only one of hundreds of pre-Baltimore catechisms examined which followed the sequential order of Trent's *Roman Catechism*: creed, sacraments, commandments. This is the same sequence found in the original edition of Baltimore.

The comparison disclosed that the four catechisms did indeed influence the manual which Spalding and de Concilio published with the council's approval, but that no one manual was its single source. Of Baltimore's 421 questions, 372 were present in the four catechisms. The following table summarizes the study.

TABLE 1

SUMMARY OF COMPARATIVE STUDY OF THE
CONTENTS OF THE BALTIMORE CATECHISM
WITH FOUR CATECHISMS IN USE
1884–1885

	Baltimore 1885	Butler 1882	Verot 1869	McCaffrey 1866	David 1825
Total number of questions-answers	421	457	212	447	743
Number of questions-answers identical to those in Baltimore	–	235	180	230	239
Percentage of each source's contribution to the to the Baltimore manual (e.g., 51% of q-a's in Baltimore Catechism are also in Butler)	–	51%	85%	51%	32%
Number of questions-answers found only in Baltimore	49	–	–	–	–

Reception of the Council's Catechism

The catechism received a cool reception when it came out in 1885. In spite of endorsement by certain diocesan synods—Cincinnati accepted it in the synod of 1886,[115] the diocese of Harrisburg in 1892,[116] the synod of Chicago in 1887,[117] Davenport in 1904,[118]—the catechism was not enthusiastically welcomed. It encountered serious resistance in many classrooms. In fact, other than approval by official diocesan assemblies, there is little evidence testifying to a favorable reception in those early years.

On the other hand, dissatisfaction with the small volume mounted increasingly during the first ten years. The ordinary of Cleveland, Bishop Richard Gilmour, was one of its earliest critics. Writing to Archbishop James Gibbons of Baltimore on April 11, 1886, he observed that he probably would be denounced for his unfavorable criticism, but he did not withdraw it. Instead, he added in an offhand manner, "Let it come."[119] What his critical evaluations were is not clear—they are not recorded in the Baltimore archdiocesan archives—but in light of his experience as a textbook author he must have felt himself a qualified judge.

The most explicit and bitter critic of the work was the anonymous author of nine articles that appeared between September 1885 and October 1886 in the *Pastoral Blatt*, a St. Louis-based monthly periodical written in German.[120] Assailing the work for its pedagogical and theological weaknesses, the critic (or critics) specified in deliberate detail examples in each of these two categories. The work was pedagogically unsuitable for children, the writer alleged, because of its incomprehensible language, its small size (children are more comfortable with a larger volume), the disproportionate number of yes/no questions (91 out of 421), the stunting of thought processes involved in questions that contain complete answers, and, finally, the monotonous sameness of the entire text, which gave equal treatment to all matters.

More importantly, according to the *Pastoral Blatt*'s critic, the catechism was theologically weak on several scores: the brevity of its treatment of God and the angels, the absence of any consideration of divine providence, only one question about the resurrection—a reference to the day it happened rather than to the significance of the event—and insufficient attention given to the Holy Spirit. The author of the last article in the series dubbed the manual the "Baltimore Catechism" in a way derivative of the "Trent Catechism," with the difference that the *Pastoral Blatt* author was acidly derisive in his naming.

As a final point, the reviewer explained in scornful terms that the title was not justifiable even in its shortened form because the catechism was published before Rome's Congregation de Propaganda Fide had approved the American council's decrees. Unlike the Trent Catechism, the content of the volume did not emerge from decrees or decisions reached during council sessions. Neither was the final copy circulated to all the bishops for a last review before publication.

The *Pastoral Blatt* critic's unrelieved negativism leaves one a little skeptical about his qualifications to assess the work. Though agreeing with his assessment in general, one cannot fail to question his total lack of objectivity. The manual surely was not starkly worse than other texts of its day. (An interesting aside is the fact that the *Pastoral Blatt's* editor, the Reverend W. Faerber, published a catechism under his own name in 1897.[121] It fared little better from reviewers than had the Baltimore manual from the pens of Faerber's selected critics.)

Dissatisfaction with the new Baltimore manual continued to spread. A 1929 article in the *American Ecclesiastical Review* admitted the volume's "many faults." Acknowledging that there was both general and explicit disapproval of it, Archbishop Sebastian Messmer of Milwaukee (bishop of Green Bay, 1891–1903; archbishop of Milwaukee, 1903–1930) defended it. He pointed out the need for uniformity in the exposition and wording of Christian doctrine, and he maintained that that particular quality was of more immediate importance than correcting any of the catechism's weaknesses.[122] Messmer's defense concurred with statements recorded in the synodal decrees referred to above, namely, that uniformity was a quality of prime importance. The desire for memorized statements in a monochromatic pattern across the United States seemed to supersede doctrinal accuracy or pedagogical know-how.

Nor was discontent with the catechism confined to verbal criticism. It was observable in another form, less direct in style but just as pointed and even more concrete: new catechisms. In that first ten-year period, at least seven new catechisms appeared bearing episcopal approval or imprimaturs in the dioceses where they were published or written. The very sanction accorded these newer manuals testifies to the bishops' joining in the pervading unhappiness with the Baltimore council's so-called text.

Unhappiness with the manual finally reached the attention of the archbishops in the country. A Paulist priest, Augustine F. Hewitt, writing from New York in 1895, voiced a sentiment held by many. Addressing his letter to Archbishop Gibbons, he observed that he had "never heard anyone express a favorable opinion of our present Catechism, and I hope it is true that the Archbishops will provide for its revision."[123]

Indeed, the archbishops did take up the matter in their meeting of that year. Minutes of the meeting reveal that inasmuch as the catechism "in its present form seems unpopular," the archbishops discussed the "advisability or necessity of revising it." They decided to poll the bishops in their respective archdioceses on the matter, questioning them "as to whether the present catechism should be revised or another catechism prepared as a substitute for the one now in use." No consideration seems to have been given to retaining the 1885 manual as it was.[124]

One year later, the matter held primacy of place on the assembly's agenda and was the first matter discussed. The 1896 minutes read: "From the reports of the various Provinces, it was evident that all the Bishops of the country were in favor of some changes while the majority recommended a *revision* of the present catechism." The archbishops resolved that a special committee be formed "to revise the catechism on lines suggested by the bishops of the country."[125]

No mention of the "catechism affair" appeared in the minutes of the archbishops' next six annual meetings, but the 1902 minutes disclose the dilemma that had halted progress. The committee "found themselves unable to offer an adequate remedy first because they knew no existing catechism which they could fully recommend; secondly, even if a proper catechism were prepared, the Board of Archbishops has no authority to order its general use."[126] And, finally, rumors circulated that the Holy See was preparing a catechism for universal use. With a seeming hint of relief, the minutes note the hierarchy's hope that Rome's projected manual would provide an answer to this country's catechism problem. It did not. When the catechism sanctioned by Pope Pius X appeared in 1905,[127] it made no pretension of becoming a universal text despite its early widespread acceptance. Nor did Pius X urge its universal use.

Strongly expressed criticisms and general dissatisfaction notwithstanding, the Baltimore Catechism gained ever-widening circulation as well as additional authoritative approval in some dioceses. Opposition, too, became more widespread, and from 1895 onwards demands for a better catechism became insistent. When no prospects of a revised or improved national catechism seemed imminent, catechists and pastors began to write their own manuals, manuals that responded to needs as their authors recognized them.

CATECHISMS AFTER BALTIMORE THREE

By the turn of the century fifteen new catechisms had appeared, most of which carried stated approval of the local bishops in whose dioceses they originated. With the exception of those by Peter Yorke, the catechisms were not distinctively different from existing manuals. Yorke, a priest of the archdiocese of San Francisco and editor of the *Monitor*, developed a graded series of manuals called *Text-Books of Religion* for the first five grades (1898). This was the earliest graded series of religion texts published in the United States. Each was presented in narrative prose with pertinent study questions and answers after each lesson. Some of these were taken from the Baltimore Catechism. The series carried the approbation of Patrick William Riordan, archbishop of San Francisco.[128]

By far the most significant single volume emerging from an episcopal editor/author during the last decade of the nineteenth century was that of Francis Silas Chatard (1834–1918), fifth bishop of Vincennes, Indiana.

Chatard published a small, thirty-eight-page volume entitled *Catechetical Instructions of Cyril of Jerusalem*.[129] In fact, the manual contained a translation of the last two mystagogical catecheses of the famous fourth-century bishop of Jerusalem. The first of the two (Lecture XXII) was a homiletic catechesis, "The Body and Blood of Christ," 1 Cor. 11:23–26; and the second (Lecture XXIII) was "On the Sacred Liturgy and Communion," 1 Pet. 2:1–5. The publication of these is remarkable on at least two scores. (1) The reflowering of patristic studies and patristic thought was still in its infancy at the time of the catechism's appearance. Renewal of interest in patristic studies is usually dated by the publication of the comprehensive collection and reprinting of the writings of the Latin and Greek Fathers by J. P. Migne. (2) These selected catecheses were addressed to adult Christians at a time – the late nineteenth century – when catechesis was considered to be reserved for children. Both catecheses were originally postbaptismal (mystagogical) and therefore intended for adult Christians. Reading them one is impressed anew with the constancy of eucharistic doctrine: "That what seems bread is not bread, even though it appears such to the taste, but is the body of Christ; and that what seems wine is not wine, although the taste so judge it, but is the blood of Christ."[130]

Meanwhile, in central Europe, especially in Germany and Austria, during the middle to late nineteenth century a ferment developed which questioned the doctrinal question-and-answer approach to catechesis. Three scholars, one of them a bishop, were responsible for this resurgence of interest and concern which in time called for a review of the early Church's practices of catechizing. They were Bernhard Galura (1754–1826), bishop of Brixen, Bernard Overburg (1764–1856), director of the diocesan seminary in Münster, and Johannes Hirscher (1788–1865), theologian at the Universities of Tübingen and Freiburg. All three men wrote catechisms[131] which gained a high degree of popularity in their respective local churches. Hirscher's pastoral concerns extended to the celebration of the liturgy, in which he called for use of the vernacular, communion under both species, and suppression of private Masses. Both Hirscher and Overburg called for a return to a historical framework as the appropriate context for catechesis. Both, too, ratified their theory by writing catechisms in that perspective. The writings of all three men had a distinct influence on Josef A. Jungmann, SJ (1889–1975), who subsequently incorporated much of their thought into his own work.

As a result of the innovative thrust and increased focus on catechesis initiated by Galura, Overburg, and Hirscher, a group of theorists and scholars began publishing the *Katechetische Blätter*, the first journal of its kind devoted to matters of catechesis. Twelve years later (1887) a similar periodical appeared in Austria with the title *Christlich-pädagogische Blätter*. Both journals have a history of publishing high-quality articles on theory, history, and pastoral studies which pertain either directly or indirectly to handing on the Christian message. Both journals, too, have enjoyed continuous publication down to the present[132] time.

4

Twentieth-Century Catechesis: Approach to Full Circle

In the context of catechesis in the U.S. Church the twentieth century opened with a kind of whimper. By the end of the third quarter of the century the whimper had changed to a healthy, articulating dialogue regarding the serious and vital nature of catechesis per se. The transition from the first to the second of these two points was neither steady nor smooth.

The Baltimore Catechism continued to serve the Church community, but it also continued to lack wholehearted, enthusiastic support and acceptance. That fact, as has been noted, surfaced frequently at the annual meetings of the archbishops. It was more clearly evident at the grass roots level.

POPE ST. PIUS X AND CATECHESIS

Because of the distinct emphasis he placed on catechesis it is important to examine briefly the role that Pope St. Pius X played in restoring catechesis to a recognized position of importance in the pastoral life of the Church.

Elected in the conclave of August 2, 1903, Giuseppe Melchiorre Sarto (1835–1914) became Pope Pius X. Two months after his coronation he set the tone and declared the ideals of his pontificate in his first encyclical, *E Supremi Apostolatus*.[1] The memorable and oft-quoted

99

passage associated with Pius X is in this document in St. Paul's words, "To restore all things in Christ (Eph. 1:10)."[2]

In this first encyclical Pius X proclaimed that the moral and social regeneration of Christendom depended on the religious formation of people. "Our first care," he wrote, "is to form Christ in those who are destined to form him in others; to train the clergy who are expected to assume leadership in teaching the faithful."[3] "Let them devote themselves to the various duties which belong to their ministry so that the lament of Jeremias may no longer be heard: the little ones have asked for bread and there was none to break it unto them (Lamen. 4:4)."[4]

The first work in which Pius X specifically addressed catechesis was his encyclical *Acerbo Nimis*, "On the Teaching of Christian Doctrine."[5] Joseph B. Collins described it as the magna carta for the revival of the Confraternity of Christian Doctrine in modern times.[6] In fact, it was the first of twenty-one documents which Pius X wrote dealing directly with catechesial matters.

The pope wrote out of a rich experience of catechizing which pre-dated his residence in the Vatican and carried over into his pontificate. As bishop of Mantua (1884–1893) he not only catechized regularly; he urged the establishment of the Confraternity of Christian Doctrine in every parish, recommended the foundation of permanent catechetical schools, encouraged diocesan clergy to foster the religious instruction of adults and children, supervised the training of seminarians, and per-mitted advanced seminary students to teach catechism on Sundays and holy days.[7] After assuming the pontifical office, he met with people who spontaneously gathered in one of the Vatican courtyards each Sunday, weather permitting, to visit, discuss, and explore with them the doctrines and practices of Christian life, "the simple truths of the Gospel."[8] As noted earlier, he was also largely responsible for the publication of the two-volume series which, at the popular level, sometimes bore his name, "The Catechism of Pius X." The official title was *Compendio della dottrina cristiana*.[9]

Though it is unlikely that he wrote any of the lessons in the cate-chisms, he was clearly the inspiration and behind-the-scenes critic of these small manuals which were based on a catechism used in the diocese of Mantua where he had been bishop. In a letter to the cardinal vicar or Rome on July 15, 1905, Pius X ordered the catechism series to be adopted in the Province of Rome and recommended its use throughout all of Italy.[10] In the United States, English editions appeared in 1906, translated by Thomas Sebastian Byrne (1874–1923), Nashville's fifth bishop.[11]

Pius X's pastoral influence was far-reaching and penetrating. He was a prolific writer and a personable man. Nothing of significance

seemed to escape him. Certainly his interests were not confined to catechesis, but he accorded that ministry a position of utmost importance in
the Church. "How many and how grave are the consequences of ignorance
in matters of religion!" he observed. "It is indeed vain to expect a fulfillment of the duties of a Christian by one who does not know them."

> We must now consider upon whom rests the obligation to
> dissipate this most pernicious ignorance and to impart in its
> stead the knowledge that is wholly indispensable. There can be
> no doubt, Venerable Brothers, that this most important duty
> rests upon all who are pastors of souls. On them, by command
> of Christ, rest the obligations of knowing and of feeding the
> flocks committed to their care; and, to feed implies, first of
> all, to teach. "I will give you pastors after My own heart," God
> promised through Jeremias, "and they shall feed you with
> knowledge and doctrine" (Jer. 3:15). Hence the Apostle Paul
> said: "Christ did not send me to baptize, but to preach the
> Gospel" (1 Cor. 1:17), thereby indicating that the first duty of
> all those who are entrusted in any way with the government of
> the Church is to instruct the faithful in the things of God.[12]

THE CONFRATERNITY OF CHRISTIAN DOCTRINE
IN THE UNITED STATES

The first Confraternity of Christian Doctrine (CCD) unit in this
country predated Pius X's election and his subsequent encouragement to
promulgate the CCD. In 1902 the parish of Our Lady of Good Counsel
in New York City organized an inter-parish Confraternity group.[13] It
owed its origin to a small number of lay persons who were concerned
about the low level of Christian knowledge prevalent among both adults
and children in the parishes. Thus they organized classes for children and
youth, especially those in public schools. Interest and zeal grew apace.
Annual training and study programs soon developed for would-be and
experienced catechists. On October 6, 1902, a *Manual of the CCD in the
Archdiocese of New York* was published carrying the imprimatur of
John M. Farley (1842-1918), archbishop-elect. The thirty-eight-page
manual expressed the timeless ideals of the Confraternity, including encouraging the recruitment of "generous teachers" and stressing the importance of adult catechesis. It also delineated the areas of service to
which nonprofessional volunteers could contribute.[14] By 1909 a diocesan
CCD congress was held. Thus the establishment of the CCD as a viable
ministry attained a degree of stability and recognition..

The early history of the CCD in the United States is also related to
the ministry of immigrants. In 1903 three lay teachers began providing

instructions classes for the mostly foreign-born Catholics in the mining districts around Pittsburgh. Their ministry mushroomed, and by 1919 five hundred teachers were involved in 153 schools of religion in the area. More than thirteen thousand children and adolescents were enrolled in their classes. John Francis Regis Canevin (1853–1927), bishop of Pittsburgh, was at the heart of this enthusiastic enterprise.[15]

Meanwhile, the movement that originated at Our Lady of Good Counsel in New York City expanded beyond the few neighboring parishes. Catechists began collaborating with each other, and by 1913 they created a vigorous foundation named *Theta Phi Alpha*. John M. Farley, the cardinal and fourth archbishop of New York, approved and encouraged the new society and its apostolate. Growing in number and activities, *Theta Phi Alpha* counted more than three thousand teachers among its members in 1929.[16]

EDWIN V. O'HARA AND THE CCD

Early in the 1920s the CCD reached out beyond urban confines when the dearth of catechesial opportunities in vast, sparsely populated farm areas was recognized by Father Edwin V. O'Hara (1881–1956), then pastor of St. Mary's parish in Eugene, Oregon.[17] O'Hara's concern for the welfare and Christian formation/education of people in rural settings became paramount in his life. Assessing the situation, he observed "food commodities are not the chief thing the farm produces. People are."[18] And for him the rural people were the most important and most neglected in the realm of social and spiritual endeavor.

Studying the existing conditions, O'Hara soon pinpointed the debilitating defect of rural life, namely, the absence of a cooperative community spirit. It was due, he explained, "to excessive individualism on the farm."[19] This, in turn, was due in some measure to the distances between family dwellings in farm areas. "Cooperative enterprises," on the other hand, "promise to build up real communities by creating common bonds of interest." Furthermore, "Cooperation is a Christian mode of industry," he maintained. "In removing destructive competition, mutual distrust, and individual selfishness, religion will have an effective aid in cooperative organization."[20]

Three things began to emerge as priorities for O'Hara: (1) the need for rural religious leaders, lay and clerical, who not only knew the land and its people but identified with both; (2) further adult religious education—"A weakness of rural life in the past has been its intellectual poverty";[21] and (3) providing opportunities for religious instruction for children — "The country Sunday school is universally conceded to be a failure."[22]

Seeking to share his views, O'Hara began to confer with like-minded individuals. By raising the consciousness of people in crucial (and political) positions he was effective in persuading the Washington-based National Catholic Welfare Conference (NCWC) to set up a "Rural Life Bureau" as a part of its structure. This occurred during a committee meeting of the Social Action Department of the NCWC which convened in Chicago in Easter week, 1920. Peter James Muldoon (1862–1927), chairman of the Social Action Department and bishop of Rockford (Illinois), was favorably impressed by O'Hara's proposal and persuaded the committee as a whole to accept it. On October 1, 1921, O'Hara officially established local headquarters for the "Catholic Rural Life Bureau" in his parish rectory at St. Mary's, Eugene, Oregon.[23] At the grass roots level he convened a meeting in St. Louis in 1923 attended by eighty rural residents and with them formed the National Catholic Rural Life Conference (NCRLC).[24]

In its earliest years the Conference provided a national forum in which problems and aspects of rural Catholics could be raised and discussed. Gradually the Conference gained status as a bona fide body, meeting annually, affirming Christian values of rural life, and becoming an effective lobbying group. At one point it defined itself as "an organization of bishops, priests, and lay persons dedicated to the economic, social and spiritual interest of the American farmers. It functions as an educational and propaganda agency within the Church for the application of the principles of Catholic philosophy to the sphere of agriculture."[25]

Responding to a nearly unanimous complaint from other rural pastors about the inadequacy of Sunday catechism classes, O'Hara initiated a search for an alternative. His own summer experiences during his youth offered a clue. Sometime in the 1890s, at his father's suggestion that he learn the language of the Norwegians who formed a large part of the population in his hometown of Lanesboro, Minnesota, Edwin participated in one of the flourishing religious vacation schools sponsored by the Lutherans. The school term was approximately a month long in July or August, and the children attended classes daily except Sundays. So O'Hara "learned Norwegian by studying the Lutheran catechism and the scriptures in that tongue."[26] The model served him well. Addressing the seventeenth annual meeting of the Catholic Educational Association held in New York City in 1920 he noted:

> In many sections the Lutherans successfully conduct rural
> religious summer schools, choosing a month in the summer
> vacation when there is a lull in the farm work. They gather

the children at the public school building or country church, and give them an intensive course of religious instruction for a month or six weeks, with sufficient review of secular branches to vary the program and prevent the day's work from becoming monotonous. Undoubtedly there are vast possibilities of organizing such summer schools for our Catholic children, and the details should be worked out on a comprehensive plan.[27]

O'Hara planned and organized a vacation school in the summer of 1921 in his parish in Eugene.[28] In fact, three rural communities in the large parish participated in the project, with sisters from the parish school in Eugene serving as instructors for one month at each of the three: College Grove, Junction City and Springfield. Teachers, pupils, and parents registered their enthusiasm for the pioneer project, and plans were made to repeat it the following and subsequent years. It was a program which "caught on" and "took off," netting interest and inquiries from other rural communities.[29] It should be noted, however, that similar religious vacation schools under Catholic auspices had been held in isolated instances prior to the Oregon experiment. Bishop William Theodore Mulloy (1892–1959) told how as a seminarian he spent his summer vacations teaching in religious vacation schools.[30] Another priest related the existence of a similar school in Kansas in 1904. What O'Hara did, however, besides organizing vacation schools in his own area, was propagate the idea and offer a forum through the NCRLC and the Rural Life Bureau in which experiences with such endeavors could be made known and shared.[31]

Like others who preceded and followed him, O'Hara acknowledged the apostolate of the press. He felt its need most acutely in agricultural regions of this country. "A field which has been practically untouched," he wrote, "is that of the rural Catholic press."[32] Applying the principle of adaptation before it was commonly held as significant, he noted, "It is true that dogmas of religion do not vary with city and country, but it is equally true that the environment in which the city Catholic lives is vastly different from the environment of his country cousin, and this difference must be reflected in the newspapers and periodicals which appeal to the various groups."[33]

With this conviction he started publishing a small four-page paper entitled *St. Isidore's Plow*. The first issue appeared in October 1922, and subsequent ones came out irregularly because of his numerous duties and the paper's low budget allotments. Two years later it became the official organ of the NCRLC under a new editor and a new name, *Catholic Rural Life*.[34]

The Apostolate Expands

Meanwhile, O'Hara was named and consecrated bishop of Great Falls, Montana, in 1930. For his motto he chose the Gospel passage, *Sinite Parvulos Venire*, "Let the little children come" (Matt. 19:14). The same text had been the theme of his homily at his first Mass a quarter of a century earlier, which testifies to the consistency of the man's apostolate: helping people grow in the understanding, appreciation, and depth of their faith-life. Throughout his episcopacy he did not lose sight of that resolve.

On January 11, 1931, O'Hara issued a pastoral letter initiating a diocesan-wide study club program based on the problems of parents as instructors of their children. It was the first formal program in adult catechesis. The bishop urged the use of *The Parent-Educator*, a textbook with discussion outlines. Although O'Hara dubbed it the "people's college,"[35] the idea and movement came to be called "The Religious Discussion Club (RDC)." The concept and program were well received, and the RDC grew steadily, ultimately expanding beyond the limits of parents' inquiries and needs. In 1935 O'Hara reported that within the past year "seven-hundred discussion clubs were engaged in the study of the early history of the Church with the Acts of the Apostles as the required text."[36]

The Confraternity of Christian Doctrine: National Level

On November 5–8, 1934, the NCRLC devoted an unusually large portion of their annual meeting to the Confraternity of Christian Doctrine. Prior to that, from 1930 to 1933, at least one session of each year's convention featured talks and discussions on practical matters pertaining to catechesis in the context of rural life and the ideals of the Confraternity. In that 1934 meeting in St. Paul, Minnesota, an entire day was given over to the CCD. At the end of that day, representatives presented a carefully worded formal request to the U.S. hierarchy that "a permanent episcopal committee" of the CCD be established and that "a central office for the [national] exchange of information" be set up.[37]

For some time there had been the growing recognition that the Confraternity was not just a rural endeavor and that it probably needed its own identity to serve adequately the Church's multiple catechesial needs. Therefore the petition proposed a friendly separation of the two organizations, the NCRLC and the CCD.[38] Later in the same month the petition was given to the hierarchy at their annual meeting in Washington, D.C. Both requests, for an episcopal committee and for a central office, were granted.

Archbishop John T. McNicholas (1877–1950) of Cincinnati, Archbishop John Gregory Murray (1877–1956) of St. Paul, and Bishop O'Hara of Great Falls were appointed to form the committee, with O'Hara designated as chairman.[39] Since 1933 Francis A. Walsh, OSB, a monk of St. Anselm's Abbey, Washingn, D.C., had been acting director with offices at the Catholic University of America. He held that position until his death in 1938.[40] The offices, however, were moved in May 1935 to the National Catholic Welfare Conference headquarters at 1312 Masachusetts Ave., NW,[41] in downtown Washington.

From 1935 to 1941 the Confraternity, independently of the Rural Life group, held its own annual "congresses." After World War II, these congresses were resumed but with less regularity than before.[42] While he lacked interest in self-glory, it is commonly held that Edwin V. O'Hara was the organizing and human inspirational force for the CCD in this country. One of his colleagues, Joseph A. Burke (1886–1962), bishop of Buffalo, once noted that "Archbishop O'Hara built the Confraternity. It is his masterpiece."[43]

CATECHISM REVISION AND BIBLE TRANSLATION

There were two more major projects that O'Hara championed and charted. The first sought a solution to the steady dissatisfaction with the "Baltimore Catechism." The second was the perceived need for a more easily understandable English translation of the Bible. As far as O'Hara was concerned, both projects were essential in order that the two works might fulfill their respective roles of assisting the entire body of the faithful, clergy and laity alike, to grow in faith, to develop and understand ever more clearly what it meant to be Catholic Christians. Thus the two projects progressed in tandem; both got their start in 1935 and reached a certain completion in 1941.

"Baltimore Catechism" Revised

In 1935, fifty years after its initial appearance, the "Baltimore Catechism" reached the point of revision. It was by no means a sudden or surprising decision.[44] As noted earlier, criticism of the manual had mounted steadily from two quarters: theologians criticized it for its doctrinal weaknesses, pedagogues for its methodological narrowness and inadequacies.

The decisive moment initiating the revision process came about almost casually. O'Hara and the apostolic delegate, Amleto Cicognani,[45] were traveling westward by train from Washington, D.C., after the 1934 bishops' meeting. In reviewing and discussing the recently concluded sessions, Cicognani remarked that "this might be a good time to study the catechism with a view to its revision."[46] O'Hara immediately discerned the timeliness of the suggestion; it was a *kairos* moment. Mentally he began laying the groundwork. In a short time he conferred with archbishops Murray and McNicholas. Concluding the consultation, the three bishops agreed that indeed it was time for the revision.

During the ensuing months a proposal was drawn up and preliminary plans were devised for executing the actual revision. The three-member committee assumed responsibility for the undertaking, but they invited, even exhorted, their peers in the episcopal conference to participate fully through questionnaires, critiques, and personal recommendations. In the summer of 1936, O'Hara, representing the episcopal Confraternity committee, invited a theologian, Francis J. Connell, CSSR,[47] to be responsible for assembling, collating, synthesizing, and organizing the material submitted by the bishops from across the country. It was deemed advisable that, if uniformity was to be achieved, one person be chosen for that task. Thus, from the vast assortment of collected material, Connell compiled a first, tentative draft which he submitted to all the bishops on October 3, 1936. Responses to this draft were mailed back, and, in light of the recommendations received, he set to work on the second draft.

In all, there were four drafts, each labeled "printed, not published." The second was sent out on January 28, 1938; the third on November 7, 1939, and the fourth on June 21, 1941.[48] The latter incorporated the suggestions recommended by Rome's Sacred Congregation of the Council. Murray, McNicholas, and O'Hara made a few minor changes and then sent the edited text to the publishers. The "Revised Baltimore Catechism" made its debut on July 18, 1941.[49] The revised "Number One" catechism for younger children was published in the fall of 1941. A first communion text appeared in October 1943.

The committee did not consider its task completed until it had "Catechism Number Three," a fuller version for the adult laity, ready for the press. This volume was, according to Francis Connell, "accomplished mainly through the personal activity of Archbishop McNicholas,"[50] the principal theologian working with Connell. The questions in this third manual were the same as those in the "Number Two" catechism, but the answers were more comprehensive and included additional explanatory material as well as pertinent scripture passages.

Revision in Perspective

Three objectives prevailed throughout the writing, editing, and selecting of content for the projected catechism: exactness, clarity, and completeness. At the same time brevity, too, was an influential norm. Connell justified this influence by contrasting a catechism with a textbook. "A textbook contains substantially all that the pupil is expected to learn; but a catechism presents only an undeveloped sketch of Catholic doctrine."[51] He illustrated this by comparing the role of a catechism to that of a map. "The map merely delineates the physical features of a section of a country; it could never of itself give the student an adequate notion of the geography of the region. So, too, the catechism of itself could never give even a bright child sufficient knowledge of the Christian Faith." In conclusion, Connell emphasized the importance of the catechist. "For this reason it is correct to say that the teacher of the catechism is much more important than the text of the catechism. A good teacher even with a catechism that is defective can accomplish much more than a poor teacher with an excellent catechism."[53]

A summary comparison of the 1885 and the 1941 manuals discloses that the revised version contained 515 questions in thirty-eight lessons in contrast to the fifty-six-year-old catechism with its 421 questions in thirty-seven lessons. The thirty-eighth lesson in the revision, "The Our Father," was an important asset with its ten questions on the meaning of each phrase in the Lord's Prayer.[54] The lesson was a significant and valuable addition on its own, but it also resumed a tradition established by the sixteenth-century manuals of Peter Canisius and Robert Bellarmine, who devoted special sections to the Lord's Prayer and prayer in general. More significantly, it resumed a tradition of the early Church which included *both* the Our Father and the creed as integral components of the catechesis of catechumens. Regretfully, the inclusion of the Our Father occurred almost as an afterthought in the last chapter of the "new" Baltimore text. The first appendix, which followed the Lord's Prayer, entitled "Why I am a Catholic," with its sixteen questions and answers, was likewise an innovative asset.

Connell, as the principal author of the revised manual, further explained and justified the major changes in the new catechism.

> The most noteworthy modification in the form of the revised Catechism is the change of the order in which the three parts are presented. The order of the Baltimore Catechism was: Creed, Sacraments, Commandments. In the revised edition the order is: Creed, Commandments, Sacraments. This seems a more logical division—what we must believe, what we must do, and the chief supernatural means to aid us to believe revealed doctrine and to obey the law of God. It is this order that is followed by most Catechisms, although the Catechism of the Council of Trent was arranged according to the plan followed by the original Baltimore Catechism.[55]

Placed in a broad perspective, the "Revised Baltimore" was not as ideal as it was hailed to be. Its weaknesses can be classified in three categories: (1) change of sequence; (2) obvious lack of awareness of or familiarity with catechesial thought elsewhere in the world; (3) little, if any, consultation with practicing catechists or theorists of the time. An exploration of each of these is in order.

First of all, the change in sequence from the 1885 text was not ipso facto an improvement. Trent's catechism and the original Baltimore manual reflected an interrelated integrity in the order, creed, sacraments, commandments (sometimes abbreviated as creed, cult, code), which was lost in the revised version. The original, despite its shortcomings, was Christocentric in a way that related to the earliest catechesis in the Church. Briefly put, the ideal of introducing the creed with its historico-narrative summary of the saving events in the God-human relationship, followed by concentration on the sacraments through which Christ's salvific events are ritually remembered and celebrated, and finally a focus on prayer and the commandments as responses to the saving realities recalled in the creed and sacraments, comprises a holistic approach which in its own way shows a kind of Christian integrity and logic. In this integrated summary the revised version's economical quid pro quo emphasis on sacraments as "means of grace" is fortunately missing in the original 1885 volume. Certainly the sacraments are of greater importance than just as "means of grace," as the "Revised Baltimore" described them.

Sequentially, the response of prayer and keeping the commandments is that of "love for love"—a reciprocal love expressing itself in prayer and in keeping the Lord's commandments in response to God's love manifested in past and present ways.

It must be noted here that some decades later (1971) the *General Catechetical Directory*[56] did *not* prescribe any particular sequential treatment of doctrinal truths. "It is right to begin with God and proceed to Christ, or to do the reverse; similarly it is permissible to begin with [humankind] and proceed to God" (#46). However, the *GCD* did insist on attention to the hierarchy of truths (#16, 27, 43, 46), and in that context pointed unmistakably to Christ as central to catechesis (#16).[57] In another section the *GCD* pointed out the "primacy of the Eucharist . . . and its supreme efficacy in building up the Church" (#58).

Viewed, then, through the prism which is Christ, each truth, historical or doctrinal, cultic, moral, or exhortatory, assumes a distinctive character in light of the whole. As Berard L. Marthaler has observed, "Catechesis has its own dynamic . . . it must be faithful to the message and helpful to those taught, expressing it in language adapted to the intelligence of the hearers" (*GCD*, #34, 35).[58]

The *GCD*'s injunction that a catechesial hierarchy of truths should address people of each age within the perspective of their cultural and social context is of extreme importance. However, it is the catechist who is primarily charged with the responsibility of discerning and relating these truths to the existential environmental and community in this manner.

> To the catechist falls the task of leading Christians from the level of symbolic consciousness to that of personal reflection and interiorization. This will not be possible if they see their function as one of mere repetition—handing on "the faith" as a neat package of doctrines articulated by remote theologians and church officials. While drawing on these resources, catechists themselves must theologize in such a way that they help to give expression to the community's understanding and experience of the mystery of God within their given cultural context and period of history.[59]

Expressed more pointedly, it is a question of the centrality of truths in the lives of particular communities and individuals, or of a theologically determined center. Karl Rahner illustrated this effectively when he observed that "the doctrine of the Trinity, in spite of its being so often extolled as the fundamental system of Christianity, plays a very modest role, if it occurs at all, in the actual life of Christians and in the teaching which they hear."[60]

The second critique of the structure and approach of the "Revised Baltimore" concerns its sharp contrast to innovative works by catechesial theorists and thinkers in both this country and in Europe. There is clear evidence of the resurgence of the historico-narrative style of catechesis being employed in catechisms during the nineteenth century in Germany and elsewhere. This style formed the backbone of the best catechesial tradition, so ably illustrated by Augustine of Hippo.[61] It was the basis of catechesis well into the late medieval period and was finally displaced during the sixteenth century when written handbooks superseded the "living word." Certain nineteenth-century efforts to restore a more ideal approach have been noted in the preceding chapter, in which the works of Bernard Overburg, Johannes Hirscher, and Bernhard Galura were singled out as farsighted endeavors to rechart the direction, theory, and methods of catechizing and return it to the comprehensive and vital role it held in the early Church. There is certain evidence that they had considerable influence on the thinking and writings of Josef A. Jungmann and Michael Gatterer (1862–1942), both of whom wrote treatises and volumes on catechesis.[62]

In this country, Virgil Michel, OSB (1890–1938), had begun working with the Dominican Sisters of Marywood in 1929 to restore the sacraments to the heart of catechesis.[63] This work was born of his studies in

Germany, where he discovered a vibrant movement to implement Pius X's ideal of restoring all things in Christ through the sacramental life of the Church. Ultimately this collaborative effort resulted in the publishing of the *Christ Life Series* in 1935.[64]

In view of the foregoing, the question arises: Why were none of these innovative/restorative emphases recognized and incorporated into the revision? Why were none of these endeavors explored? Was it a lack of awareness, or did the theological community regard such isolated thrusts with suspicion, as disruptions of the existing "tradition" of catechisms? These are not just rhetorical questions, and they are not easily answered.

A third critique, related to the second, questions the lack of consultation with catechists actually engaged in the ministry of catechizing at the time. There was at least one U.S. precedent for such a practice, in the work of Peter Yorke who invited and consulted with catechists, mostly sisters, who were engaged in catechizing. He listened to them, questioned their observations, and incorporated their suggestions into his manuals, *Text-Books of Religion.*[65]

When one places the two Baltimore manuals, the 1885 and the 1941 editions, side by side, one is truly hard put to cite one as superior to the other. While the earlier catechism had greater promise and potential, it realized neither, while the second had its redeeming merits. Unfortunately they had one thing in common — a certain leveling of the total content to an equality of importance. For example, in the 1941 catechism question 37, "What are angels?" receives as much emphasis as 132, "Which are the chief moral virtues?" and 356, "Why does Christ give us His own body and blood in the Holy Eucharist?" One could select similar examples from the 1885 catechism. One of the most significant defects in the earlier manual is the brevity of the attention paid to the central mystery of Christianity, the Resurrection of Christ, which is treated only in question 89:

> Q. On what day did Christ rise from the dead?
> A. Christ rose from the dead, glorious and immortal, on
> Easter Sunday, the third day after His death.

This leaves one with the realization that a question-and-answer catechism probably cannot carry the oversized burden which has been expected of it.[66] In the larger view, one must gratefully acknowledge the advances made by the contemporary catechetical movement sanctioned and affirmed by the Second Vatican Council, with its emphasis on directories rather than catechisms as the major sources and guides for catechesis and its special recognition of the Christian community, which, with its witness and service capabilities, is regarded as the principal catechist.[67]

New Translation of the Bible

The major themes of the "Study Clubs," as the "Religious Discussion Clubs" had come to be called, were based largely on the life of Jesus Christ and frequent explorations of writings in the New Testament. A growing enthusiasm for reading the Scriptures developed from such experiences. Study Club members had cultivated a greater appreciation for Catholic literature in general, but particular interest in New Testament reading grew apace.

Edwin O'Hara was not unaware of this growing interest and enthusiasm. As time progressed, he became convinced of the need for an improved, more easily readable version of the New Testament, one that would update the translation of the then current 350-year-old English translation called the "Challoner-Douai-Rheims."[68]

After the 1935 CCD Congress in Rochester, New York, O'Hara conferred with his two episcopal colleagues, McNicholas and Murray. The three decided to take steps toward revising the Challoner text of the Bible. In effect this meant "Americanizing" the centuries-old English version of the Latin Vulgate.[69]

O'Hara took the initiative. He addressed a letter to sixteen scripture professors teaching in selected seminaries in the United States. He asked two things of them: (1) to comment on the advisability of a revision based on the Challoner text and (2) to participate in a meeting to discuss the matter of a revision.[70] Fifteen scripture scholars responded to the invitation and met on January 18, 1936, at the Sulpician Seminary (now Theological College), Catholic University, Washington, D.C. Shortly after assembling, the group agreed on both the opportuneness and the advisability of the revision. At a second meeting in April of that year guiding principles for the revision were accepted and the project was set up. An editorial board was formed and work began. Five years later, on May 18, 1941, the first U.S. Catholic edition of the New Testament was released.[71] It soon came to be known as "The Confraternity New Testament." Shortly thereafter work began on the Old Testament. Then, on September 30, 1943, Pope Pius XII's encyclical *Divino Afflante Spiritu*[72] appeared, inviting and instructing Catholic scholars to work directly from the original languages. This added a new dimension to the Old Testament project. A team of scholars coordinated by chairman Edward P. Arbez, SS, and including such authorities as Louis Hartman, CSSR, Stephen Hardegen, OFM, and Patrick W. Skehan started its work.[73] The objective was a four-volume edition: I, Genesis to Ruth; II, the remaining historical books; III, Job to Sirach; and IV, the Prophetic Books. No deadlines were set, but the men worked steadily and faithfully. Volume I was published in 1952, volume III in 1955, volume IV in 1961, and volume II, Samuel to Maccabees, in 1969. St. Anthony Guild Press of Paterson, New Jersey, published all four.[74]

O'Hara's contribution to scripture scholarship expanded beyond the contents and bindings of books and his encouraging people to familiarize themselves with Sacred Scripture. He was not content to initiate projects and then abandon them to their own unguided destinies. He stayed with each one and faced the difficulties and hurdles that each encountered. James Gerard Shaw reported that "twenty years after he called that first meeting in Washington . . . O'Hara was still poring over proofs, meeting with translators, editors and publishers, and winnowing suggestions. He had read proofs on every single one of the successive publications of the revised catechism and of the revised and newly translated Bible.[75]

On thing led to another. As the Rural Life Conference had fostered the formal, nationalized organization of the Confraternity of Christian Doctrine, the latter in turn made possible other independent bodies. The Catholic Biblical Association of America (CBA) was one of these. It began in 1936 on the occasion of the annual CCD Congress being held in New York City (October 3-6). The group of scripture scholars and those engaged in the revision of the New Testament convened and drew up a statement of purpose and ideals. The immediate objective was to expedite the revision which was under way, but the major long-term purposes were (1) "to place at the disposal of the bishops a group of biblical scholars to work out questions on Sacred Scripture" and (2) "to afford an opportunity for those interested in Scripture to advance their knowledge of it." Officers were elected, and the prospects of publishing a quarterly journal to serve as organ of the body were considered and approved.[76] Eighteen years later (1954) the CBA honored O'Hara with the following resolution: "Be it resolved we . . . name him officially what he has always been in fact, the Founder of the Catholic Biblical Association."[77]

The outstanding characteristic of O'Hara's genius was probably his comprehensive, holistic grasp of Christian life and ideals. He knew that the mystery of Christ was the heart of what it means to be Christian and that the sacraments, with the Eucharist at their center, offered full participation in that life; that prayer and praise was the language of those who were one in, through, and with Christ; that Scripture was an essential source for understanding and appreciating God's love for humankind; and that catechesis was an additional and continuous means of grasping the core of doctrinal truth. "To restore all things in Christ," the motto formally adopted by Pius X, was echoed and lived in the life of Edwin Vincent O'Hara.

O'Hara died en route to the First International Congress of Pastoral Liturgy, held in Assisi, September 10-22, 1956. His paper, "The Observance of Holy Week in the United States in 1956," was delivered by Leo F. Dworschak, auxiliary bishop of Fargo (North Dakota).[78] In his address O'Hara cited the positive effects of the restored Holy Week rites and took the opportunity to plead for further "break-throughs." He urged the use of the vernacular in the liturgy, stressing its importance for the community's fuller participation in the central act of worship in the Church.

O'Hara had assumed a dominant, but not dominating, role of leadership in the Confraternity and in related bodies whose apostolates endeavored to assist people and clergy in their growth in faith.[79] However, he was not alone in these undertakings. With Murray and McNicholas he formed an effective and dedicated team. The three collaborated in joint efforts, yet each worked individually on particular projects. A survey of the annual proceedings of the Confraternity Congresses discloses the numerous addresses each gave on a wide variety of topics, often two or more different talks at a single gathering. They were committed and zealous, recognizing decades before the Second Vatican Council that catechesis holds a legitimate "pride of place" among episcopal responsibilities.

CCD: MINOR LEAGUE FOR MAJOR MOVES

The Confraternity of Christian Doctrine became a forum in which bishops, clergy, and others could emphasize and direct catechesial concerns, priorities, and approaches. The periodic congresses offered a platform for idea exchanges, inspiration, and encouragement that extended far beyond the assembly halls. For many, these congresses provided the means of introducing fresh vigor, enthusiasm, and even pride in the Church's life. Furthermore, the Confraternity welcomed apostolates related to, but not specifically, catechesis as such. Just as the CCD had fostered the more serious study of Scripture with the organizing of the Catholic Biblical Association, so did it afford a setting and opportunity for the better understanding and appreciation of the Church's sacramental life and liturgical practice[80] and for the significance of culture and environment to valid expressions of Christian living. The Confraternity encouraged ecumenism, explored the relationship of findings in the human sciences toward realizing human potential, and emphasized the value of communications media. All of these were presented in the overall perspective of one's growth in faith.

The Congresses in Retrospect

In retrospect, it is possible to assess the congresses with quite positive acclaim. One of the most valuable merits of the periodic assemblies was the experience and image of "church" which they projected and realized. Gathered to celebrate the Eucharist together and reassembled to address and listen to one another, they perceived and discovered anew that they were indeed the Church alternately learning and teaching. As Bishop So-and-So addressed the body—comprised of married and single people, sisters, brothers, priests, and other bishops, all dedicated to promoting growth in understanding and in faith—one surveyed the listeners and was awed at that *ecclesia*. At the next session, several hours later, the bishop would be among the attentive listeners as Mr. Craig or Miss Marks or Mrs. Tinney or Sr. Rosalia or Father Smith or another bishop addressed the gathering. It was a rare experience, that recognition of the Church as a body of tacitly acknowledged "unfinished Christians" learning from each other. It was a realization of what the early Church knew and what the late-twentieth-century Church is rediscovering—that indeed the *ecclesia*, the community of believers, is the primary catechist.

That community catechizes implicitly and explicitly. That same community from episcopal shepherd to newest and/or youngest member was (is) alternately the *ecclesia docens* and *ecclesia discens*. All were open to learn from, to share with, to search for the fullness of meaning in the reality of their being Christian. No one was "too big" in status or "too small" in importance to participate in those rally-like congresses. "The apostolate does not belong to bishops alone," someone observed.[81] It was evident that the bishops did not see themselves as "too magisterial" to learn from others. Nor did they, on the other hand, hesitate to fulfill their own role as formal catechists when the occasion arose.

An additional value of the congresses was the opportunity they provided for catechists in parochial schools to participate alongside those who, on a weekly basis, catechized children outside the parish school setting. Both groups profited from their informal exchanges with each other and from the formal papers presented at the sessions.

Robert E. Lucey, Archbishop of San Antonio

Notable among Church leaders active in the Confraternity was Robert E. Lucey (1891–1977), second bishop of Amarillo (1934–1941) and later archbishop of San Antonio (1941–1969). Besides serving on the episcopal committee of the Confraternity for twenty-five years (1946–1971), he brought to catechesis his special concern for social justice. This was shaped by the presence of large numbers of Mexican-Americans in the metropolitan area which he served. Though he is probably best remembered as a "champion of social justice"[82] with regard to the life and plight of Mexican-Americans in his archdiocese and beyond, he was an innovator in the sphere of catechesis on two scores: (1) the aspect of cultural differences and their influence in catechesis, and (2) the value of modern communications media in transmitting the Christian message

Regarding the first, Lucey was largely responsible for the broadening out of this country's CCD movement to include ideas, practices, thrusts, and exchanges from the Church in other countries of the western hemisphere. It was through his influence that the first Regional Inter-American Catechetical Congress was held in San Antonio, October 23–25, 1947. It was also through him that the 1961 congress added a new, international dimension to its gatherings, which included contributions from leaders in nations south of the Rio Grande.[83]

With farsightedness Lucey insisted on the merits of modern technology in shaping and proclaiming the Good News. In June 1969 he graciously hosted an "International Study Week of Mass Media and Catechetics" in San Antonio.[84] Lucey seemed to exemplify the conviction which emerged, according to Alfonso Nebreda, from that study week: "The Church must once again have recourse to the gift of tongues with this difference: in addition to Hebrew, Aramaic and Latin, it must master the language of the sound wave, the image and the computer."[85] In this vein Lucey himself addressed the participants of the International Catechetical Congress in Rome on September 23, 1971.

> Religion must be actively associated with a worldwide satellite network. . . . Today, radio and TV programs are inferior. Tomorrow, a world network will provide programs of many kinds. The world audience will select the programs which please it best. Our script writers must give humanity the finest information and entertainment or lose the contest for men's minds. That would be a tragedy. Either we shall have trained men and women for religious education through the modern media of communication or the Church will face disaster.[86]

Whether or not Lucey placed exaggerated emphasis on the potential of electronic media may be questioned. One could justifiably argue that person-to-person contact is irreplaceable and of prime importance. On the other hand, when one considers the extensive and persuasive media contacts made by contemporary fundamentalist evangelicals, one is forced to acknowledge the effectiveness of that means of communication. Undoubtedly it is not a matter of either-or but of the wise employment of both. What it does say in this context is that Lucey was a man of his own time with a "tomorrow" vision.

In fact, Lucey's catechesial concerns were comprehensive. His two-pronged, innovative direction only partially conveyed his total conviction of the importance of catechesis. He took seriously the Second Vatican Council's statement addressed to bishops that "catechetical training is intended to make men's faith become living, conscious and active . . ., [that] bishops should see to it that . . . children, adolescents, young adults and even grownups" (n. 14) be provided catechetical opportunities. Furthermore, the bishops "should encourage institutes, special meetings in which priests can gather . . . for the acquisition of deeper knowledge of ecclesiastical subjects especially scripture, theology, the social questions of major importance and new methods of pastoral activity" (*Christus Dominus*, 16). Lucey determined to implement these injunctions.[87]

On June 15, 1967, he circulated a letter to the clergy in the diocese announcing that he had invited "two of the world's best exponents of biblical-liturgical catechetics—Father Johannes Hofinger, S.J. and Father Alfonso Nebreda, S.J.—to conduct a special archdiocesan institute for the people and clergy of San Antonio during July 14–16, 1967."[88] The preregistration blank carried Lucey's statement.

> Today effective teaching methods are being developed and the Vatican Council has given us new and fascinating aspects of old religious truths which must be taught to the people of God. The laity must do a substantial portion of that task not only because there are not enough priests in the world to teach religion to the people but also, and particularly, because the layman must share his spiritual treasures with his neighbor.
>
> If anyone should remark that in the 20th century it seems strange that priests and laity should be taking courses in the teaching of religion we can only reply that the Church in the modern world has much unfinished business.[89]

In his opening address, a five-page introduction to Alfonso Nebreda, Lucey presented a sort of position paper defining his view of the role, scope, significance, and privilege of the ministry of catechizing.[90] Reading it one realizes anew that catechesis is not, and has never legitimately been, confined to children.

> My dear teachers, you must instruct children and adults to communicate personally with Christ warmly, sincerely, intelligently. . . . When we insist on the dynamics of Christianity, when we teach our people to love God in their neighbor, then with joyous hearts they will see the image and likeness of God in the faces not only of their friends but in the faces of the lowly, the poor, the unlovely and because they have learned to love Christ in their neighbor, the religion of Christ will be triumpahnt.[91]

The Kerygma and "Other Sheep"

On Monday, April 13, 1932, the day sometimes called "Other-Sheep-Monday," a young priest stepped onto the lawn in front of the country courthouse in Oklahoma City, Oklahoma, and began to tell the loiterers and passersby about God's word and God's Son, Jesus. It was early evening and a "first" for that southwestern state's capital. It was no accident that it occurred on "Other-Sheep-Monday," as the young preacher labeled it, for the Gospel passage assigned for that day's reading was John 10:16, in which Jesus told his followers that "there are other sheep I have that are not of this fold, and these I have to lead as well. They too will listen to my voice and there will be only one flock and one shepherd." The most startling thing about the event was that the loiterers interrupted their conversations or their naps and the strollers stopped their ambling. All listened. Furthermore, that experience became a weekly event on Mondays through the spring and summer months of that year.[92]

The speaker was twenty-seven-year-old Stephen A. Leven, assistant pastor at nearby St. Joseph Cathedral. Accompanying him was a fellow priest, Victor J. Reed, who addressed the street congregation on alternate Mondays. It was a "first" in another way: the beginning of a twenty-seven-year apostolate of street preaching in the southwest. But Leven and Reed had "practiced" elsewhere before engaging in that "revival approach" in Oklahoma.

In fact, the idea was not original. It was initiated by the two men's bishop, Francis Clement Kelley, who had planted the idea when, in 1926, he visited the American College in Louvain, Belgium, where the two, along with other Oklahomans, were engaged in studies preparatory to their ordination to the priesthood.[93] Kelley's enthusiasm was derived from his recent visit to London and his encounter there with the work of the Catholic Evidence Guild, a movement which got its start in the wake of World War I. The objective of the guild was to teach anyone who was willing to listen about Catholicism.[94] The guild sponsored training sessions for prospective preachers. These sessions were serious classes in theology, Scripture, and philosophy followed by examinations in the respective subject areas.[95] Some technical training in open-air communications, coping with hecklers, responding to genuine inquiries, etc., was also included.

Kelley expressed the hope that the Oklahoma seminarians he visited would take advantage of their nearness to England, go over during the vacation months, learn the ways and means of street preaching, and take their newly gained information and expertise back home with them. Three Oklahoma priesthood students took his suggestion. One of them was Stephen A. Leven (1905–1983), who later (1969) became the third bishop of San Angelo, Texas.[96] Another was Victor J. Reed (1905–1971), who became Oklahoma's fourth bishop in 1958. A third was Charles A. Buswell (1913–), who was bishop of Pueblo, Colorado, from 1959 to 1979. It was Leven, however, who was the foremost proponent, organizer, and advocate of this apostolate. It was chiefly through his tireless zeal and enthusiasm that street-corner *kerygma* became an accepted and effective means of bringing the Christian message to countless uninformed or poorly informed people.

The Oklahoma City experience initiated years of intensive street preaching by Leven and others. Different responsibilities curtailed Reed's involvement in this apostolate though he retained his interest in it. As to Buswell, Leven himself testified to the fact that he was a "truly great street-preacher."[97]

The idea spread beyond the state's limits. In 1939 Leven hosted the "First Institute of Street Preaching" in Tonkawa, Oklahoma, the small rural town in which he was then pastor, which welcomed a number of out-of-state participants. At Bishop O'Hara's request, Leven later organized and directed similar institutes at the College of the Ozarks in Carthage, Missouri, where facilities could accommodate a larger number of participants.

It must be clarified here that priests were not the only preachers in these "curb-service Christian doctrine" sessions. At the invitation of Sr. Thomas Aquinas, OP, Leven addressed the student body at Rosary College, River Forest, Illinois, in 1933. There he described the evangelical apostolate in which he was engaged. As a result students volunteered to assist the priests and "to do street-preaching" under Leven's direction. According to personal accounts, these experiences were as beneficial to the young women as to the street-corner listeners.[98]

Leven's street-preaching apostolate came to a gradual halt in 1959. He maintained that advances in ventilation and communication were the "maladies" that led to its demise.[99] Prior to their allurement, on hot summer evenings people escaped the indoor heat by finding nonstrenuous activities and entertainment outside their homes. A gathering crowd attracted curiosity. Once "caught," people stayed to inquire and to learn.

When air conditioning and the television set made staying at home irresistible, street preachers were generally left in isolation. Nonetheless, Leven maintained that the idea and the practice had a timeless value. "Street-preaching," he once said, "is the way that St. Paul converted the Gentiles."[100] What was called for was new media to replace the outdoor preacher. One might observe that Lucey and other proponents of the use of contemporary communications media later employed the Pauline approach in catechizing.

Street-preaching was by no means restricted to the southwestern areas nor to rural parts of the nation. Kenrick Seminary in St. Louis introduced it into the training program for priesthood students in the late 1930s.[101] It also became popular enough to be included as one of the "exercises" that seminarians did in certain cities on the East Coast and elsewhere. It is reported that other future bishops were also involved in the activity. Albert Fletcher (1896–1979), bishop of Little Rock, Ernest Leo Unterkoefler (1917–), currently bishop of Charleston, and John Joyce Russell (1897–), retired bishop of Richmond, were among those who became engaged in the apostolate at different times.[102]

Another prelate-to-be who was influenced by Hyde Park's Catholic Evidence Guild but whose apostolate took a somewhat different direction was Fulton J. Sheen (1895–1979). Sheen spent the summer of 1925 and part of 1928–1931 street-preaching in England. His autobiography, *Treasure in Clay*, includes a picture of him street-preaching in Alabama.[103] It was apparently a good "novitiate" for his later twenty-two years on the air (1930–1952) in NBC's "Catholic Hour" radio program and his years in the television series "Life Is Worth Living," which ran from 1951 to 1966.

CROZIER AND INK CATECHESIS

There is a well-known Latin dictum attesting to the importance of the written word: *Verba volant scripta manent* (words fly away, the written remains). Ever since the first letters were written and collected in what we call the "New Testament," the ministry of promulgating the Good News as well as that of nurturing and stimulating the faith-life of Christians has relied on both the spoken and the written word. It continues to do so. For some Church leaders, the written word was (and is) a medium with which they were more comfortable and more gifted. Some of their writings qualify as catecheses inasmuch as they were directed to believers with the intention of stimulating and inducing growth in faith.

Francis Clement Kelley (1870–1948), the second bishop of Oklahoma City-Tulsa (1924–1948), was one of the "greatest home missioners of his age," according to James P. Gaffey, his biographer.[104] He was also one of the most prolific writers among U.S. bishops. Writing "was the heart of his artistic life" and a medium with but one purpose: the "overpowering desire to promote the interest of the Church."[105] At times the literary quality lessened because of his "constant penchant to moralize,"[106] but for the most part the mettle of his prose and overall style, branded "Kelley-esque," was exemplary, commanding the respect of literary figures of his own time such as H. L. Mencken, Eileen Duggan, and others.[107]

If one considers catechesis as that which contributes to the ever deepening faith-life of Christians, the majority of Kelley's works were indeed catechesial. Two of his books were more ostensibly didactic,

Letters to Jack (1917) and *The Epistles of Father Timothy to His Parishioners* (1924).[108]

More innovative and significant in catechesis per se was the address he gave at the CCD Congress in St. Louis in October 1937. Entitled "Let the Eternal Magnet Do His Work,"[109] the presentation was an exhortation to reconsider approaches currently employed. In it he touched on initial evangelizing and its follow-up catechizing, and urged in both a "new" apologetic which centered on Christ.

He insisted that engaging in controversial issues was not the way to win or to convince and should be avoided when introducing an inquirer to Christian realities. "Vainly we begin by controversy," he cautioned, since it would lead only to bitter discussion and defensive stance.

The ideal is to "begin with Christ." "Let him be transfigured before men. Let him be transfigured in men. Men's hearts must be new Tabors."[110] The approach was "new" yet based on the oldest catechesis of apostolic and early Christian times. The address rang with overtones of the catechetical renewal under way in Germany and stimulated the year before (1936) by Josef A. Jungmann's classic work, which in turn was based on the nineteenth-century insights of Johannes Hirscher, Bernard Overburg, and others. Kelley's call for catechists to center on Christ, to shift to what has become identified as the "kerygmatic approach," indicates that the bishop perceived the more comprehensive and ideal direction catechesis ought to have been taking. It is highly unlikely that Kelley was aware of Jungmann's volume.[111] It was not widely circulated in non-German-speaking countries, and it was not translated into English until twenty-six years later as *The Good News Yesterday and Today*.[112]

Another quality of Kelley's writing theory relates well to contemporary catechesial practice, namely, story telling. Often he combined two literary forms, story telling and editorializing. His fiction was never without a cause, and sometimes the cause overweighted the story; but just as often the story carried the message gracefully. At this writing, in the early eighties, story telling is enjoying a resurgence of appreciation that dates back to Jesus' use of parables. Kelley maintained that a good and engaging story could keep the attention of nearly everyone and at the same time communicate powerful messages. He urged its use.[113]

One final observation before leaving this Prince Edward Islander-turned-Oklahoman is in order. Like nineteenth-century prelates such as John England, Benedict Fenwick, and others, Kelley recognized the value of a periodical to promote causes and to inform the faithful. *Extension* was the organ for the Extension Society which Kelley had founded (October 18, 1905) as a mission organization to assist and support (morally and otherwise) the Church in the neglected mission areas of the

United States. The first issue of *Extension Magazine* appeared in April 1906.[114] Kelley was its editor. The magazine grew steadily in subscriptions and in popularity, gradually surmounting publication costs and other difficulties. Its contents gave readers a sense of pride and confidence as well as an opportunity to express their generosity to the missions. It also afforded Kelley a forum for literary expression.

John Francis Noll (1875–1956), fifth bishop of Fort Wayne (Indiana), was a man who as cleric and bishop used writing and editing as "evangelizing and catechetical tools."[115] Concern for correcting the false notions of non-Catholics which led to prejudice against Catholicism resulted in his first booklet, *Kind Words from Your Pastor* (1904). Zeal for his fellow Catholics and their growth in faith urged him, in 1908, to begin publishing *The Family Digest*, a magazine for circulation in parishes.[116] Four years later (1912) he began publishing a newspaper, *Our Sunday Visitor*, which would serve in both apostolates, that among non-Catholics and that among the Catholic faithful themselves. This periodical has enjoyed uninterrupted publication from that day until the present time. A third periodical, which he introduced for a more specialized readership, first appeared in 1925 under the title *The Acolyte*. It, too, has enjoyed continuous publication, though its name was changed to *The Priest* in 1945. Noll's articles and columns in both *Our Sunday Visitor* and *The Priest* addressed and explained doctrinal issues.[116]

In addition Noll wrote several books and numerous pamphlets (approximately 150 in all). Among the most widely read among Catholics and non-Catholics alike were *Father Smith Instructs Jackson* (1913) and *Our National Enemy Number One: Education Without Religion* (1942).

Fulton Sheen, though best known for his oral presentations in both radio and television, also wrote more than fifty volumes of book-length studies. These ranged from theological treatises to philosophical probings, from contemporary social issues to spiritual matters.

Paul J. Hallinan (1911–1968), Atlanta's first archbishop, was "a true leader," according to Joseph L. Bernardin.[117] And he was that with grace and a natural ease which made being with him a privilege. "He was a humble yet secure man who never held back because he was afraid of personal repercussions his stand might have."[118] He took strong positions on social issues such as racial discrimination and war.

In the Catholic world Hallinan was perhaps best known for his vital concern with the Church's liturgy and with the general ignorance of the faithful regarding the central act of their Christian lives. He deplored the fact that "we still take our liturgy as we take our athletics — from the comfort of a grandstand seat."[119] But Hallinan was not a single-issue bishop. For him being a genuine Christian (bishop, cleric, parent, or youth) meant that "today we are all liturgists" and "today we are all catechists."[120] "There will always be need for specialization but the tight compartment walls are falling. . . . We are all catechists informing — but much more than that, *forming* — others in faith, initiating children, young people, and adults and bringing them to a genuine conversion in which they will remain."[121]

Hallinan insisted on "reading" and interpreting correctly the signs of the times. Nothing, he added, should be foreign to the Church. He did not bury his head in the sand, "never retired from the world and its problems because of fear. On the contrary, he was always out front, ready to meet the challenge no matter what it might be."[122] In an address to the Catholic Adult Education Commission he forthrightly illustrated the need for wisdom and for the intelligent perception of current events.

In another context he pointed out that the spirit of the post-Vatican II Church is one of sharing and unity, that the walls which previously created divisions — whether of adult scholars or school children — are falling and, indeed, must fall. Addressing the Confraternity Congress in Pittsburgh in 1966, he insisted that the distinctions which favored one group over another within the Church had to be eliminated. "The 'second-class citizenship' of the public school student must be replaced by 'the special affection and faithfulness' the [Second Vatican] Council calls for."[123]

Pointedly he turned to the hierarchy and proposed an "Agenda for Bishops." "What does the Church expect of us bishops in the matter of religious education?" he asked. Then he responded to his own question by citing the council document addressed to bishops: "We are required to announce the Gospel of Christ to men . . ., expound the whole mystery of Christ to them." He implied that the Church is saying to its bishops that they must "use all the means at hand, preaching and catechetical instruction; spread the Gospel of Christ through public statements well-disseminated through the news media; train the catechists properly for their task; in the exercise of authority, govern, promote and guard the entire liturgical life" (*Christus Dominus*, 13).[124] He added, "It seems to me that three great questions of religious education face every bishop: 1) *Should we not lead the breakthrough of this Maginot Line*, the dying catechism . . .? 2) *Is not a bad CCD worse than none at all?* 3) Finally, beyond the new avenues of necessary facts and the pools of better teachers, *we bishops are at a formidable point of decision.*"[125]

He then proceeded to enlarge on each of the "great questions."

(1) *Should we not lead the breakthrough of this Maginot Line,* the dying catechism, rote methods, non-liturgical structures? Is it not our task to shatter the old formats and give free rein to new teachers who know liturgy and know pupils? Recent far-reaching studies . . . do not find present CCD effective.

The truth is—we just don't know the facts. We are in no position to take a stand in the great conceptual debate on Catholic education. To get these facts we must enter the two-way street of research, experiment, and free options. I submit that our first task is to get the facts we need.

(2) *Is not a bad CCD worse than none at all?* A class that travels only one-way streets of instruction will not really love our Lord. It will only hear his voice. Father John E. Corrigan, in a recent article in *Worship*, has coined one of the classic understatements of all time: "Our concept of faith has all too often been overly cerebral." Only the teacher who loves his faith and his pupils can change that. We must find such cate-chists, train them, compensate them. There are fine religious communities ready to prepare them for us.

Even the poor parish can make a start. Periodicals like *Worship, Lumen Vitae,* and the reports of the Society for Sacred Doctrine are very helpful. Under Father Sloyan's direc-tion at the Catholic University of America, and at such centers as Fordham and Manhattan, and in summer programs at Manhattanville, to name only a few, there are places of cate-chetical dynamism where religion is taught as an art. The best minds in the field are at work.

(3) Finally, beyond the new avenues of necessary facts and the pools of better teachers, *we bishops are at a formidable point of decision.* We must give equal billing to all channels of reli-gious education—like concern, teacher-quality, facilities and opportunities to the pupil wherever he is found. Child and youth must be instructed and formed in the parochial school, the school of religion, or any other facet of Confraternity education. A proportionate budget is essential. Although allowing for the existing physical plant, the building must be seen as serving, not just the pupils of the parish school, but those in public schools, young adults, and the general public.

The "second-class citizenship" of the public school stu-dent must be replaced by "the special affection and faithful-ness" the Council calls for. One obvious start is a diocesan Secretary for Education responsible for all religious instruc-tion and formation. Another step is the professional training of catechists. A third is a paid full-time director for the parish school of religion.

But there are a hundred little ways we must explore, to keep these pupils from becoming the Oliver Twists of educa-tion. The First Communion Day should know no distinctions;

public school boys should serve at the altar, girls at other work; picnics and outings can be arranged on days when all can attend. The rector of our Cathedral, Bishop Joseph L. Bernardin, has told his people that "separate, but equal treatment" is over: "Sacramentally, socially and recreationally, they are a single body of boys and girls, and we welcome them all as one."[126]

In a broader context he offered some suggestions. "1) One obvious start is a diocesan Secretary responsible for all religious instruction and formation. 2) Another step is the professional training of catechists. 3) A third is a paid full-time director for the parish school of religion."[127]

Hallinan had encouraging and helpful words for catechists: "The catechist is today's prophet — gently sometimes sharply, guiding the young, disdaining easy, old-style methods, refusing to be discouraged." Carrying the analogy further, he explained:

> The prophets of Israel helped their people to stop clamoring after idols. They urged them on to God, loving them and wanting their full development. These rugged witnesses found that they could not turn aside for an easier path. And only hope in God held them to their mission. . . . It is a high and noble role, to share with Isaiah, Daniel, Hosea and Habakkuk the delicate burden of opening men's minds to God. It is not easy.
>
> And yet you have this consolation — the entire Church is watching and praying for you. . . . As you climb the teaching ladder to the summit of divine worship, there is one overriding consideration, one grand design — to make God felt in the minds and hearts of men.[128]

In terms of academic preparation Raymond A. Lucker (1927-) is unique among the U.S. bishops: both of his doctoral dissertations deal with catechesis. In 1966 he earned a doctorate in sacred theology (STD) from the Angelicum in Rome. His dissertation was a comparative and historical study, "The Aims of Religious Education in the Early Church and in the American Catechetical Movement."[129] Three years later he earned a Ph.D. at the University of Minnesota with a 357-page dissertation entitled "Some Presuppositions of Released Time."[130] This background undoubtedly had some effect on his being selected in 1968 to serve as director of the department of education at the United States Catholic Conference, where he was influential in shaping policy and setting directions in catechetics until 1971, when he was named auxiliary bishop of St. Paul and Minneapolis.

Lucker's talks and writings addressed issues of the day and prospects of the future. He presented one of the major papers at the 1971 International Catechetical Congress in Rome, calling attention to the potential which modern media of social communications have for the Church's ministry of the word. "The media of social communications can be involved at every level of religious education, especially at the human development level and at the level of theological understanding but also at the critical level of faith experience."[131]

In another context Lucker illustrated the importance of the laity in catechesis, anticipating in this two points made in the GCD in 1971: the stress on adult catechesis[132] and the insistence that the faithful as a whole are catechists.[133] Lucker qualified the realization of the people as catechists by specifying that it was directly related to their understanding of themselves as being the Church. Relying extensively on Pius XII's addresses and writings, Lucker strengthened his points.[134] He quoted the pontiff frequently. "The consecration of the world is essentially the work of the laity . . ., of people who are intimately a part of economic and social life."[135]

> The needs of our times require that the laity . . . procure for themselves a treasure of religious knowledge, not a poor and meager knowledge, but one that will have solidity and richness through the medium of libraries, discussions, and study clubs; in this way they will derive great benefit for themselves and at the same time be able to instruct the ignorant, confute stubborn adversaries, and be of assistance to good friends.[136]

Emphasizing the point, Lucker quoted Pius XII again. "I can write encyclicals, I can speak over the radio. But I cannot go into your homes, into the mines and shops. These places are closed to us. If the laity do not translate the doctrines of Christ into the spheres of political, social, economic, educational, professional, and recreational life, no one else can; no one else will."[137] In other words, catechesis takes place in the actual world of the lay person.

In a final thrust Lucker called for an assessment of discussion clubs in the context of their apostolic formation of adult participants. He highlighted the fact that they had moved away from their original purpose, and, though change could be good, the time had arrived for an evaluation of their contemporary direction and objectives.

Lucker was named bishop of New Ulm (Minnesota) in 1975. His concern for and involvement in the ministry of catechesis has not waned.

AN OVERVIEW

In retrospect it becomes clear that the recognition of catechesis in the U.S. Church during the first six decades of the twentieth century was closely linked to the development of the Confraternity of Christian

Doctrine. Through the tireless efforts of Edwin O'Hara and numerous committed and dedicated people across the nation the ministry of cate-chizing experienced a new impulse which brought it into clearer focus as an important and vital apostolate. It could not be left exclusively to the schools, though it certainly belonged there. Gradually catechesis became acknowledged as an ecclesial responsibility, not confined to schools, not limited to children and youth, not restricted to question-and-answer manuals, and not the exclusive preserve of the clergy and hierarchy. Nonetheless, the bishops acknowledged their leadership role in catechesis.

In 1934 the U.S. bishops, at their annual November meeting, corpo-rately acknowledged their responsibility when they established a special Committee of Bishops to coordinate, regulate, oversee, and encourage the apostolate of catechizing through the Confraternity. Bishops John T. McNicholas, archbishop of Cincinnati, John G. Murray, archbishop of St. Paul, and Edwin V. O'Hara formed the charter committee with O'Hara designated as chairman. "This was the grain of mustard seed that grew into the mighty tree of the CCD, its roots penetrating every diocese of the country and its benevolent branches shading and refreshing all who thirst for the lifegiving and consoling teaching of eternal truth."[138]

One of the earliest decisions of this first episcopal committee was to open a National Center in Washington, D.C. Such a center was viewed as an essential element in serving the Church. According to Ruth C. Rock, "There was no escaping the logic that the National Center was to be what its name implied, a center that would gather in and give out, for the ser-vice of the bishops and diocesan Confraternity directors, the fruits of the best thought and experience in the field of religious instruction. . . . This was therefore the very heart of the plan."[139]

In the course of its nearly forty years of existence (1934–1973) the episcopal committee, through the center, served as coordinator and clearinghouse, as energizer and confirmer of general and specific endeavors connected with catechizing. During those years at least twenty-two bishops served on the national committee. O'Hara, McNicholas, and Murray served as the committee from 1934 to 1940. In time the committee expanded from three members to five, to eight, and finally to twelve.

Among the prelates (besides O'Hara, McNicholas, and Murray) who served on the committee were James E. Kearney, bishop of Rochester; Gerald P. O'Hara, bishop of Savannah–Atlanta; Chester H. Winkelmann, bishop of Wichita; Matthew F. Brady, bishop of Burlington and later of Manchester; Robert E. Lucey, archbishop of San Antonio; Wm. Theodore Mulloy, bishop of Covington; Wm. P. O'Connor, bishop of Superior and later of Madison; Charles D. White, bishop of Spokane; Charles P. Greco, bishop of Alexandria; Joseph P. Dougherty, bishop of Yakima; Josef M. Gilmore, bishop of Helena; Hugh L. Lamb, bishop of Greensburg; Joseph T. McGucken, bishop of Sacramento and later archbishop of San Francisco; Sidney M. Metzger, bishop of El Paso; Hubert M. Newell, bishop of Cheyenne; John J. Carberry, bishop of Lafayette, later archbishop of St. Louis; Christopher J. Weldon, bishop of Springfield; and John J. Wright, bishop of Worcester and later of Pittsburgh. Bishop Charles P. Greco was chairman of the committee from 1966 until 1978 when the center closed and the committee ceased functioning as a body.

5

The 1970s and a Forward Thrust

A SURVEY OF CATECHETICAL EVENTS

From a worldwide perspective the twentieth century might legitimately be called a "catechetical century," a time of catechetical resurgence. For the first time in the Church's history specific concentration on the ministry of catechizing came into prominence in different parts of the globe. Its roots were in nineteenth-century Germany and Austria, with such leaders as Bernhard Galura, Bernard Overburg, and Johannes Hirscher. Their efforts were joined to advances in learning theory made by psychologists and educationists such as Germany's Johann F. Herbart (1776–1841), Switzerland's Johann H. Pestalozzi (1746–1827), and others. As a result of their studies the nature and process of learning and related procedures in teaching were reexamined and altered. Innovative methods were introduced and popularized in the schools.

Little by little the progressive practices spilled over into extraschool settings. Catechists took note of the changing procedures and began to adopt them. They also collaborated with each other and formed small, local catechetical societies. By 1900 the several small societies and local groups, expanded in size, conviction, and collaboration, formed what in retrospect may be called a catechetical movement.[1] By that time catechesis as a ministry had lost its earlier comprehensive concept and was more narrowly identified with question-and-answer handbooks for children in formal educational settings. Therefore, educational methodology was considered the logical area in which to assess practical catechesis and to develop improvements.

The best-known of such endeavors was the "Munich Method," so named for the city in which its originators resided.[2] That method advocated two principles: (1) careful adherence to self-contained units of information (doctrines) and (2) the text-developing approach, in which the catechist was to employ an example that would relate and appeal to the particular children whom he or she was addressing. From that starting point the catechist was to develop the text of the lesson and to assist the children in understanding the matter and incorporating it into their lives.[3]

Catechetical Congresses

Beginning in 1903 regional catechetical congresses were held in European centers—in Vienna, Salzburg, Munich, Budapest, Milan, Luzerne, and other cities. These congresses served to encourage the movement, broaden the search for methodological advances, and give catechesis increased emphasis. Enthusiasm and interest grew. In 1912 the first "international" catechetical congress was held in Vienna (September 8–11). With an attendance of 800 participants, the congress thoroughly explored instruction theories and ended by affirming the tenets of the Munich Method.[4] Before the assembly dispersed, plans were made for a second congress. However, World War I intervened, and it was sixteen years before the second international congress was held. In the meantime Pope Pius XI had set up a catechetical office (*Officium Catecheticum*) in the Sacred Congregation of the Council. That office was established through Pius's recommendation in his *motu proprio, Orbem Catholicum*, of June 1923.[5] Catechesis received further attention when the Sacred Congregation for Seminaries and Universities charged the bishops of the world to prepare diocesan seminarians to give religious instruction. Seminaries were advised to introduce teacher training into the curriculum and to provide opportunities for practice teaching.[6]

In 1928 (August 6–10) Munich hosted the second international congress. That congress retained much the same spirit, enthusiasm, and participation as the Vienna congress had done before it, emphasizing methodology and encouraging catechists.[7] Furthermore, it approved the procedures that Maria Montessori had introduced into the teaching field.[8] P. Mario Barbera, a member of the Vatican's *Officium Catecheticum*, attended the Munich Congress.[9]

The third international catechetical congress was held in Rome, October 10–14, 1950. This gathering has sometimes been regarded as quasi-official inasmuch as it was assembled in the "Eternal City" and included addresses by high-ranking Church officials.[10] At least four U.S. churchmen were among the participants: Bishop Edwin V. O'Hara of Kansas

City, Bishop Matthew Brady of Manchester, Bishop Jacob McNulty of Newark, and Fr. Claude Sons, OSB, of Shawnee, Oklahoma. O'Hara presented a paper describing the vitality of the Confraternity of Christian Doctrine in the United States.[11] The concluding remarks by Pope Pius XII deviated from the prevalent concentration on methodology.

> Most people know all the sacraments; they know about the person of Christ, as well as about Our Lady, Peter and Paul, Adam and Eve, and a good many others. They know enough about the commandments of God and of the Church.

> But what is lacking among the faithful, is a sense of unity, seeing it all as a whole, an understanding of the wonderful message of divine grace. All they retain of Christian doctrine is a string of dogmas and moral precepts, threats and promises, customs and rites, tasks and duties imposed on Catholics. . . . Both our teaching and our catechisms are too much in the nature of theological treatises.[12]

According to Josef Jungmann, who also participated in the congress, "The main root of today's religious malady is to be sought in an extensive misunderstanding or nonunderstanding of the Christian message."[13] He illustrated this point in a commentary on Luke's Gospel. In narrating the experience of the disciples at Emmaus (Luke 24:13-30), he questioned and explained:

> What was his [Christ's] remedy for the dullness of faith of those disciples? A vital understanding of the Scriptures as they unfolded his role of suffering servant in the Father's merciful plan of salvation. And the result? Their hearts were aflame with a joyous, enthusiastic faith that leapt into action and enkindled the spirits of others! We witness the very same process in the experience of the Apostles on Pentecost.[14]

> There would seem to be a law here that has not been sufficiently appreciated at all times in our religious teaching: that it is not enough to show the necessity and reasonableness of faith, nor enough to expound every point of doctrine and every commandment down to the very last division; but that it is singularly important to achieve first of all *a vital understanding* of the Christian message, bringing together "the many" into a consistent, unified whole, that then *there may be joyous interest and enthusiastic response* in living faith.[15]

In brief, what was needed, according to his former student, Johannes Hofinger, was a better grasp of the core and substance of the Christian message.[16]

From the Gospel accounts Jungmann had turned to the practice of early Christianity, "the Church's springtime." His doctoral dissertation, completed at Innsbruck in 1923, had been a study of the treatment of grace in catechesis and in the kerygma during the first two centuries of the Church's existence.[17] He urged a return tradition — Scripture and liturgy — as the source for catechesis and life. Heralding, preaching, and living the Good News, the kerygma, became his theme. "Before Karl Barth could accuse Catholic theologians of keeping 'a very strict silence' on the subject of preaching, this silence was already broken by the *Good News* of Jungmann."[18] Barth,[19] in fact, had little if any influence on Jungmann, who claimed his own findings in patristic writings along with the studies of nineteenth-century thinkers as his sources and mentors.

Jungmann was no superficial theologian: he was comprehensive and holistic in his view of Christian thought, life, and practice. Nor did he conceive of theology as inimical to catechizing and preaching. For the pastor and the catechist the three were interdependent. It was, in fact, according to Jungmann, the responsibility of both pastor and catechist to study seriously the progress of the Church's theological thought, use it as a winnowing instrument to extract particular insights and nuances in Scripture and tradition, and communicate them to the faithful of every age.

One did not address adult and youthful inquirers in the same language and with the same images that one used to exchange insights with one's theological colleagues. And, in fact, Jungmann decried the almost total concentration on childhood catechesis, observing that, in effect, instruction limited to childhood can achieve only incomplete results.[20]

Josef Jungmann's discoveries were transmitted to the faithful in the United States through his own visits to this country in the early 1950s for summer courses at the University of Notre Dame, through the circuit lectures of his former student, Johannes Hofinger, and through U.S. scholars who studied at Innsbruck or kept abreast of the thought and findings of European thinkers.

During the 1950s and 1960s a healthy sense of uneasiness with the prevailing practice of catechizing resulted in a mushrooming search for a "new" catechesis in the large parochial and private schools across the land. Teachers looked for opportunities to probe more deeply into theological, historical, and celebration depths of Christian truths. Summer and academic-year programs in religious studies swelled. Meanwhile institutes and programs developed. An international center, Lumen Vitae (Brussels, Belgium), had opened its doors in 1946. Numerous U.S. students helped fill its classrooms. The well-established department of Religious Education which opened in 1937 at the Catholic University of America grew proportionately as well, as did similar programs at other universities.

International Study Weeks

Meanwhile international study weeks began to be held periodically. Unlike earlier gatherings, these were not called "congresses." The Catechetical Office (*Officium Catecheticum*) in the Sacred Congregation of the Council had decreed in 1924 that every catechetical "congress" which was not diocesan should seek permission from the Sacred Congregation and submit programs of the proposed congress for approval.[21] Since the international gatherings, as projected by Hofinger, their instigator and director, were exploratory forums for the exchange of thought, practice, and insights, they were named "study weeks."

In 1956 the Institut Saint-Ignace in Antwerp hosted 400 representatives from thirty-two nations for a twelve-day session entitled "Catechesis for Our Time."[22] At least one U.S. representative, Gerard S. Sloyan of Catholic University's Religious Education Department, participated in this meeting. Three years later, September 12–19, 1959, a second major study week was held, in Nijmegen, Holland. It was convened by the initiative and under the direction of Johannes Hofinger from the Institute of Missionary Pastorate of Manila. The accent was on the needs of the missions, but the focus was on the Church's worship as central to the life and formation of the true Christian. Cultural and environmental diversities surfaced among the representatives, but there was a unanimity in vision and practice.[23]

The most significant of these study weeks was held in Eichstätt, Bavaria, July 21–28, 1960.[24] It, too, owed its origin and organization to Johannes Hofinger. One hundred and eight persons, sixty of whom were bishops, gathered from widely separated points around the world. U.S. participants numbered eleven clergymen (no bishops) and one sister, Sr. Maria de la Cruz Aymes-Couck.[25] The full assembly gathered in the small Bavarian town where, in the eighth century, Saints Boniface and Willibald had been familiar figures.

The twenty-eight presentations were in-depth explorations of (1) methodology, (2) the ramifications and tradition of the kerygma, (3) Scripture and catechesis, (4) the centrality of worship to Christian life, (5) the adult catechumenate, and (6) the preparation of catechists. Beyond the diversities projected by representatives from far-flung nations, fundamental problems and issues appeared strikingly similar: the critical and essential task of catechesis, practical directives, and adaptation of the message to unique circumstances. Basic principles of catechesis were identified and assessed. In the end the body approved the kerygmatic renewal and at the same time affirmed that worship, the Eucharist, is the heart of Christian community and that catechesis embraces a four-fold presentation of the faith: through liturgy, Bible, systematic teaching, and the testimony of Christian living.[26]

In brief, the Eichstätt gathering seemd to echo Jungmann's summarizing words:

> A kind of faith as is illuminated in the Roman liturgy as heir to Christian antiquity ought to be unfolded with equal and greater clarity, in the actual teaching of the faith. Sermon and catechesis, religious art and the organization of service ought to strive jointly to promote a consciousness of the faith upon which the liturgical and sacramental life may be based, and from which a joyful Christian faith can arise. This will be possible only when out of the many accretions of the centuries the one single message, the kerygma of the early Church, is once again allowed to emerge. To accomplish this, Christ must be restored to the centre of the faith. The restoration of the kerygma to its full power and clarity is, therefore, a principal task of modern pastoral work.[27]

Seemingly the pinnacle had been attained, the direction set, and all was well. In truth, however, there was no cause for complacency. The message and its proclamation could brook no static stance. Insights of the faithful and the findings of scholars would continue to uncover new facets of the mystery and learn more secrets of its beauty, which would both alter and direct further explorations. One very essential reality was already overlooked, namely, that the good news, the kerygma, reached people in their own settings, and, according to the principle of adaptation, their unique environmental and cultural circumstances had a determining effect on the way in which the word was received, comprehended, and communicated. In the following study weeks—Bangkok in 1962, Katigondo, 1964, Manila, 1967, and Medellin, 1968—the critical question arose repeatedly: "Are we to go on reiterating Christ's message in the very kerygmatic form which was used by the apostles? Surely times have changed!"[28]

Bangkok, Katigondo, Manila, Medellin

At the Bangkok meeting, the concept of preevangelization came to the fore as missionaries and catechists alike explored the necessity of starting where people are with their particular values and milieux, instead of proclaiming the Gospel truths in some prepackaged form. Even the four Gospel accounts testify to a respect for the specific group each evangelist addressed. In short, Bangkok uncovered a heretofore unexamined dimension.

Missionaries formed the largest proportion of conference participants, and their questions gave direction to the sessions. Theodore Stone from Chicago described the process as "positive apologetics" which "proceeds from a true understanding and appreciation of whatever is good and acceptable in (peoples') culture. It consists in taking due consideration of the person with whom we speak and in removing the personal concrete obstacles which prevent one's ready acceptance of the kerygma (message)."[29]

Two years later (August 26–September 1, 1964), on the African continent, another international study week opened in Katigondo, Uganda. Like the congresses at Nijmegen, Eichstätt, and Bangkok, the planning and arrangements were made by Johannes Hofinger. More than 100 participants collected at the major seminary in Katigondo. Once again attention was paid to the cultural circumstances and the dominant characteristics of those being evangelized and catechized. In the main the principles of Bangkok were upheld,[30] with attention given to the specific needs and unique values and traits of African nations. It was the anthropological phase reiterated and exemplified.

The Manila conference (April 1967) in the Philippines also confirmed the tenets of Bangkok and Katigondo but with a more confident and explicit tone. What Eichstätt had been for the kerygmatic renewal, Manila was for the anthropological thrust. In fact, the two formed an almost natural progression and, in retrospect, were acknowledged as complementary to each other.

According to one commentator:

> The Study Week in Manila may be referred to in years to come as a culminating point of this new concern with man and his world, just as the Eichstätt meeting is looked upon as a climax of the kerygmatic phase of the catechetical movement. The strong emphasis placed, in the papers and discussions of the Manila meeting, on approaching man as we find him, on the anthropological orientation of catechesis, gave this meeting its peculiar character. But it must always be remembered that this deep concern for man never distracts from the Mystery of Christ: it rather opens for Christ the door to man.[31]

The 1968 study week at Medellin, Colombia (August 11–17) brought yet another aspect to light. This meeting, which attracted 200 participants, was convened principally by the heads of fifteen institutes, regional and international, with the specific intention of arranging some cooperation between existing pastoral institutes and faculties of theology in seminaries or universities.[32] At the time few of the institutes were qualified to grant degrees, diplomas, or certificates. Yet there was an increasing demand for such specific qualifications in order to raise academic standards, improve the state of catechesis in general, and focus on the discipline of catechetics across the board. What they accomplished may have led to that, but no such specifications emerged in the final conclusions. What did surface was a stark reality that previous study weeks had not confronted: the political, social, and economic order of the late twentieth century is often hostile, contradictory, and even impervious to both the message and the ideal life of Christianity. The turbulent and sometimes destructive socioeconomic conditions existing in many Latin American countries served to illustrate this. These conditions were also prevalent in other areas throughout the world. The assembly agreed that it was unrealistic to present a message of salvation while disregarding existent cacophonous "noises" that deafened or muted the transmission of the word. Theoretically and ideally the Christian message always takes into consideration the existential realities of peoples' lives, but when these realities deliberately and pointedly militate against freedom and legitimate options, a third aspect of the ministry must come into play, namely, a grappling with these elements in the social order which obscure or prevent Christian truth from being experienced.

The saving word has to be spoken in a variety of circumstances, some of which may be inimical to it. The word *will* get through to those who will to hear it. Circumstances charge catechesis with the responsibility of being inventive and creative in penetrating the morass. Msgr. Joseph Bournique from France reminded the group that Christianity is future-oriented, not complacent in recreating a past. It calls on society "to create a new civilization . . . not that Christianity marches in one direction and the human in another. But that one is incarnated in the other."[33] Furthermore, it is imperative for the Christian community to be discerning enough to direct or redirect the course which a given society is taking. Christianity has something to say to human society. It "says . . . 'Your plan must be centered on Christ' and on his values."[34] In another session, Paulo Friere, the exiled Brazilian educator, was cited. "To educate," he insisted, "is not to introduce someone into a ready-made world, but to help him transform the world."[35] One speaker warned that the church must pause and examine its own position lest it be an integral part of, or at least ancillary to, the very structure that deserves condemnation. "She cannot claim to be blameless when around her thousands are starving," François Houtart said. "She cannot say that she is only concerned with spiritual matters." That kind of scrutiny, he pointed out, does not apply only to the southern continent of the western hemisphere but "to the Universal Church, as much to Europe as to other continents." However, "it must be diversified according to different concrete situations."[36]

The Medellin study week drew up seventeen conclusions which addressed not only the situations and circumstances of Latin American but also those beyond its continental boundaries. The sixth conclusion illustrated in part the scope of the ideals addressed by the assembly.

> We want to stress the demands of pluralism in the joint pastoral effort. The situations in which catechesis evolves are very diverse: from those of the patriarchal type, where traditional forms are still accepted, to those of the most advanced contemporary urban civilizations. One of the aims of the study week has been to stress the richness existing in the diversity of view-points and of forms which exist in catechesis. It is impossible, in view of this, to think in terms of a universal catechesis of the monolithic type. The increasing pluralism, while a sign of life and energy, demands a new type of unity which must be expressed in a new form of words. The Study Week desires that collaboration at all levels be intensified and that the national and international exchanges be multiplied so as to promote this unity of faith in diversity.[37]

"Catechesis lives," according to the twelfth statement, "in permanent tension between continuity and rupture."[38] In conclusion, "the living and operative presence of Christ in the human community . . . urges everyone to be co-responsible through reflection."[39]

Finally, the assembly made an earnest appeal to John Cardinal Villot who was then president of the Pontifical Commission for Clerics[40] and had served as honorary president of the Medellin study week. The assembly's appeal to him was twofold, but it focused on the catechetical directory on which his commission in Rome was working.

> 1. That *in the Committee for the International Catechetical Directory*, the conclusions reached by the delegates of the International Study Week at Medellin be utilized in discussions and deliberations.
>
> 2. That the International Directory when completed be presented to the National Hierarchy of each country *not* as a normative document, but that it be promulgated in such a way that it leaves the national hierarchies free to exercise that flexibility of approach and expression so clearly indicated by the exigencies of this moment in history.[41]

Reflecting on four decades of catechetical congresses and study weeks, from 1938 to 1971, held in the United States and in various other parts of the world naturally evokes a search for comparisons. Despite the poet's scorn—"comparisons are odious"—one cannot fail to recognize the clear distinctions between the two sets of conferences. They served two distinct purposes and personnel. The Congresses in the United States during that period provided a much-needed sanction for the people involved in catechizing, especially in nonschool settings. They also provided catechists a means of mutual support, exchange, and witness during a time when they needed all the encouragement, inspiration, and idea-exchanging they could get from each other. The emphasis on methodology and ideology predominated. A parochial and private school system had become increasingly strong and was, in the eyes of many, the only ideal setting for catechesis, with CCD classes viewed as second-best substitutes. Basically catechesis was equated with the knowledge of doctrines imparted in classrooms.

Confronting more widely diversified groups of Christians from equally varied geographical regions, the international study weeks adapted to multiple needs and inquiries on a worldwide basis. Nudged by haunting dissatisfaction with what had become a too exclusively defined catechesial concept, they explored and challenged the corpus as well as the contemporary concept of catechesis. In the long run their inquiries and findings directed the Church into a more realistic and at the same time more authentically traditional understanding of catechesis.

From 1962 to 1965 the conciliar participants of the Second Vatican Council and the "students" of the study weeks encountered each other in pen and in person to the mutual advantage of both groups and to the benefit of the Church as a whole.[42] The most concrete evidence of this is the *General Catechetical Directory* promulgated by the Sacred Congregation for the Clergy in 1971.[43]

ADVANCES IN CATECHETICAL THEORY AND PRACTICE IN THE 1970s

The decade of the 1970s was an unusually rich era for catechesis on a global scale. In addition to the surfacing and swelling of interest in catechesis at both the parochial and episcopal levels, seven events marked the seventies as special for the U.S. Church. They were (1) the promulgation of the *General Catechetical Directory* (1971); (2) the International Catechetical Congress held in Rome, September 20–25, 1971; (3) the "National Congress of Religious Education" in Miami Beach, Florida, October 27–30, 1971; (4) the publication of *To Teach as Jesus Did* (1972) and (5) *Basic Teachings for Catholic Religious Education* (1973); (6) the 1977 synod, "Catechesis in Our Time," held in Rome, September 29, 1977; and (7) the publication of *Sharing the Light of Faith*, the National Catechetical Directory promulgated by the U.S. bishop in October 1979.

The first, second, and sixth events had universal import, while the remaining ones were more specifically related to the United States.

In general, the seventies summarized and climaxed a worldwide movement that had been pulsating in the Church's life for decades at many levels — grass roots and among scholars, pastors, and bishops. In one sense the movement called for a restoration of catechesis to a vibrancy known in the early Church, but it was not a nostalgic attempt to duplicate previous practices. Each era carries its own characteristics, assets, and needs. The call was for the principle of stable values in a contemporary mode.

THE *GENERAL CATECHETICAL DIRECTORY*

The innovative idea of a directory in the field of catechesis was both startling and energizing for the Church. Startling, because it was a break with existing practice which had long identified the pastoral ministry of catechizing with children, classrooms, and question-and-answer handbooks (catechisms).[44] It was energizing in the sense that it expanded the boundaries of catechesis beyond the accepted confines and structures that had identified catechesis with formal education and returned it to the holistic, integral concept that focused on a comprehension of the Christian mysteries such as the early Church had experienced. Further, the *Directory* affirmed the "revolutionary" theories about catechesis that had emerged from seminal thinkers during the previous century, for example, that the objective of catechesis is faith, mature, informed faith, that catechesis is based on revelation, is lifelong, with particular emphasis on adults, that it is both a responsibility and a ministry that involves the entire Christian community.[45]

The *Directory* owes its immediate origin to the Second Vatican Council, though it had roots in events and developments that either predated or coexisted with the council's sessions. Vatican I's unimplemented proposal for a universal catechism was one of the former.[46] The fact that no common catechism had been promulgated in the wake of Vatican I led some bishops to conclude that the Second Vatican Council was the logical time and place to act on that "unfinished" business of the earlier council. Others, however, had contrasting ideas, for example, Pierre Marie Laconte, bishop of Beauvais, France, who proposed that the council sponsor and promulgate a catechetical directory that could serve as a guide for the diverse populations that comprise the Catholic Church throught the world.[47]

The Vatican II Preparatory Commission, *De disciplina cleri et populi christiana*, after extended and deliberate consideration, came to the conclusion that, due to the diverse plurality of worldwide Christian communities with their respective cultural, environmental, and geographical differences, a single catechism for the universal Church was not feasible (*nonexpedire*). Instead, the commission affirmed the proposal for a directory which could better serve the whole Church and foresaw that such a volume would establish rules and general norms concerned with the goal of catechesis along with the major doctrinal tenets and phrasing of formulas.[48]

The proposal received further support when the general directive, or "mandate" (*mandatum generale*), as it came to be called, in the bishops' document, *Christus Dominus* (1964), prescribed a general directory which would treat "the catechetical education of the Christian people, and should deal with fundamental principles of such education, its organization and the composition of books on the subject" (#44).[49]

After the final session of the Second Vatican Council, it fell to the Sacred Congregation for the Clergy to implement the mandate. For fifteen months, June 1966 to August 1967, committees in that congregation worked at the rationale, design, structure, and corpus of the proposed directory. They called on and collaborated with special committees of theologians on the ideal contents. In January 1968, John Cardinal Villot, prefect of the Congregation for the Clergy, invited the suggestions, critiques, viewpoints, and written participation of the presidents of episcopal conferences throughout the Catholic world. In May of that year an international commission of eight experts convened in Rome to continue work on the project. Monsignor Russell Neighbor from the United States Catholic Conference represented the U.S. hierarchy. By April 1969 a tentative draft was compiled and ready for a "trial run." Copies were sent to each of the national episcopal conferences for their critiques and reactions. After incorporating the recommendations submitted into the circulated draft, the volume was given to a special theological commission for its assessment and then to the Sacred Congregation for the Doctrine of the Faith.

In this final stage of composition, the "Addendum" on first confession and communion was added. Finally, the Congregation for the Doctrine of the Faith approved the completed text on February 24, 1971. Authorized publication date was April 11, Easter Sunday, 1971. Two months later, June 17, 1971, John Cardinal Wright, prefect of the Sacred Congregation for the Clergy since April 4, 1969, formally introduced the *Directorium Catechisticum Generale* at a public news conference.[50]

A Parenthesis

Of related but parenthetical interest is the proposal of U.S. bishops to compile a "source book" for use among catechists, pastors, and bishops in this country. This proposal, of the Bishop's CCD Committee, was the

outgrowth of a project initiated in 1963 to replace the "Baltimore Catechism" (published in 1885, revised in 1941), which was a source of widespread dissatisfaction. Joseph T. McGucken, archbishop of San Francisco,
as chairman of the Bishops' CCD Committee, proposed it to the U.S.
bishops at their annual meeting, held that year on November 11, 1963,
amidst Vatican II sessions in Rome. The episcopal assembly accepted the
proposal for a "source book," and McGucken announced the decision on
January 10, 1964. The idea gained support and some enthusiasm among
catechists and others. However, after a three-year period of study and
work the project was ultimately abandoned. No reasons were given. It is
possible that the similarity between the proposed "source book" and the
general directory then being composed in Rome was enough to terminate
the plan.[51]

Reception of the GCD in the United States

One indication of the reception the *Directory* received in this country is found in reviews in the periodicals which critiqued and assessed it.
The major religious journals reviewed it and accorded it a deserved spot-
light.[52] A certain amount of the initial response placed exaggerated emphasis on the "Addendum" which dealt with first confession and first
communion. Similar to the postscript at the end of a letter which, like an
afterthought, calls for special attention, the "Addendum" threatened to
overshadow the greater worth of the volume as a whole.

John Cardinal Wright, in the *Homiletic and Pastoral Review*, wrote
a seventeen-page article delineating the import of first confession and
first Eucharist as prescribed in the "Addendum," pointing out the formative and corrective influence which preparation for and reception of
those sacraments possessed.[53] In a later interview Wright mitigated his
position, insisting that the passages in the *GCD*, including the "Addendum," were intended as guidelines, not binding prescriptions. Meeting
with English-speaking delegates attending the International Catechetical
Congress in Rome in September 1971, Wright clarified his position, saying, 'The point I would like to underscore is that we were setting guidelines, that we were not legislating. We are not a legislative body."[54] That
stance was in keeping with the recommendations made to Cardinal Villot
by the Medellin assembly in 1968 that the *Directory* not be a rigidly pre-
scriptive document.[55]

Thomas Sullivan, then associate superintendent of schools for the
archdiocese of Chicago, put the issue in a clearer perspective in his comprehensive review of the *Directory*. He stressed the fact that neither
Quam singulari (1910)[56] nor the Code of Canon Law *demands* that
children receive the sacrament of penance before first reception of the

Eucharist. "The precept of canon law regarding mandatory annual confession has been consistently interpreted as obliging only those who have been guilty of serious sin. There is general agreement that children of the customary age for first Communion are normally incapable of serious sin."[57]

By far the most significant and comprehensive written response to the *Directory* was that of Berard L. Marthaler in his book *Catechetics in Context*,[58] a work written specifically "to help put the directory in perspective." In addition, his 293-page work endeavored "to relate the Directory to contemporary issues and problems in catechesis."[59] Marthaler provided a detailed history of the work along with an insightful and illuminating commentary on the entire text.

In the main, the reception of the *Directory*[60] was heartening. Its appearance heralded a new era in catechesis for the Church as some traditional principles were revived and an age-old ideal image of the Church as a whole came into clearer focus. Two things were outstanding and challenged the status quo: (1) citing adult catechesis as the model and norm (*GCD*, #20), and (2) charging the Christian community as a body with its role in catechizing, which is to be "every day conscious of its duty . . . to be a sign of the wisdom and love of God that was revealed in Christ," by "taking an active part in the undertaking of projects, in making decisions, and in carrying out what has been decided" (#107).[61]

Furthermore, the *GCD* clarified the objective of catechesis: "catechesis is . . . that form of ecclesial action which leads both community and individual members of the faithful into maturity of faith" (#21). This implied the lifelong nature of catechesis in its relation to faith and the continuous process of conversion which is "always present in the dynamics of faith. Catechesis is one means of deepening that faith conversion" (#18, 22). In brief, the objective of catechesis was not knowledge per se but knowledge insofar as it informs faith.

The *General Catechetical Directory* reintroduced aspects of catechesis which had not received special attention for centuries. Essentially it called for a more comprehensive and permeating role for catechesis in the Church's life, a role it had known in the early Church, as manifested in the writings of Augustine of Hippo, Cyril of Jerusalem, Ambrose of Milan, John Chrysostom of Constantinople, and others.

INTERNATIONAL CATECHETICAL CONGRESS, ROME, SEPTEMBER 1971

Five months after the *Directory* appeared, hundreds of participants from around the world gathered at the Lateran University in Rome for a congress on catechetics. The Congregation for the Clergy, on May 2, 1969, presented four motives for convening the international assembly at that particular period in the Church's history. "It appeared," according to John Cardinal Wright, then prefect of the Sacred Congregation for the Clergy, "not only useful but very necessary."[62]

The first motive Wright cited was to highlight the emerging problems and difficulties encountered in the ministry of the word of God in post-Vatican II pastoral renewal. Second, he mentioned the relationship of catechesis to the existing problems of justice (and injustice) in the world. Undoubtedly this issue was in the forefront of people's minds inasmuch as the third Synod of Bishops was scheduled to convene shortly after the catechetical congress ended and had "Peace and Justice" as its theme. A third motive for the congress was the need for an international "fraternal exchange of experiences and opinions concerning the subject of cate-chetics."[63] The proposed exchange was intended for people active in the field and for those whom serious study had marked as "experts." Finally, the fourth motive given was to provide an opportunity to reflect on the recently published *General Catechetical Directory* "and to calm discussion of so-called vital problems concerning the christianization of the world and the maturing in faith of the ecclesial community."[64]

The U.S. representation numbered twenty,[65] three of whom were bishops and fourteen of whom were official representatives of the United States Catholic Conference. The bishops were Robert E. Lucey, former archbishop of San Antonio and an ardent proponent of contemporary catechesis, William E. McManus, then auxiliary bishop of Chicago, and Raymond A. Lucker, then auxiliary bishop of Minneapolis-St. Paul.

The U.S. delegates were forthright in making their views known. All three bishops addressed the assembled participants. Lucker presented a formal paper, "Catechesis and the Media of Social Communication."[66] Of particular importance is the fact that Lucker was the one episcopal representative who had done formal research in catechetics.[67]

Both Lucey and McManus presented interventions. Lucey called attention to the potential which modern communications media offer the Church in its catechetical ministry. "Perhaps we can find some excuses for our failure in the past to 'make disciples of all the nations' (Mt. 28:19), but from here on there isn't going to be any excuse," he maintained.[68] He related that challenge to the current and promised availability of communications via satellite in the space age.

In an enthusiastic tone McManus addressed the assembly on the matter of the bishops' role in catechesis. His optimistic intervention projected the positive influence that the congress could have on the episcopacy.

> I will bring to my fellow bishops in the United States, a message full of hope, optimism and joy. . . . I hope that bishops, while they themselves renew and invigorate their

> faith through the process of catechesis, will be surrounded by
> catechists like those here, while the collaborative work of pre-
> paring national catechetical guidelines is undertaken. Cate-
> chists, in turn, should be ready to give bishops a generous
> measure of kind and patient assistance.[69]

In addition to the bishops' contributions, eleven of the U.S. delegates addressed the congress in prepared papers or interventions.[70]

When the congress ended twenty-eight stated conclusions summed
up the six days' work. They revealed a unanimity of concerns, objectives,
and desired projections on the part of the participants from the widely
diversified cultures around the world. The twenty-eight points were
grouped under four major categories: (I) the necessities, difficulties, and
possibilities of the ministry of the word in catechetical matters of our
present day (nine points); (II) the nature, goals, and process of catechesis
in the Church's pastoral activity (eight points); (III) the object or content
of catechesis and the mutual relationship that exists between sources of
catechesis (seven points);[71] and (IV) conclusions specifically related to
the third-world countries and drawn up by their delegates.[72] In addition,
reports and conclusions from diverse language groups, such as French,
German, Italian, and Spanish, were also included.[73] Completing the
report were resolutions from the English-speaking participants representing Australia, Canada, England, Ireland, and the United States. Their
resolutions were grouped into six main areas: (1) The *General Catechetical Directory*: Points for a Commentary; (2) Adult Religious Education
and the Education of Parents; (3) Formation of Catechists; (4) Sacraments of Initiation; (5) Relationship between Revelation and Experience
and between Catechesis and Theology; and (6) Education of Clergy.[74]

In retrospect one cannot fail to note the hopeful spirit that prevailed
as the congress came to a close. It was not an unrealistic optimism but
one tempered with the experience of continuous work in the ministry and
a recognition that improvements and changes take time, patience, dedication, and prayer.

CCD Congress, Miami, October 1971

The same spirit and enthusiasm seemed to carry over a month later
when many of the representatives from the Rome gathering met again at the
CCD Congress in Miami Beach, Florida, October 27–30, 1971. The congress had been planned and was sponsored by the National Center for the
Confraternity of Christian Doctrine in Washington, D.C. Its theme, "Continuing Christian Development in a Changing World," employed the
acronym "CCD" to good advantage. An estimated 8000 people attended.[75]

Four bishops presented papers at the meeting. Bishop McManus, with echoes of the Rome congress ringing in his memory, spoke of "The Teaching Mission of the Church" (October 28, 1971). William D. Borders, the bishop of Orlando, addressed the large assembly on the subject "Religion and Personal Spiritual Values" (October 29, 1971). In the afternoon of the same day Gerard Louis Frey, bishop of Savannah, pointed out the importance of "Evaluating and Accrediting Religious Education Programs" (2:00 PM). Emphasizing a theme stressed in the *General Catechetical Directory*, Bishop Raymond A. Lucker spoke on the necessity of "Building a Community of Faith" (October 30, 3:30 PM).[76]

One of the most significant events of the Miami meeting was an un-scheduled, off-the-record session called by Bishop McManus when he gathered a number of participants, most of whom had been at the Rome congress, to discuss the possibility and importance of initiating steps to produce a national catechetical directory for the United States. McManus also played an outstanding role in the subsequent planning and composition of the work until it finally appeared in 1979.

In terms of catechesis the decade of the 1970s was off to a fine start by the time the Miami congress wrapped up the details of its four-day session and business resumed its practice "as usual." The year 1971 had witnessed the publication of the *General Catechetical Directory*, a signif-icant international congress in Rome, and an enthusiastic rally-like gathering in Miami. But the decade was young. Before the seventies ended the U.S. bishops were to promulgate two small works on cate-chesis: *To Teach as Jesus Did* (1972) and *Basic Teachings* (1973). A ma-jor work, *Sharing the Light of Faith*, the national catechetical directory for the U.S., would close the decade with a flourish in 1979. In addition to that, at the international level, another event would make history when, in 1977, representative bishops from around the world would meet in Rome for the fifth episcopal synod, "Catechetics for Our Time." At least six U.S. bishops contributed to the synod. In relation with it Pope John Paul II published his work *Catechesi Tradendae* (1979). Each of these events or works will be treated below.

To Teach as Jesus Did (1972)

To Teach as Jesus Did, subtitled "A Pastoral Message on Catholic Education,"[77] was the product of the Bishops' Committee on Education chaired by Bishop William E. McManus.[78] The fifty-seven-page docu-ment originated as a pastoral interpretation of Vatican II's Declaration on Christian Education, *Gravissimum Educationis*.[79] Although it was primarily and explicitly concerned with those agencies and instruments "which are commonly recognized as 'educational' " and aimed at achieving "what are commonly recognized as educational objectives," the pastoral in some ways related more to catechesis than to formal education as it is identified with schooling. One friendly critic observed: "It would have been more satisfying if elements found in catechetical practice using liturgy and ritual, the parish life, etc. . . . had been included in the message. Something is lost of the freedom and creativity which catechetics requires, however, when it is considered under the rubric of education."[80] No doubt the greatest single and enduring part of the work was its delineating the threefold educational mission of the Church: teaching (*didache*), building up the believing community (*koinonia*), and serving (*diakonia*) (#14, 118). With that triple emphasis the bishops called for an expansion of educational vision beyond the programs, structures, and brick-and-mortar of existing institutions. This may, indeed, be the document's most lasting contribution.

Basic Teachings (1973)

Although it was not a direct descendant of the ill-fated "source book" of the late sixties, *Basic Teachings* had a distant relationship to that proposed work. In the process of evolving thought and discussion of needs for the proposed source book, agreement had centered on several aspects, one of which was a concentration on doctrinal points considered essential to catechesis.

During their annual November meeting in 1970 a number of bishops had complained about the lack of such content in religion manuals and textbooks in current use. In response to the complaint, John Cardinal Krol, archbishop of Philadelphia, introduced a resolution to the episcopal body:

> that there be established a committee of bishops charged to prepare a positive statement of irreducible doctrinal principles to serve as a guide to publishers and religious educators so that they will have available a syllabus of those doctrines of the Church without which adequate catechesis is impossible. This action was meant to be a positive assertion of the teaching role of the bishops, stressing what ought to be taught when the Catholic faith is presented.[81]

The resolution was approved. A committee of five bishops was appointed to carry out the project: John F. Whealon, archbishop of Hartford, chairman; John McDowell, auxiliary bishop of Pittsburgh; William E. McManus, auxiliary bishop of Chicago; Clarence E. Elwell, bishop of Columbus; and John Graham, auxiliary bishop of Philadelphia. The committee considered a variety of approaches, finally settling on chapter two of the *GCD*, "The More Outstanding Elements of the Christian Message," as a general outline for the volume.

Basic Teachings went through several versions and as many name changes during the three years of its composition. During that time consultations were held with the total episcopal body and prospective users (parents and religious educators), as well as with the Sacred Congregation for the Clergy in Rome. Significant additions were made to the original outline, such as "Importance of Prayer," "Participating in the Liturgy," and "Familiarity with the Holy Bible." "The Beatitudes" were added to the Ten Commandments as particularly important in teaching morality (Appendix A).

The volume appeared in 1973.[82] Its publication must be credited especially to the work of Archbishop John Whealon who shepherded the small volume through the sometimes rocky terrain of multiple critics and less-than-verdant pastures. He was indefatigable in assessing suggestions, refining issues, and determining the extent of the corpus. More than any other single person he was responsible for the thirty-six-page manual.

SHARING THE LIGHT OF FAITH (1979)

"*Sharing the Light of Faith* belongs to a new genre of Church documents called 'directories' which have appeared since the Second Vatican Council."[83] This is one of the introductory observations made by Berard L. Marthaler about the *National Catechetical Directory for Catholics of the United States*.[84] The volume was compiled at the juncture of two imperatives: (1) the conviction that such a work was needed—a need recognized by the bishops in 1966 when they decided to sponsor a "source book"; and (2) the prescription of the *General Catechetical Directory* that "the specific task of applying the principles and declarations contained in the *General Catechetical Directory* to concrete situations properly belongs to the various episcopates and they do this by means of national and regional directories."[85]

At their annual November meeting in 1971 the bishops authorized the appointment of an ad hoc committee to do a feasibility study on developing a national directory. Joseph McKinney, auxiliary bishop of Grand Rapids, chaired the committee. Of special import is that the decision to appoint the ad hoc body was the result of Bishop William McManus's initiative.

Following the Miami meeting McManus had turned to Bishop Joseph L. Bernardin, then member of the executive committee and general secretary of the National Conference of Catholic Bishops and the United States Catholic Conference. The two bishops invited a consultant,

Berard L. Marthaler, chairman of the Department of Religion and Religious Education at Catholic University, to attend. Knowing that the agenda for the annual bishops' meeting was already set and a decision to proceed with a formal proposal was out of the question, the three agreed that the most promising procedure was to request the appointment of a committee to study the possibility of composing a directory. The project was then proposed and sanctioned by the 1971 plenary body of bishops and McKinney's ad hoc committee was formed.

McKinney's committee met, conferred, and studied the pros, cons, and possibilities. Having concluded that a directory was possible and important, the group proposed three guiding principles and a working structure. The principles which the committee felt should shape the directory were:

> 1. The broad directives of the *General Catechetical Directory* should be adapted and applied to the needs and conditions of the United States.
>
> 2. Taking into consideration established principles of Sacred Scriptures, the human sciences, contemporary theology and the teachings of Vatican II, the national directory should give priority to pastoral concerns. It should give special prominence to liturgy.
>
> 3. The national directory should be the fruit of the widest consultations feasible, so that the process by which it is developed has an educational value, and at the same time create an environment which will assure broad acceptance of the finished product.[86]

The ad hoc committee then concentrated on drawing up implementation plans. In that context they recommended a tripartite working structure consisting of two committees and a project director.

> 1. A Policy and Review Committee comprised entirely of bishops who would oversee the project, and, on a regular basis, set policy and review progress on the composition of the directory.
>
> 2. The second committee, "the Directory Committee," was the working body charged with managing, consulting and drafting the text. That committee, broadly representative of pastorally oriented individuals from different constituencies, was to include laywomen, laymen, religious women and men, parents, pastors, and bishops.
>
> 3. The project director was to be, in effect, the executive officer of the working committee, responsible for the progressive activities of the project and to serve as liaison with the Committee on Policy and Review.[87]

Eight bishops made up the Policy and Review Committee: John F. Whealon, archbishop of Hartford, who chaired the committee; William Cardinal Baum of Washington (D.C.); John R. Quinn, archbishop of

Oklahoma City; Clarence E. Elwell, bishop of Columbus; Raymond Lucker, bishop of New Ulm; William McManus, then auxiliary bishop of Chicago (later [1976], bishop of Fort Wayne); and John J. Ward, auxiliary bishop of Los Angeles. When Bishop Elwell died in 1973, Rene H. Gracida, auxiliary bishop of Miami, succeeded him. As a representative of the Eastern Churches, Basil Losten, auxiliary bishop of the Ukrainian Archeparchy of Philadelphia, joined the committee a short time after the original group had formed.

The fourteen-member Directory Committee included four bishops, four priests, three lay people, two sisters, and one brother. In addition to Archbishop Whealon, who served ex officio on the committee, there were William D. Borders, archbishop of Baltimore, Mark Hurley, bishop of Santa Rosa, and Kenneth J. Povish, bishop of Lansing. Miss Mary Baylouny of West Paterson, New Jersey, Mr. Thomas C. Lawler of Alexandria, Virginia, and Mrs. Joan O'Keefe of Northbrook, Illinois, represented the laity at large. Sr. Celia Ann Cavazos, MCDP, of San Antonio, Texas, Sr. Anne Marie Mongoven, OP, of Madison, Wisconsin, and Bro. Cosmas Rubencamp, CFX, of Richmond were the religious sisters and brother on the team. Rev. James Lyke, OFM, of Memphis, Tennessee, Rev. William A. Wassmuth of Boise, Idaho, Msgr. Seely Beggiani, rector of the Maronite Seminary, Washington, D.C. and Rev. John Zeyack of the Byzantine Eparchy of Passaic, New Jersey, were the four priests. All persons on the committee had had experience of one kind or another in catechetical endeavors and were qualified to serve. Brother Rubencamp was elected by the committee to serve as chairman, a position he held until 1975 when he resigned that post but remained active on the committee. The group chose Father Wassmuth to succeed him.

Finally, the project director was named, Msgr. Wilfrid Paradis of Manchester, New Hampshire. Sr. Mariella Frye, MHSH, of Pittsburgh was named associate project director.

At their spring meeting, April 1972, in Atlanta, the bishops in plenary session approved the ambitious proposal. They endorsed the procedures as presented, especially that of broad representation of the directory committee and the innovative projection of wide consultation. From the beginning and throughout the next seven years the bishops made it clear that the directory was to serve and reflect the Church in the United States. Simultaneously they also clarified that they were not only interested in the work but held themselves responsible for it at every stage of its development. It was indeed their directory. What shall not go unmentioned is the dedication and leadership of Archbishop John F. Whealon in his steadfast attention to the work. The chart included here summarizes the progress of the enterprise and may prove more helpful than a detailed narration of events.

SHARING THE LIGHT OF FAITH Progress Chart

Bishops approved directory project, April 1972; published, March 1979.

Dates of Progressive Stages	Basis for Consultation	Demography of Consultation	Number of Recommendations Received	Results and Consequences
I. Consultation I December 1973 March 1974	Preliminary outline of projected topics for proposed directory	Broad selection of consultants from every Catholic diocese, every identifiable national society or agency (Catholic or non-Catholic) concerned with catechesis/religious education	17,000	First draft drawn up based on the recommendations submitted (First draft completed, December 1974)
II. Consultation II January 1, April 1975	First draft	Same as above	76,335 86% of the dioceses responded	Thorough revision of the preliminary text. Second draft composed.
III. Consultation III January 1977– March 15, 1977	Second draft	The second draft was sent to each diocesan office for critique and evaluation. It was not disseminated to the broad population that previous consultations included. The third consultation went to each diocese which in turn disseminated the draft and tallied their own responses and suggestions.	90% of the dioceses responded	Another revision; mostly minor changes. Policy and Review Board made further minor changes. Third draft ready, July 1977 That draft sent to every bishop well in advance of Nov. 1977 meeting

Dates of Progressive Stages	Basis for Consultation	Demography of Consultation	Number of Recommendations Received	Results and Consequences
IV. Stage IV November 14–17, 1977	The "penultimate" draft submitted to bishops	Plenary Session of bishops during their 1977 November meeting in Washington	300 amendments proposed during the four-day session. Some approved, other amendments rejected.	Bishops as a body amended and approved the draft. Balloting: 216–12
V. Early 1978	The draft approved by bishops at November 1977 meeting, sent to Rome	Sacred Congregation for Clergy (Rome) critiqued the draft, made recommendations.	Emendations in four areas: (1) treatment of revelation (Art. 50); (2) catechesis for the sacrament of reconciliation; (3) circumstances for giving general absolution (#124); (4) clarification of the nature and form of priesthood (#132, 93).	
VI.	Emendations made according to recommendations	Sacred Congregation for the Clergy		Rome approved the amended version, Oct. 30, 1978
VII. March 1979				*Sharing the Light of Faith* published (182 pages)

On November 17, 1977, at the conclusion of their annual meeting, the bishops approved the directory as they had amended it in the course of their four-day gathering that year (see chart, pp. 150–51). Early in 1978 the amended draft (actually the fourth edition of the directory) was sent to the Sacred Congregation for the Clergy in Rome. Approval of the volume was subsequently given in a letter dated October 30, 1978, and addressed to Archbishop John R. Quinn, then chairman of the National Conference of Catholic Bishops in the United States. Archbishop Maximino Romero de Lema, who signed the letter, commented that the Sacred Congregation of the Clergy found the directory to be "outstanding for its ecclesial spirit, its clarity of expression, . . . its solid argument and flexibility."[88] The Congregatio pro clericis, however, called for the reworking of four points: (1) the treatment of revelation, (2) the matter of catechesis for the sacrament of reconciliation, (3) the circumstances of general absolution, and (4) the specific nature of priesthood. After the draft was revised to incorporate these recommendations, it was sent to the printer and appeared in bound form in March 1979.[89]

Archbishop Jean Jadot, then apostolic delegate to the United States, praised the volume with obvious enthusiasm, calling it a "remarkable document" and one of the first directories in the world to be composed and endorsed by a national hierarchy and, in fact, the first in any language to be approved by the Holy See. Jadot considered it "remarkable" on another score, namely, "because it was established by a broad consultation,[90] the widest in the history of the Catholic Church in this country and possibly the world, and has brought about a consensus among large numbers of persons in all walks of life."[91]

When it appeared in the spring of 1979, *Sharing the Light of Faith* represented the U.S. Church in numerous ways. In its 182 pages, which included the "Foreword" written by Archbishop John R. Quinn, eleven chapters, a conclusion, two appendices, notes, and index, it reflected the pluralistic, diverse, and cross-cultural characteristics of a people who knew themselves to be Church. It further represented, through the consultations, the involvement of numerous individuals from all segments of the religious population of the United States. This in itself is a tribute to the bishops of the United States who obviously recognized appreciatively the *sensus fidelium* of the Church in this country and the fact that God is not restricted in his channels of revelation.

The work has outstanding strengths, as Jadot had indicated. It also has some glaring weaknesses.[92] After all, it is a human document. Notable among its shortcomings are (1) the failure to incorporate references to the catechumenate for children as recommended by the *Rite of Christian Initiation of Adults* (1974); (2) the absence of attention to catechesis on peace in a strife-torn era of human history; (3) omission of the beatitudes—references were made to them in three places (#100, 105, 176), but, unlike the ten commandments, they were *not* presented as a model in the volume; (4) the text itself is irregular in its prose. In places the tone is clearly juridical and authoritative; elsewhere it is more inviting and inductive. Certain passages seem to emerge from the pages of theology manuals, while the language of others is more biblical and appealing.[93] In brief, the objective of catechesis is not knowledge per se but knowledge insofar as it informs or deepens faith.

In a significant study, James P. Lyke, auxiliary bishop of Cleveland, emphasized indigenization, pluralism, and inculturation as they relate to the U.S. Black community in the Church's contemporary catechesis. His work reviewed the overall state of Black spirituality and catechesis in existential situations, indicating critical biblical and doctrinal teachings which deserve special treatment and inclusion. Entitled *The Black Perspective on the National Catechetical Directory*, it was the first such work to be done in response to the directory's encouragement to "seek out viable alternatives" to distinct situations.[94] Of note, too, are Lyke's qualifications for the study. As a Black priest, a serious scholar, and a dedicated member of the "Directory Committee' which worked on the National Directory, he was eminently qualified to execute the study. Lyke was consecrated auxiliary bishop of Cleveland on August 1, 1979.[95]

In summary, the assets of the volume clearly outweigh its shortcomings. In a sense it is descriptive of the 1979 position of the U.S. Church vis-à-vis its pastoral ministry as a whole. *Sharing the Light of Faith* reflects the marks of plurality, cultural multiplicity, and yet unity that characterize the episcopal body and the people the bishops represent and lead. Furthermore, *Sharing the Light of Faith* brought the Church in the United States to a new threshold, not only in terms of catechesis but especially in terms of its own self-awareness as an identifiable witness to Christian presence in the world.[96]

CATECHESIS FOR OUR TIME: SYNOD, 1977

Six weeks before the U.S. bishops met for their final assessment and approval of *Sharing the Light of Faith*, the fifth post-Vatican II synod began in Rome, September 30, 1977.[97] It was a month-long study of the subject "Catechesis for Our Time." In relation to the final stages of the U.S. national directory, it was timely. For the bishops who represented the U.S. Church in the synod it was a continuation of the five-year study of catechesis in which they were already engaged for the composition of the directory. In another sense it was a total immersion process that served them well in their participation in the final draft of the directory scheduled for the bishops' November meeting a little more than a month away.

The U.S. prelates who represented the Church of this country were Archbishop Joseph Bernardin, John Cardinal Carberry, Archbishop Stephen Kocisko (Ruthenian Rite, Pittsburgh), Bishop Raymond Lucker, Archbishop John Whealon, and Timothy Cardinal Manning, who had been appointed to the synod by Pope Paul VI. They, in turn, were accompanied by *periti*, advisors, and assistants, including Rev. Lorenzo Albacete, Francis Buckley, SJ, Sr. Mariella Frye, MHSH, Msgr. Wilfrid Paradis, Rev. James P. Roache, and Russell Shaw. Sr. Maria de la Cruz Aymes-Couck of San Francisco, a member of the Special Secretariat for the synod, was also present.

Prior to their flight to Rome and the opening session of the synod, the U.S. delegates had prepared for the assembly by consultations and studies of the issues facing the Church in its catechesial ministry. A major gathering assembled for this purpose took place at Mariottsville, Maryland, on March 13–16, 1977.[98] There, a number of professional catechists and theorists convened with certain of the delegates to study the role of catechesis in the contemporary Church. On August 1–2, 1977, the four elected bishops, Bernardin, Carberry, Lucker, and Whealon, met with Buckley and Albacete in St. Louis as guests of Cardinal Carberry.[99] At this meeting the group drafted four main areas of interest they considered important to place on the agenda: (1) community, (2) doctrine/message, (3) service, and (4) worship. Clarification of expectations and the possible structure and procedures of the coming synod were also considered. At this preparatory meeting, too, the group decided unanimously to appoint Sr. Mariella Frye as an official advisor to the synod.[100] Sister Frye thus became the first woman to serve as an official delegate of the U.S. bishops in a synod.

The goal of the synod was to provide "a new impulse to catechesis in the Church," according to Aloisio Cardinal Lorscheider, archbishop of Fortaleza, Brazil, and "Rapporteur" (general relator or reporter) of the synod by the appointment of Pope Paul VI.[101] While there were sharp differences, ideologically and culturally, among the synodal participants, there was a unifying basis and vision which bonded the body. The differences should not surprise even a casual observer if one considers the diverse geographic, linguistic, and cultural backgrounds of the assembled prelates.

The synod opened on Friday, September 30, 1977, with a state-of-the-Church message. The discussions were formally introduced on the morning of October 1 with an address on the synod's theme by Cardinal

Lorscheider, who played a leading role throughout the entire event. "It is important to arrive at a unified approach despite the need for pluralism," he observed in his opening presentation.

> There are certain lines which must be followed in seeking this unity as regards the very definition of catechesis. . . . If catechesis is part of the prophetic mission of the Church which announces the message of Christ, then it has its roots in baptism. Therefore it cannot be reduced solely to instruction nor is it simply the reading of the scriptures, nor is it [just] preparation for the liturgy, nor the reading of theological literature, nor is it simply initiation into social and economic activity. In catechesis we cannot separate the knowledge of faith from the celebration of the faith in the sacraments and its profession in daily life. It is from here that the civilizing character of catechesis arises. Hence there also arises the right to free expression in civil society.
>
> Finally it is necessary to note that the norm of catechesis is the Gospel and the Credo.[102]

Archbishop Bernardin was the first U.S. prelate to address the body. His intervention, which took place on that first full day of the synod, explored the theme, "The Inner Spirit of Catechesis."[103]

Bernardin related catechesis to evangelization, pointing out that "both catechesis and evangelization have their origin in the activity of the word of God." Both, too, are integrally related to conversion—evangelization to an initial turning-to-God and catechesis as "a continuing process of conversion in the life of the believer. From this fundamental event, catechesis draws applications which, adapted to the concrete situation of believers, enable them to respond to the word of God." He continued:

> Within the catechetical enterprise itself, much of the polarization that threatens its success could be overcome by the evangelical synthesis of components of the mystery of redemption which many have come to fear as incompatible: a Christ-centered catechesis and a church-centered one; a church-centered catechesis and one centered on our social responsibilities; community and individual; word or sacrament; Bible or magisterium. All of these find their synthesis through a catechesis that is truly evangelical. . . . To be a Christian is to be incorporated into the "new man" which is a reality already created by God and offered to us with Christ Jesus as the basis, measure and goal. . . . Since life in Christ, one and indivisible, is communicated to all believers, the new man is a corporate reality; it is always lived in community. . . . Every act prompted by grace engages the entire community, and it is at the same time an activity of the word of God. The community's responsibility for evangelization and

catechesis is based on this insight. Through such activities, the church reproduces itself.[104]

In a subsequent intervention Bernardin reemphasized the coorporate responsibility of the ecclesial community in catechesis. "Catechesis must not be reduced merely to transmitting information."[105] "Prayer, community and service are key elements in the entire process of bringing Christian faith, love and responsibility to maturity," he wrote in his statement. He pointed out that there are misunderstandings, varying emphases, and communication gaps among the people and scholars. It is imperative that such gaps be bridged among bishops, theologians, catechists, and the faithful. Since, ideally,

> catechesis fosters initiation into a community, we must take care that there really is a community which welcomes those being catechized, a community recognized and valued as a true Christian community, with all this implies.
>
> . . . There are four groups which ought to be in constant catechetical dialogue: bishops, theologians, catechists, and faithful. These categories overlap. All must be practicing believers. Some bishops are theologians and all should be catechists. But within the believing community, special types of conversion are needed.[106]

Before the synod closed on October 29, U.S. bishops and their associates presented eleven more interventions. On October 5, Archbishop Whealon emphasized the need to relate catechesis to the realities of the everyday life of people with problems that vary in each setting. "A catechesis according to human problems," he said, "becomes generally speaking a catechesis on the example and the imitation of Jesus Christ. And the ultimate hope of any man or woman facing life's problems is to be placed in the resurrection of Our Lord Jesus Christ. That resurrection we celebrate every Lord's Day and we present it in catechesis."[107]

In his intervention Bishop Lucker maintained that the essential issue in the catechesis of children and youth is the catechesis of adults. Pointing to the lifelong nature of catechesis as it relates to faith, Lucker concluded that "young people need adult witnesses, people who express their beliefs in their daily lives by what they do and say and love."[108]

Cardinal Carberry made an oral intervention on October 4 in which he stressed the importance of "The Blessed Virgin and Popular Devotions in Catechesis."[109] Cardinal Manning's intervention called for special catechesis for people in unique circumstances such as those incarcerated in detention institutions, handicapped persons, etc.[110] Archbishop Kocisko addressed the need for a distinctive catechesis directed to those who have left the Church. Inasmuch as, according to Kocisko,

more individuals leave the Church over points of discipline than of doctrine, it falls on catechesis to make distinctions between what the Church
teaches and what is Church discipline.[111]

John Cardinal Wright, a U.S. cardinal and at the time prefect of the
Vatican Congregation for the Clergy, reminded the assembly that the
renewal of catechesis does not depend principally on a revised teaching
method, "the manner of formation or transmission of doctrine."[112] Instead, a "key" to renewing catechesis is to recognize the vertical and hori-
zontal characteristics of the Church. Central to that reality is the mystery
of Jesus Christ: "the mystery of Christ appears in the history of men and
of the world—a history subject to sin—not only as the mystery of the in-
carnation but also as the mystery of salvation and redemption."[113]

Finally, in terms of episcopal interventions, a paper drawn up by the
National Conference of Catholic Bishops of the United States and submitted to the synod addressed the issue of pluralism in contemporary
times. In accord with a theme found in the national catechetical directory
then being composed, the bishops emphasized a particular responsibility
of catechesis toward ecumenism and an appreciation of freedom. Catechesis should, they maintained, give people "a clear sense of their Christian identity" along with an understanding of and respect for the beliefs
and convictions of others. The statement stressed that "all people, believers and nonbelievers alike, are created in God's image and likeness
and therefore worthy of the deepest respect and esteem. The Catholic
Church champions the dignity of the human vocation and holds out hope
to those who do not know anything higher than earthly existence."[114]

In the context of catechesis for children and youth, according to the
bishops' intervention, the Church has a responsibility to prepare the
young "to live in a world where many people have different beliefs or no
belief at all."[115]

The bishops' advisors and associates played a significant and tireless
role in the preparation and delivery of interventions. Together with the
episcopal delegation they conferred as a body, composing, critiquing, and
editing the respective presentations. Their varying experiences and expertise
lent a high degree of credibility and validity to the U.S. interventions.

Albacete, out of his combined academic background in physics and
studies in theology, presented an intervention on "The Church and Its
Relationship to Science, Technology and Industry."[116] Later, he injected
a somewhat different but important emphasis into the deliberations with
his statement on "Catechesis for Racial, Cultural and Ethnic Groups."[117]
His third paper, "The Mass Media and Catechesis,"[118] added a uniquely
contemporary tone.

Francis Buckley, relying on his rich experience in the field, intervened with papers on "Catechesis for Children and Youth in a World of Religious Pluralism"[119] and "Theological Content of Catechesis for Young People."[120] Frye's presentations were written statements on "Family Catechesis"[121] and "Catechesis for Respect for Human Life."[122] Her final intervention, "Women in Catechesis," earned well-deserved attention considering the enormous responsibility which women have borne in catechesial programs in the United States.[123] Paradis presented "The Qualities of Catechists"[124] and "The Role of the Parish Priest in Catechesis."[125]

On October 21 the synod presented its carefully worked through "Thirty-four Points"—statements synthesizing the synod's perception of ideals, priorities, and emphases in catechesis. The points were grouped into six areas: the (1) nature, (2) contents, (3) manner, (4) recipients, (5) context, and (6) agents of catechesis.[126]

Assessments of the synod were mixed in their emphases. Donald R. Campion, Jesuit observer from the United States, commented that "catechesis is not a topic that produces drama, tension and enthusiasm but it did allow the bishops to endorse the principles of renewal."[127] Both participants and observers gave the United States delegation high marks. Paradis observed that the pages of L'Osservatore Romano, which faithfully and steadily summarized the activities of the synod, especially the oral and written interventions, carried more contributions from the U.S. participants than from any other single national group.[128] One scholar, according to Wilfrid Paradis, openly stated that the Americans were "considered the best organized and are presenting some of the best papers of the Synod."[129] Archbishops Bernardin and Whealon both reported that some of their fellow bishops complimented them for the position of leadership the U.S. bishops were taking in the synod.

Campion made some astute observations of the synod in his articles in America. "A major achievement of this synod," he wrote, "will be seen to have been its careful evaluation implicitly of one of the most important aspects of postconciliar renewal in the church, that in the field of catechesis."[130] "What happens when the synod members go back to their posts?" Campion questioned. Putting this in context, he added: "The 1977 synod is . . . an education for the bishops as well as a means of providing counsel to the Pope."[131]

At least one U.S. prelate confirmed Campion's statement about its being an educational experience. On October 19, Cardinal Carberry sized up his own impression with an enthusiastic statement declaring that "now he had a far better understanding of catechesis" and that one of the first things that he would do on his return to his archdiocese would be to speak to his diocesan director of religious education. "In a sense, I believe, this generation of bishops is only now coming face-to-face with some of the long-range impact of Vatican II. They must deal with the deeper implications of statements that found their way into the council's pronouncements but that have yet to be adequately explored for their pastoral bearing."[132]

In reflecting on the decade of the 1970s — from the early anticipation of the *General Catechetical Directory* (1971) to the publication of *Sharing the Light of Faith* (1979) along with intervening events and publications — the U.S. bishops could justifiably count the 1970s as a ten-year span rich with major catechesial contributions which could have a lasting influence on the faith life of the people who comprise the Church in the United States.

6

In Perspective

Putting all available factors in perspective, one concludes that the Church in the United States has achieved a new threshold of self-realization in the ministry of catechizing. From the days of John Carroll down to and through the publication of *Sharing the Light of Faith*, the bishops of this nation have sought to assist the faithful (including themselves) in realizing the vocation, the meaning, and the challenge of being Roman Catholic Christians in the particular, multi-diverse circumstances of life in the United States.

In the late eighteenth century, catechesis was identified principally with the three "c's"—catechism, children, and classrooms. The early U.S. bishops along with the faithful accepted that status quo. Sensitive to the unique cultural circumstances of their respective dioceses, U.S. bishops wrote or commissioned the writing of manuals that were applicable to their regions. It probably did not occur to anyone to approach catechesis without a trusty manual, a catechism, in hand. When, in the nineteenth century, the multiplicity of such manuals appeared to be a problem, the bishops determined to authorize and sanction a common, uniform catechism. The 1885 "Baltimore Catechsim," along with its 1941 revision, was the result.

In the twentieth century an embryonic, innovative ferment began to develop. Its roots were deep in nineteenth-century European scholarship, with a renewed interest in the patristic period and the spirit of the early Church,[1] more critical scripture studies, and a vibrant, growing realization of the meaning and reality of church *qua* church.[2] Rather than being a nostalgic looking back, it was a serious effort to capture the spirit and ideals of the early Christian Church and examine current practice and principles in light of those findings. St. Pius X (1903-1914) aided this move through his pastoral exhortations and decrees. *Instaurare omnia in Christo* — "To restore all things in Christ" — became a motto for him as well as an inspiration for many Church leaders and thinkers. It served as an inducement to reassess priorities of practice and understanding. Out of this spirit of rediscovery and renewal the contemporary catechetical renewal was born.

CATECHESIS: A MINISTRY

In conclusion, it is important to observe the status of catechesis at the beginning of this last fifth of the twentieth century, to survey the nature of catechesis, its objectives and tasks, and the significance which U.S. bishops accord it.

Catechesis is a form of ministry of the word, "a ministry which," according to the *General Catechetical Directory*, "is absolutely necessary for the proper fulfillment of the Church's mission in the world."[3] Its objective is that of nurturing, developing, assisting the process of the maturing faith-life of the believing body. Catechesis presumes faith, however seminal or advanced that faith may be. It endeavors to make a conscious contribution to increasing the faith of believers to an ever deeper and more comprehensive level. As Archbishop Raymond G. Hunthausen of Seattle observed, "Faith is the beginning and goal of . . . catechesis."[4] Hunthausen seems to echo a Pauline conviction found in the Apostle's letter to the Romans: "For in the gospel is revealed the justice of God which begins and ends with faith" (Rom. 1:17).

Related to this, the thread of conversion, too, is woven into the fabric of catechesis. As the *GCD* stated, "the element of conversion is always present in the dynamism of faith" (*GCD*, #18).

The concept of conversion currently explored in theological and scriptural studies and used in catechesis does not refer only to a once-in-a-lifetime experience like Paul's en route to Damascus. Conversion is a continuing process, a rediscovery of the Risen Lord and growth in the faith-life initiated by him — a "dynamic process rather than a *fait accompli*."[5]

In light of previous practice, when memorizing questions and answers was accepted as the sole form of catechesis, it appeared important to emphasize the role of knowing and the acquisition of knowledge in relation to catechesis. In 1960 François Coudreau, a French scholar, summarized this relationship.

A certain pedagogy of religious instruction can convey religious information—what might even be called "religious beliefs"—without developing believers. It can transmit Christian truths without making a person live by faith. All catechesis must beware of this temptation or illusion. It is so easy to remain on the level of knowledge or beliefs. It is ever so much more difficult to pass to the level of conversion and faith. All of us need always fear that we are only producing "knowers" when we should really be producing "believers."[6]

In fact, the aim of catechesis is not knowledge as such, but a living faith that responds to God's message. However, catechesis of its nature does not denigrate knowledge, information, and intellectual pursuit. On the contrary, as a ministry catechesis necessarily requires a thorough and in-depth comprehension of the truths and mysteries of Christianity. Furthermore, those responsible for catechesis seek to dialogue with other scholars in the fields of theology, Scripture, and the human sciences in order to grasp ever more accurately varying aspects of the message and meaning which different approaches disclose. Catechesis, theology, scripture study, and all forms of pastoral ministry are interdependent, with the common good of the whole Church as their objective. The ideal is for an ever better-informed, knowledgeable faith, with a clear emphasis on *faith*. As Bishop Kenneth Povish has said, "Contemporary catechesis stresses the Scriptural dimension of faith that embraces more than intellectual acceptance of certain truths." "This approach," he added, "incorporates liturgical and para-liturgical experiences; it recognizes the ecumenical stance of the Church today; it reflects the theological and cultural milieu of the late twentieth century."[7] "Mature faith is to *know* Christ's resurrection as a reality and to accept its meaning for salvation."[8]

Knowledge has its own role to play in catechesis and in faith, because, according to Berard L. Marthaler, faith "in its fullest sense implies knowledge, love, trust, fidelity, and other virtues. . . . Inceptive faith . . . needs to be nurtured by life-long catechesis." As a matter of fact, "both knowledge and experience are essential to the Act of Faith."[9]

In their directory, *Sharing the Light of Faith*, the bishops perceived the integral relationship between catechesis and revelation, the "loving self-revelation of God and the response of humankind" (*SLF*, #48). Together the two constitute a profound dialogue. "Catechesis calls attention to this dialogue and seeks to shed light upon it" (*SLF*, #61). Although there was some struggling for accuracy of expression and terminology during the composition of the directory, the undergirding and permeating theme of revelation perdured.[10]

Pope John Paul II confirmed the role of catechesis in relationship to revelation to his 1979 exhortation, *Catechesi Tradendae*.

It is on the basis of revelation that catechesis will try to set its course, revelation as transmitted by the universal Magisterium of the Church, in its solemn or ordinary form. This revelation tells of a creating and redeeming God, whose son has come among us in our flesh and enters not only into each individual's personal history, but into human history itself, becoming its center. Accordingly, this revelation tells of the radical change of man and the universe, of all that makes up the web of human life under the influence of the good news of Jesus Christ. If conceived in this way, catechesis goes beyond every form of formalistic moralism, although it will include true Christian moral teaching. Chiefly, it goes beyond any kind of temporal, social, or political "messianism."[11]

It seeks to arrive at man's innermost being (*CT*, #52).

Tasks of Catechesis

Another strong asset of the bishops' directory was the delineation of the four major tasks of catechesis. In no other single document had the four been so clearly stated, although there was pointed reference to them in different works of previous periods.[12]

The fundamental tasks of catechesis, according to *Sharing the Light of Faith*, are (1) to proclaim the message of Christ, (2) foster community life and participate in efforts to develop and form community, (3) serve and motivate others to serve people, and (4) assist in encouraging and leading people to worship, to pray.[13]

One easily recognizes the bishops' reliance on their earlier work, *To Teach as Jesus Did* (1972), with its emphasis on the first three of these tasks, teaching (*didache*), community (*koinonia*), and service (*diakonia*). Of larger significance is that the delineation of these tasks broadened the scope of catechesis from its more confining four centuries' association with schools, children, and question-and-answer manuals to a more comprehensive concept of catechesis as being churchwide, lifelong, and charged with keeping the Gospel message alive and vibrant.

Adult Catechesis — Normative

One of the initially startling statements of the *General Catechetical Directory* when it first appeared was that "catechesis for adults . . . must be considered the chief form of catechesis. All other forms which indeed are always necessary are in some way oriented to it" (#19).[14] It was neither the first such statement nor was it without precedent in practice, but it *was* a sharp distinction from prevailing practice. Bishop Edwin V. O'Hara had recognized the importance of nurturing adult inquiries and developing means to respond to them and thus had begun the study clubs with which he has been identified. However, when one looks for a normative precedent for adult catechesis, one turns quite naturally to the New Testament. James, Paul, and the other Apostles directed their evangelizing and teaching to adults.[15]

There are, however, within modern times, both models and exhortations to focus the ministry of catechesis on the adult population of the Church. In his 1905 encyclical *Acerbo nimis*, Pope St. Pius X had addressed emphatic remarks to the subject of adult catechesis. The need, Pius maintained, is great and continuous for adults, including those "tottering with age." For, "in matters of religion, the majority of people in our times must be considered uninstructed."[16]

Pope Pius XII had also addressed the subject.

> The needs of our time, then, require that the laity too procure for themselves a treasure of religious knowledge, not a poor or meager knowledge, but one that will have solidity and richness through the medium of libraries, discussion clubs; in this way they will derive great benefit for themselves and at the same time be able to instruct the ignorant, confute stubborn adversaries and be of assistance to friends.[17]

Added to this mosaic of excerpts extolling adult catechesis, is an address given by Archbishop Paul J. Hallinan in April 1962 to the Catholic Adult Education Commission. In his insightful and engaging style he encouraged his listeners to inquire and pursue a better understanding of Christianity and its mysteries despite the air of existing complacency which often hinders the intellectual growth of adults.

> Our educational process has developed an occupational disease. We want philosophy without tears, theology without dogma, poems in anthologies, and novels in digest. Are we willing today to struggle with ideas, sacrifice for ideals, suffer for consequences? . . . Knowledge is a pyramid that leads to God. The senses and the intellect dig down and stretch out far. . . . We must have God's assistance. It comes through faith. And once God has spoken, not only does the fact of God become more clear, everything else does too. Faith unlocks the tower of the Trinity, the Incarnation and the Redemption. But it is not only a tower; it is also a lighthouse. These mysteries, revealed by God, cast a fine light over human affairs, and over biological facts and psychological theories, and over everything else. . . . To be informed, responsible, loyal, and apostolic, these are the hallmarks of the [adult] Christian.[18]

In this final section it is important to call attention to the bishops' recognition of the responsibility which women have assumed in catechesis in the U.S. Church. In the international forum of the 1977 synod, the bishops of this country paid particular tribute to those women who serve and have served as catechists. They urged their fellow bishops from around the world to recognize the potential that the Church has in Catholic women.[19] Prior to this, in 1937, Archbishop Robert E. Lucey had acknowledged the Church's debt to women, especially to sisters, for their generosity and dedication in that sphere.[20] Bishop Charles Buswell echoed much the same theme in 1967 when he emphasized the tireless work of religious women who, by their lives and example, exemplified the spirit of Vatican II.[21] Archbishop Paul Hallinan, in a slightly different tone, observed:

> We will never grasp woman's role until we see that she is a person with human needs, not a biological deviation, a social appendage, or an economic competitor.
>
> It's an old saying that "It's a man's world!" Contemplating its present messed-up state, what woman would ever claim it? More likely she would say, "He can have it." Society was meant to be human but we have dehumanized it. Both men and women are made for God, both here and hereafter . . . If we stop dehumanizing, depersonalizing and defeminizing women, they will emerge as free, rational human persons. They are people, too.[21]

A FUTURE THRUST

One of the seven conclusions which the congressional body of the International Catechetical Congress of 1971 projected called for national catechetical centers. According to that congress, such centers are

> a vital need for the quality of the work at the regional, diocesan and local level. . . . Institutions cannot rest content with carrying on that which exists today. From them is demanded an effort of prevision, of anticipation about what could be the situation twenty years from now. This effort of prevision goes side by side with the task of programming and evaluating what catechesis is achieving today. At all levels catechetical activity should be understood as a task subject to periodic revision, both concerning its directives and guidelines, and its institutions, in such a way as not to be surpassed by the transformation of society and the Church.[23]

From 1934 until 1978 the Church in the United States had such a center directed by an episcopal committee which served the Church and the catechetical ministry well. While the 1970s were rich in the results of ad hoc committee work, the 1980s face a questionable future in regard to catechesis with no one episcopal committee charting the course or opening the avenues for channeling ideas, suggestions, and projections from the faithful. There is no single committee charged with the continuous concern and responsibility for this ministry which is increasingly recognized as significant to the Church's life and growth at all levels, at all ages. As one scholar expressed it, "catechesis is for the entire faithful, it is not only for the youth and classrooms; catechesis is a people term, not just a school 'word.'"

Bishop Hunthausen summarized it well when he addressed his own diocese. "As your bishop and chief catechist, I am convinced," he said, "that what we studied in the 70's must now happen in the 80's."[24] His message extended beyond the boundaries of the archdiocese of Seattle as he continued: "It is clear that the church in general, and the American church in particular, has done its homework very well. We now know the facts, the theories, the skills. A primary task of the 80's will be to put into action what our documents spell out in theory."[25]

Notes

Introduction

1. *Christus Dominus*, #13, *AAS*, 58 (1966), 678-679; See *The Documents of Vatican II*, ed. Walter M. Abbott (New York: Herder & Herder, 1966), 405.

2. *Catechesi Tradendae, AAS*, 71 (1979), 1277-1340; see *Catechesi Tradendae — On Catechesis in Our Time* (Boston: Daughters of St. Paul, 1979), 13.

3. Félix Antoine P. Dupanloup (1802-1878) wrote *Le catéchisme chrétien ou exposé de la doctrine de Jésus Christ offert aux hommes du monde* and a major work on the ministry of catechizing, *L'oeuvre par excellence — entretiens sur le catéchisme* (1868). Richard Challoner (1691-1781) wrote and published *The Catholick Christian Instructed in the Sacraments, Sacrifices, Ceremonies and Observances of the Church* (1737) and *Abridgement of Christian Doctrine: Revised and Enlarged by R. C.* (1772). James Butler II (1742-1791) published *A Catechism for the Instruction of Children* in 1777. In 1802 the four archbishops of Ireland adopted this manual as a "General Catechism for the Kingdom." See Patrick Wallace, *Irish Catechesis — The Heritage from James Butler II, Archbishop of Cashel, 1774-1791* (Ann Arbor, Mich.: University Microfilms, 1975), 95-116. George Hay, bishop of Edinburgh, Scotland (1729-1811), wrote *The Sincere Christian Instructed in the Faith of Christ* (ca. 1780). He was responsible for the publication of the first Catholic Bible in English printed in Scotland (1796-1797).

4. Boniface of Mainz (ca. 674-754) wrote "Catechetical Statutes" (ca. 745). See P. Joseph Hartzheim, ed., *Concilia Germaniae*, Tome I. Boniface is also credited with the writing of *Aenigmata*, a moral catechesis in acrostic hexameters. See Ernst L. Dummler, ed., *Poetae Latini Aevi Carolini, Tome I* (Berlin: Verlag Weidmann, 1881), 316-320. Pirmin of Reichenau (d. 754) wrote *Scarapsus*, a missionary manual of catechetical instruction composed between 718 and 724.

5. Gregory of Nyssa (ca. 335-394) delivered his well-known *Oratio Catechetica Magna* ca. 382. See *The Catechetical Oration of Gregory of Nyssa*, ed. James H. Srawley (Cambridge: Cambridge University Press, 1903). See Cyril of Jerusalem (ca. 350-394), *Lectures on the Christian Sacraments*, ed. F. L. Cross (London: SPCK, 1966); Ambrose (ca. 339-397), *The Mysteries*, Fathers of the Church, vol. 44, trans. Roy J. Deferrari (Washington, D.C.: Catholic University of America Press, 1963); Augustine, *The First Catechetical Instruction*, trans. Joseph P. Christopher, Ancient Christian Writers, vol. 2 (Westminster, Md.: Newman Press, 1962); John Chrysostom (ca. 349-407), *Baptismal Instructions* (Mystagogical

catecheses), trans. and annotated by Paul W. Harkins (Westminster, Md.: Newman Press, 1963); Theodore of Mopsuestia (350–428), "Commentary of Theodore of Mopsuestia on the Lord's Prayer and on the Sacraments of Baptism and the Eucharist," *Woodbrooke Studies*, vol. 6 (Cambridge, 1933). Ignatius of Antioch (d. 110) wrote letters to the churches in six cities in Asia Minor. These epistles included warm, personal greetings and concerns for the people in those places as well as exhortations and doctrinal statements of Christian truths.

6. George Delcuve, SJ, "What the Catechisms Say of the Holy Spirit," *Lumen Vitae*, 17 (1962), 241.

7. *Of Singular Benefit* (New York: Macmillan, 1970).

8. James A. Burns, CSC, *The Principles, Origin and Establishment of the Catholic School System in the United States* (New York: Benziger Bros., 1912); James A. Burns, CSC, Bernard J. Kohlbrenner, John B. Peterson, *A History of Catholic Education in the United States* (New York: Benziger Bros., 1937); Albert C. Koob, *What's Happening to Catholic Education?* (Washington, D.C.: National Catholic Education Association, 1966); Neil G. McCluskey, SJ, *Catholic Education in America—A Documentary History* (New York: Bureau of Publications, Columbia University, 1964); William J. McGucken, SJ, *The Catholic Way in Education* (Chicago: Loyola University Press, 1962); Emmett McLoughlin, *American Culture and Catholic Schools* (New York: Lyle Stuart / Polyglot Press, 1960).

9. *Theological Dictionary of the New Testament*, 3:638; James I. H. McDonald, *Kerygma and Didache* (Cambridge: Cambridge University Press, 1980), a study of the articulation and structure of the earliest Christian message.

10. "Catechesis," *The New Schaff-Herzog Religious Encyclopedia*, 2:440; "Catechesis," *NCE*, 3:208–218; "Catéchese," *Dictionnaire de Théologie Catholique*, 2, 2:1877–1895.

11. See Gerard S. Sloyan's essay, "The Relation of the Catechism to the Work of Religious Formation," in *Modern Catechetics* (New York: Macmillan, 1962), 63–101.

12. See Franz Arnold, "The Act of Faith, A Personal Commitment," *Lumen Vitae*, 5 (1950), 251–255; André Liégé, *Consider Christian Maturity* (Chicago: Priory Press, 1966); Gabriel Moran, *Catechesis of Revelation* (New York: Herder & Herder, 1966), 30–40; 107–110; *General Catechetical Directory* (hereafter, GCD), #3, 4, 15, 21, 36; *Sharing the Light of Faith* (hereafter, SLF), #33, 172–203, 32, 47; *Catechesi Tradendae*, 19, 20, 4, 18, 28.

13. GCD, #19, 20, 75, 79, 101, 107; SLF, #172–203, 227, 228, 213, 224, 243; Jacques Audinet, "Catechesis: The Church building the Church within a Given Culture," *Our Apostolate*, 24 (1976), 132–156; Mary Charles Bryce, "The Interrelationship of Liturgy and Catechesis," *American Benedictine Review*, 28 (1977), 1–29; Berard L. Marthaler, "Socialization as a Model for Catechetics," in Padraic O'Hare, ed., *Foundations of Religious Education* (New York: Paulist Press, 1978), 64–92; "Message of the People of God," part ii, #7–17, from the synod of 1977, *L'Osservatore Romano* (Eng. ed.), November 3, 1977, 5–6; Pierre Ranwez, "General Tendencies in Contemporary Catechetics," Gerard S. Sloyan, ed., *Shaping the Christian Message* (New York: Macmillan, 1958), 112–130.

14. See Raymond J. Jansen, *Canonical Provisions for Catechetical Instructions*, (Washington, D.C.: Catholic University of America Press, 1937). Jansen cites synods, councils, and regulations which call attention to the importance of

catechesis in specific and general terms from the Council of Nicaea in 325 through the late 1930s.

15. See John Tracy Ellis, *American Catholicism*, 2d rev. ed. (Chicago: University of Chicago Press, 1972), 1–40; Clifford Olmstead, *History of Religion in the United States* (Englewood Cliffs, N.J.: Prentice-Hall, 1960), 25–39.

16. *Sharing the Light of Faith*, the National Catechetical Directory for Catholics of the United States (Washington, D.C.: United States Catholic Conference, 1979).

17. Fridericus Streicher has collected the three catechisms of Peter Canisius into two volumes, *Catechismi Latini et Germanici* vols. 1 and 2 (Rome: Pontificia Universitas Gregoriana, 1936).

18. The most recent English translation of Trent's catechism is that by John A. McHugh and Charles J. Callan, *Catechism of the Council of Trent for Parish Priests* (New York: Joseph F. Wagner, Inc., 1923).

19. The first of Bellarmine's two catechisms, *Dottrina Christiana Breve* (a compendium of Christian doctrine), written in Italian, appeared in Rome in 1597. For complete text, see *Dottrina christiana breve, composita per ordine di N. S. Papa Clemente VIII,* in *Opera Omnia Roberti Bellarmini*, 12:257–282.

20. Auger wrote two catechisms: *Catéchisme et sommaire de la religion chrétienne* (Lyon, 1563) and *Petite catéchisme et sommaire de la religion chrétienne* (Paris, 1568). At one time Auger was hailed the "Chrysostom of France."

21. It is interesting and significant to point out that in 1892 the diocesan synod of the Apostolic Vicariate of Arizona recommended the use of Jerome Ripalda's catechism for the Spanish-speaking Catholics in that area. See Carlos Sommervogel, *Bibliothèque de la Compagnie de Jésus* (1890), 1:603–608.

22. Roderick MacEachen, "The Catechism: Its Origin and Development," *The Catholic University Bulletin*, 27 (1921), 11–16. See also Guy de Bretagne, "History of the "Textbook," *Lumen Vitae*, 5 (1950), 470–476; Jean Claude D'Hotel, *Les origines du catéchisme moderne* (Paris: Aubier, 1966).

23. See André Fossion, SJ, "La catéchèse scolaire d'hier à demain," *Nouvelle Revue Théologique*, 112 (1980), 3–21; Mary Charles Bryce, "Evolution of Catechesis from the Catholic Reformation to the Present," in *A Faithful Church*, edited by John H. Westerhoff III and O. C. Edwards, Jr. (Wilton, Connecticut: Morehouse-Barlow, 1981), 204–235.

24. Francis J. Donohue, 'Textbooks for Catholic Schools Prior to 1840," *The Catholic School Journal*, 40 (March 1940), 65.

25. The Rare Book Collection, Mullen Library, Catholic University of America, Washington, D.C., has a large number of such catechisms among its holdings.

26. Andrew White, *Relatio Itineris in Marylandiam* (Baltimore: John Murphy, 1874). See also John Gilmary Shea, *History of the Catholic Missions among the Indian Tribes of the United States, 1529–1854* (New York: P. J. Kenedy, 1883), 490.

27. Clifton E. Olmstead. *Religion in America: Past and Present* (Englewood Cliffs, N.J.: Prentice-Hall, 1961), 98. Gerald Shaughnessy puts the figure at 23,000 in 1785 and indicates its rise to 27,000 in 1789. See G. Shaughnessy, *Has the Immigrant Kept the Faith?* (New York: Macmillan, 1925), 36.

28. *The Official Catholic Directory* (New York: P. J. Kenedy & Sons, 1981), "General Summary," 4.

Chapter 1

1. Eleanor Darnell Carroll was his mother and Daniel Carroll, his father. John, the fourth of seven children, was born in Upper Marlboro, Maryland. For further

information, see Peter Guilday, *The Life and Times of John Carroll* (Westminster, Md.: Newman Press, 1954), 2-3; Annabelle M. Melville, *John Carroll of Baltimore* (New York: Charles Scribner's Sons, 1955), 1-2.

2. Guilday, *John Carroll*, 31.

3. Ibid., 32 n. 12.

4. Albert Henry Smyth, ed., *Writings of Benjamin Franklin* (New York: 1905-1907), 6:447; Guilday, *John Carroll*, 103 n. 18. See Carl Van Doren, *Benjamin Franklin* (New York: Viking Press, 1938), 542.

5. Melville, *John Carroll*, 68-69.

6. *Ex hac apostolicae*, the papal bull elevating Carroll to the bishopric. See *The John Carroll Papers*, ed. Thomas O'Brien Hanley (Notre Dame: University of Notre Dame Press, 1976), 1:454. Guilday calls it "the most venerable of all papal documents which have been sent by the Holy See to the Church in America," Guilday, *John Carroll*, 357. The bull is cited in its entirety on pp. 358-361.

7. Cited in Melville, *John Carroll*, 86.

8. *NCE*, 3:152.

9. Melville, *John Carroll*, 212.

10. Ibid., 198, 201, 204-205, 213.

11. "Report to the Roman Congregation—To Caesar Brancadoro," *The John Carroll Papers*, 2:264.

12. "Bishop Carroll's Pastoral Letter," in Hugh J. Nolan, ed., *Pastoral Letters of the American Hierarchy, 1792-1970* (Huntington, Ind.: Our Sunday Visitor Press, 1971), 6.

13. Cited in Peter Guilday, *A History of the Councils of Baltimore* (New York: Macmillan, 1932), 64.

14. John Gilmary Shea, *Life and Times of the Most Reverend John Carroll* (New York: John G. Shea, 1888), 2:398; also cited in Guilday, *Councils*, 62. Simon Bruté was the first bishop of Vincennes (1834-1839).

15. Guilday, *Councils*, 62-63.

16. See *Concilia Provincialia Baltimori* (Baltimori: Joannem Murphy & Socium, 1851), 11-24. "The value of the decrees of 1791 were [*sic*] of such a high nature that the Fathers ordered the Statuta of 1791 to be reprinted at the head of those passed by the Council of 1829" (Guilday, *John Carroll*, 446).

17. *Concilia Provincialia*, #4, p. 13; #15, p. 17; #16, p. 20.

18. Hugh J. Nolan, ed., *Pastoral Letters of the American Hierarchy, 1792-1970* (Huntington, Ind.: Our Sunday Visitor Press, 1971), 6-15. See also Peter Guilday, ed., *The National Pastorals of the American Hierarchy, 1792-1919* (Washington, D.C.: National Catholic Welfare Conference, 1923), 1-16.

19. See Guilday, *National Pastorals*, #3, p. 3; Nolan, *Pastoral Letters*, p. 6.

20. Nolan, *Pastoral Letters*, #3, p. 7.

21. Ibid., #11, p. 10.

22. Ibid., #22, p. 14.

23. *Abridgement of Christian Doctrine—Part First, Short Catechism*, prescribed by Pope Pius X, translated by T. Sebastian Byrne (Rome/New York: Fr. Pustet & Co., 1906); *Abridgement of Christian Doctrine—Part Second, Larger Catechism*, prescribed by Pope Pius X, translated by T. Sebastian Byrne (Rome/New York: Fr. Pustet & Co., 1906.

24. Molyneux was born in Lancashire, England, and entered the Society of Jesus in 1757. He taught at the Jesuit School in Bruges, Belgium, where John Carroll

was enrolled, and the two men became close friends. Molyneux was sent to the United States in 1771, arriving in Philadelphia on March 21 of that year. He later became the first superior of the restored Society of Jesus in the United States.

25. Archives of the Archdiocese of Baltimore (hereafter, AAB), K5–K17, LI. See Charles J. Carmody, "The 'Carroll Catechism'—A Primary Component of the American Catechetical Tradition," *Notre Dame Journal of Education*, 7 (Spring 1976), 76–95.

26. *A Catechism of Christian Doctrine by Laurence Vaux, D.D.*, reprinted from an edition of 1583 with an introductory memoir of the author by Thomas Graves Law (Manchester: Chetham Society, 1885).

27. In an introductory section "To the Christian Reader—The Author to the Reader," Vaux concludes with a citation of his sources: "And what I have set furth in this little booke . . . I have collected and translated out of the Scripture, . . . out of the bookes of D. Petrus de Soto, and D. Canisius, adding here and there some sentences of the ancient Fathers, S. Cyprian, Athanasius, Ambrose, Hierome, Damascene & S. Bernard. God send the eares to heare which shall learne it, and them, that neede not learne it, because they knowe it, to take it quietly when they read it, knowing that I haue made it for the simple, and ignorante, and not for the fine felowes, and learned" (p. 7). Of particular interest is Vaux's attributing each of the twelve articles of the creed to one of the Apostles; see pp. 11–12.

28. *Abridgement of Christian Doctrine* was first published in 1649.

29. J. D. Crichton, "Religious Education in England in the Penal Days (1559–1778)," in Gerard S. Sloyan, ed., *Shaping the Christian Message* (New York: Macmillan, 1958), 81. See also J. D. Crichton, "Challoner's Catechism," *The Clergy Review*, 63 (1978), 140–146; Bernard Pickering, "Bishop Challoner and Teaching the Faith," ibid., 65 (1980), 6–15; J. D. Crichton, "Richard Challoner: Catechist and Spiritual Writer," *The Living Light*, 18 (Summer 1981), 103–111.

30. See Edwin H. Burton, *The Life and Times of Bishop Challoner* (London: Longmans Green & Co., 1909), 161; Pickering, "Bishop Challoner," 10.

31. The volume was published by L'Ecole Economique in New York, a school founded for children of refugees of the revolution in the French West Indies. Founders included General Jean Victor Moreau, Baron Jean Guillaume Hyde de Neuville, Bishop Jean Cheverus, and others. See *Memoirs of Baron Hyde de Neuville*, trans. and abridged by Frances Jackson (St. Louis: B. Herder, 1913), 246.

32. Fénelon exerted wide influence and innovative range throughout his life. He was one of the first persons to demonstrate the value of the education of girls. His first important work, *Traité de l'education des filles*, appeared in 1687. The volume was a pioneering work which emphasized the dignity of women and their right to education. Fénelon was accused of quietism at one point but after a long and difficult time was exonerated.

33. *Catechism on Foundations of the Christian Faith*, 3.

34. Part I, 28.

35. Part II, 33–35.

36. Two earlier editions of Hay's catechism had already appeared, but only that of 1809 carried Carroll's approbation "with some alterations in the language." See George Hay, *An Abridgement of Christian Doctrine* (Philadelphia: Matthew Carey, 1803; Baltimore: Geo. Dobbin & Murphy, 1809).

37. Melville, *John Carroll*, 280.
38. Ibid., 210–212; Guilday, *John Carroll*, 723–728. Reuter and his involvement in the U.S. Church is treated at length by V. J. Fecher, SVD, in *A Study of the Movement for German National Parishes in Philadelphia and Baltimore (1787–1802)*, Analecta Gregoriana, vol. 77 (Rome: Gregorian University Press, 1955).
39. Bellarmine's first catechism, *Dottrina cristiana breve*, appeared in 1597. Within two years it had been translated into sixty different languages and dialects. Because of its conciseness and clarity it gained widespread acceptance, but inasmuch as it had originated in Rome it enjoyed a kind of preferential esteem in that city.
40. Cited in Guilday, *John Carroll*, 724.
41. Ibid., 724.
42. Fridericus Caesarius Reuter, *Katechetischer Unterricht für die Christl. Katholische Jugend* (Baltimore: Gedruckt ben Samuel Saur, 1797), 30.
43. Ibid., 41; unpublished translations by Margrit Banta (1980).
44. Ibid., 95.
45. Ibid., 106.
46. *Carroll Papers*, 2:260.
47. Ibid.
48. See "Plan of Organization," in Guilday, *John Carroll*, 166–168.
49. John Carroll to Charles Plowden, Belgium, September 23, 1783; *see Carroll Papers*, 1:78.
50. See John Gilmary Shea, *Memorial of the First Centenary of Georgetown College*, Washington, D.C. (Washington, D.C.–New York: P. F. Collier, 1891). Georgetown opened its doors to students in September 1791; see p. 15 (Sulpician Archives).
51. Elizabeth was the daughter of Richard Bayley and Catherine Charlton Bayley. She married William Magee Seton in 1794, and they had five children. William died in 1803, and Elizabeth turned to a life of generous charity.
52. Seton arrived in Baltimore on June 15, 1808. See Annabelle M. Melville, *Elizabeth Bayley Seton, 1774–1821* (New York: Charles Scribner's Sons, 1960).
53. The pope, of course, later condemned the Civil Constitution. For a brief account, see John McManners, *The French Revolution and the Church*, Church History Outlines, 4 (London: SPCK, 1969), and for a longer study, André Latreille, *L'église catholique et la révolution française*, Tome I: *Le pontificat de Pie VI et la crise française (1775–1799)* (Paris: Editions du Cerf, 1970).
54. Charles G. Herbermann, *The Sulpicians in the United States* (New York: Encyclopedia Press, 1916), 16–19; Joseph W. Ruane, *The Beginnings of the Society of St. Sulpice in the United States (1791–1829)* (Washington, D.C.: Catholic University of America Press, 1935), 20–26.
55. Ruane, *Society*, 39–43.
56. Olier (1608–1657) founded a community for the training of priests located in the parish of St. Sulpice in Paris; it has been identified with the patron of that parish ever since. Olier is sometimes called a leader of the French school of spirituality. A copy of his *Catéchisme chrétien* is among the holdings of the Sulpician archives, Baltimore, Md. See Jean Jacques Olier, *Catéchisme chrétien pour la vie intérieure et journée chrétienne*, annotated by François Amat (Paris: Le Rameau, 1954).
57. Richard is one of the most interesting figures in early U.S. church history. On June 24, 1792, he arrived in Baltimore from France and was sent to Illinois, later

to the missions of Wisconsin, Minnesota, and Detroit, Michigan. Through his interest in education he established a number of primary and secondary schools. He promulgated the use of Fleury's catechism. Furthermore, he was largely responsible for the founding of the University of Michigan in Ann Arbor. In 1823 he was elected as a nonvoting delegate of the Territory of Michigan to the House of Representatives—the first Catholic priest to serve in Congress. He died in Detroit during a cholera epidemic in 1832. See F. Woodford and A. Hyma, *Gabriel Richard: Frontier Ambassador* (Detroit: Wayne State University Press, 1958).

58. For Maréchal's episcopacy, see below, Chap. 2.

59. DuBourg became administrator of the diocese of Louisiana in 1812 and three years later, September 24, 1815, was ordained bishop there.

60. David figures somewhat prominently in catechetics in the next period.

61. An English translation of the original work: Félix Dupanloup, *The Ministry of Catechising* (London: Griffith Farran, 1890). Dupanloup became bishop of Orleans, France, in 1849.

62. *L'oeuvre par excellence* was the French title of Dupanloup's work first published in 1868. The work describes the catechetical method developed by Jean Jacques Olier. The history of the "Method" is summarized and described in Joseph Colomb's study, "The Catechetical Method of Saint Sulpice," in Sloyan, ed., *Shaping the Christian Message*, 91–111. See also Joseph Colomb, "Quelques réflexions sur la méthode catéchistique," in *La Doctrine de vie au Catéchisme* (Paris: Société de Saint Jean l'Evangeliste, 1955), 1:16–27.

63. Dupanloup, *Ministry*, 2.

64. Ibid., 483.

65. Ibid., 485.

66. Ibid., 200.

67. See "Message to the People of God," #25, in *L'Osservatore Romano* (Eng. ed.), November 17, 1977, 6. Also, "The Written Interventions—The National Council of Catholic Bishops of the USA," *L'Osservatore Romano*, November 3, 1977, 7.

68. Colomb, "Method," 100–101.

69. See AAB, 8 A–K 1, p. 3.

70. The present writer has been unable to locate this catechism. None of the early Americana collectors cite its location, and Flaget's letter to Carroll concerning it seems to be the sole evidence for its existence.

71. In a letter to Leonard Antonelli, Congregation of Propagation of the Faith, April 23, 1792, Carroll referred to the need for a division of the large diocese. See *Carroll Papers*, 2:29.

72. See *Catéchisme historique contenant en abrégé l'histoire sainte et la doctrine chrétienne*, nouvelle edition (Lyon: Jean Marie Bruyset, Imprimeur Librairie, 1767). Fleury's first edition was published in Paris in 1683. It carried the approbation of the bishop of Meaux, J. Benigne Bousset, 1683. See the assessment of his catechism in Claude D'Hotel, *origines du catéchisme moderne*, 356–367.

73. Fleury, dissatisfied with the skeletal truths contained in sixteenth-century catechisms, prefaced his manual with a detailed explanation of its corpus and use. He was caustically critical of the pedagogical approach and the "very dry" (p. viii) catechisms children were subjected to. He found it incomprehensible "to interrogate a child before we have taught him anything, . . . to make him deliver the whole doctrine" (p. viii) before teaching him the engaging story of God's care for

humankind through the ages. His catechism contains brief chapters of scriptural narratives. Following each narrative is a series of questions and answers reviewing and, hopefully, reaffirming the lessons. His first chapter is about God's creating the universe and humans. Thus, the first question after the well-told creation story is "Who made the world?" See the Irish version, *An Historical Catechism . . . by Monsieur Claude Fleury* (Dublin: Ignatius Kelly, 1753). The introduction is 60 pages long.

74. Annabelle M. Melville, *Jean Lefebvre de Cheverus, 1768–1836* (Milwaukee: Bruce, 1958), 54–55. The whereabouts of this catechism is unknown to the present writer. It is likely that it was hand-written and not published.

75. See William Augustine Leahy, "The Archdiocese of Boston," in William Byrne, ed., *History of the Catholic Church in the New England States* (Boston: Hurd & Everts Co., 1899), 1:35.

76. See Robert H. Lord, John E. Sexton, and Edward T. Harrington, *History of the Archdiocese of Boston, 1604–1943* (New York: Sheed & Ward, 1944), 594.

77. *Ibid.*

78. Ibid.

79. Ibid., 650. Recorded in Joseph Finotti, *Bibliographia Catholica Americana* (New York: Catholic Publishing House, 1872), 39.

80. *Monthly Anthology and Boston Review*, 4 (February 1807), 71–77.

81. Ibid. (April 1807), 187–190.

82. "Ut incommodis ex Catechismorum varietate ortis obviam eamus, statuimus Catechismun [sic] Revmi. Archiepiscopi Baltimorensis auctoritate olim editum, in hoc Dioecesi ab omnibus Sacerdotibus adhibendum in edocentis pueris, donec alius, sedis Apostolicae approbatione munitus, in communem totius provinciae usum editus fuerit." *Acta Synodi Diocesana Philadelphiensis Primae, Philadelphiae* (Philadelphia: F. Pierson, 1832), #9, p. 13; first diocesan synod, May 15, 1832.

83. Joseph Rosati (Epis.), *Synodus Diocesana S. Ludovicinis,* April 1839, pp. 22–23.

84. *A Short Abridgement of the Christian Doctrine; Newly Revised and Augmented for the Catholic Church in the Diocese of Boston* (Boston: Thomas J. Flynn & Co., 1843). On the title page the following citation is found: "Published with the approbation of the Rt. Rev. B. Fenwick." See Raymond J. O'Brien, "History of Our English Catechism," *Ecclesiastical Review*, 91 (1934), 594.

85. See *First Plenary Council of Baltimore*, 1852, 33rd decree. The catechism committee "would suggest that the extensively and favorably known catechism of . . . Carroll be submitted to the . . . Holy See"; O'Brien, "Catechism," 594.

86. Charles Carmody listed 22 editions (or printings). This in itself testifies to the high regard in which it was held. See Carmody, "'Carroll Catechism'," 84.

87. Cited in Melville, *John Carroll*, 202.

Chapter 2

1. John Lingard, *Catechistical Instructions on the Doctrines and Worship of the Catholic Church*, sec. ed. (New York: P. S. Casserly and Sons, 1841), 48–49. The question reminds one of Finley Dunne's "Mr. Dooley Books." In one of these volumes Dooley was asked: "Are you Roman Catholic?" "No, thank God," Dooley retorted emphatically, "I am a Chicago Catholic."

2. Clifford Olmstead, *History of Religion in the United States* (Englewood Cliffs, N.J.: Prentice-Hall, 1960), 430. One manifestation of hostility was the

development of Know-Nothingism, a movement which developed in the last half of the nineteenth century in response to the heavy German and Irish, chiefly Catholic, immigration. The large number of immigrants caused alarm among native-born citizens who feared the threat of a Roman takeover by the newcomers. That alarm expressed itself in outbursts against the foreigners, especially the "papists." The alarm was further nurtured at that time by the publication of *Awful Disclosures of the Hotel Dieu*, written by Maria Monk (assisted by unscrupulous ministers) about life in a convent. See Ray Allen Billington, *The Protestant Crusade, 1800-1860. A Study of the Origins of American Nativism* (New York: Macmillan, 1938; Rinehart & Company, Inc., 1952).

3. Edward Wakin and Joseph F. Scheuer, *The De-Romanization of the American Catholic Church* (New York: Macmillan, 1966).

4. Oscar Handlin observed that "the national interest was never revealed as an ideal above and beyond all the individuals in the nation. It was rather discovered by realistic compromise achieved through free discussion and open exposition of all diversities of opinion and interest involved." See "America Recognizes Diverse Loyalties," cited in Joseph H. Fichter, "The Americanization of Catholicism," in Thomas T. McAvoy, ed., *Roman Catholicism and the American Way of Life* (Notre Dame, Ind.: University of Notre Dame Press, 1960), 116. See also Currin V. Shields, *Democracy and Catholicism in America* (New York: McGraw-Hill, 1958), 1-28.

5. Fichter, "Americanization," 116.

6. Sometimes the two were closely associated, as when trusteeism in Charleston was at an explosive high and Ambrose Maréchal, third archbishop of Baltimore, appealed to the Holy See with the recommendation that Georgia and the Carolinas be erected into a separate diocese with Benedict Fenwick as bishop. Rome looked on the recommendation favorably, and on June 18, 1820, initiated the procedure to establish the diocese of Charleston. Contrary to Maréchal's suggestion, however, Rome nominated the parish priest, John England, of Bandon, Ireland, the first bishop of Charleston.

7. John Tracy Ellis, *American Catholicism* (Chicago: University of Chicago Press, 1956), 40-50. Thomas T. McAvoy presented a fuller and more plausible explanation of the discord in his article, "The Formation of the Catholic Minority in the United States, 1820-1860," *Review of Politics*, 10 (1948), 13-34.

8. Ellis, *American Catholicism*, 45. A previous incident of lay trustees trying to choose their own pastor occurred in New York in 1785. The Germans in Philadelphia did not attempt to elect a pastor until 1789. See Vincent Fecher's study, cited above, Chap. 1, note 38.

9. Ellis, *American Catholicism*, 45.

10. The first four were: Luke Concanen, an Irish Dominican, first bishop appointed to New York, who died in Naples (June 19, 1810) before reaching his see; Michael Egan (1761-1814), first bishop of Philadelphia, from Limerick; John Connolly (1750-1825), second bishop of New York, from County Meath; Henry Conwell (1745-1842), second bishop of Philadelphia, from County Derry.

11. See Peter Guilday, *Life and Times of John England* (New York: Arno Press & New York Times, 1969), 2:48ff. See also Patrick Carey, *An Immigrant Bishop: John England's Adaptation of Irish Catholicism to American Republicanism* (Yonkers, N.Y.: U.S. Catholic Historical Society, 1982).

12. See Sebastian G. Messmer, ed., *John England's Works* (Cleveland: Arthur H. Clark Co., 1908), 7:9-44. See also the five-volume collection, *The Works of*

the Right Rev. John England, edited by Ignatius A. Reynolds (Baltimore: John Murphy & Co., 1849). Reynolds succeeded England as second bishop of Charleston.

13. Dated July 12, 1820, this pastoral appears in full in Guiday, *John England*, 1:291–293.

14. See ibid., 1:305.

15. *The Constitution of the Roman Catholic Churches of the States of North-Carolina, South-Carolina and Georgia* . . ., (Charleston: Burges & James, 1840), #14, p. 9. Guilday gives a careful description and assessment; see *John England*, 1:343–379.

16. *Constitution*, 32–36.

17. See Carey, *Immigrant Bishop*, 58

18. Leon LeBuffe, *Tensions in American Catholicism, 1820–1870* (Ann Arbor, Mich.: 1973), 59.

19. England's address to the thirteenth convention in South Carolina, January 1837; quoted in *U.S. Catholic Miscellany*, XVI, 225; see Guilday, *John England*, 1:377.

20. Messmer, *England's Works*, 4:302.

21. APF, Scritture riferite nei Congressi, America Centrale, vol. 5 fols. 578^r–581^r, January 27, 1820, pamphlet of G.M. Mazzetti re: status of Archdiocese of Baltimore.

22. Ibid., fols. 563^r–577^r, January 26, 1820, document of G. M. Mazzetti on the difficulties and evils besetting the Church in Virginia, Carolina, and Georgia.

23. England related his initial establishment of the Charleston "Book Society" in his *Diurnal*, April 26, 1821. See also Guilday, *John England*, 1:317; Dorothy Fremont Grant, *John England, American Christopher* (Milwaukee: Bruce, 1949), 79; and John Gilmary Shea, *History of the Catholic Church in the United States* (New York: John G. Shea, 1890), 3:316.

24. For this letter, dated March 6, 1821, see Reynolds, ed., *Works of England*, vol. 4.

25. March 9, 1821.

26. *Diurnal of Rt. Rev. John England, First Bishop of Charleston, 1820–1823*, (Philadelphia: American Catholic Historical Society, 1895), 16.

27. *Catechism of the Roman Catholic Faith, Published for the Use of His Flock*, by the Right Reverend Father in God, John, Bishop of Charleston (Charleston: Hoff Printing Office, 1821). A photostatic copy of the catechism is among the holdings of the Rare Book Collection, Mullen Library, Catholic University of America, Washington, D.C.

28. These questions are cited from an 1807 copy of the "Butler Catechism." See Dr. James Butler, *A Catechism for the Instruction of Children* (Twentieth Edition) (Dublin: R. Conolly, 1807), 7.

29. APF, Scritture riferite nei Congressi, America Centrale, vol. 8, fol. 85^{rv}, April 14, 1823, England to Cardinal Consalvi. England sent his missal, catechism, and pastoral letters to Propaganda Fide. He also explained his proposal for a commentary on Sacred Scripture. He described the situation in his diocese, requesting that the principal patron of the diocese be St. Finbar.

30. Fuller's letter as published in the *Courier*, followed by England's detailed reply, is found in Messmer, *England's Works*, 4:159–176.

31. The advertisement ran in the *Miscellany* in 1822 on June 5, p. 1; June 12, p. 16; June 19, p. 24; June 26, p. 32; July 3, p. 40; July 10, p. 40; and July 17, p. 56.

32. The title page of the 1873 edition is missing from the photostatic copy available to this writer and thus the publisher is unidentified. No by-line or credit is

given to the editor of this volume either. There is a letter in the Charleston diocesan archives critiquing the edition and suggesting improvements which would make the catechism more appealing to children. See Aloisius M. Folchi, Pastor, St. Peter's, January 15, 1873, ADC tem 54-G-7. The present writer has compared the 1822 edition with that of 1873 and finds some differences, most of them minor, with the exception of the three questions-and-answers cited here.

33. *The Roman Missal* by the Right Rev. Doctor England (New York: William H. Creagh, 1822), preface, iii. England's copyright on this volume was secured September 13, 1821.

34. Ibid., xxiii.

35. Messmer, *England's Works*, 5:315-316.

36. Guilday, *John England*, 1:330.

37. Ibid.

38. Ibid., 332.

39. See AAB 16-J-7. England wrote this letter from Raleigh, North Carolina.

40. Guilday, *John England*, 1:331. See also "Letter from the Right Reverend John England, D.D., to the Honorable William Gaston, LLD," in *American Catholic Historical Society Records*, 18 (1907), 378.

41. *The Roman Missal* by the Right Reverend Doctor England, late bishop of Charleston (Philadelphia: Eugene Cumisky, 1843).

42. See Olivier Rousseau, *The Progress of the Liturgy* (Westminster, Md.: Newman Press, 1951), 207.

43. Guilday, *John England*, 1:458.

44. Ibid., 461.

45. Ibid., 473.

46. England's diary dates from July 10, 1820, to December 5, 1823.

47. In all there are fifty-one references to his catechizing, explaining, instructing. Throughout, one perceives the profound respect England had for people of all walks of life. One entry (June 7, 1821) describes giving instructions to "three catechumens, persons of color," a description he employed for the nonwhites in his diocese.

48. Edward McSweeney, "Ecclesiastical Charleston," *American Ecclesiastical Review*, 32 (1905), 500.

49. Cited in Reynolds, ed., *Works of England*, 2:358; Guilday, *John England*, 1:467.

50. Guilday, *John England*, 1:338.

51. Charles George Herbermann, *The Sulpicians in the United States* (New York: Encyclopedia Press, 1916), 77.

52. Columba Fox, *The Life of the Right Reverend John Baptist David* (New York: United States Catholic Historical Society, 1925), 51. Consult also Charles Lemarié, *Mgr. J.-B. David, 1761-1841, Etudes sur les missionaires bretons dans le Middle West Américain*, vol. 1: *Les origines religieuses du Kentucky* (Angers: C. Lemarié, 1973).

53. Fox, *David*, 51-52. Seminary life was modeled on the program and spirit of St. Sulpice in Paris. See ibid., 52; Herbermann, *U.S. Sulpicians*, 163.

54. Herbermann, *U.S. Sulpicians*, 163; Fox, *David*, 96-108.

55. Raymond J. O'Brien, "The History of Our English Catechism," *Ecclesiastical Review*, 91 (1934), 591-592.

56. *Catechism of the Diocess [sic] of Bardstown*, Printed by the Authority of the Right Reverend Benedict J. Flaget (Bardstown, Ky.: N. Wickliff & S. Bailey,

1825). A copy of this manual is among the holdings of the Rare Book Section, Mullen Library, Catholic University of America, Washington, D.C.

57. APF, Scritture riferite nei Congressi, America Centrale, vol. 8, fols. 741^{rv}-742^{rv}, S. T. Badin to Propaganda Fide, December 15, 1826. This folio includes a copy of David's catechism submitted to Propaganda Fide by Badin, vicar general, Bardstown. Badin clearly credits David with its authorship.

58. A copy of the Boeswalt edition is in the Rare Book Collection, Mullen Library, Catholic University of America, Washington, D.C.

59. O'Brien, "Catechism," 591.

60. Herbermann, *U.S. Sulpicians*, 181.

61. Ibid., 183.

62. Dupanloup, *Ministry of Catechising*, ix. Dupanloup's work postdates Maréchal's lifetime, but it is considered a faithful disclosure of Sulpician principles, ideals, and practices in catechetics.

63. Olier (1608-1657) founded the Society of the Priests of St. Sulpice in 1642 in a suburb of Paris. The society was named for the patron saint of the parish church where Olier was pastor. The special purpose of the society is "to prepare young men in seminaries for ecclesiastical life and for Holy Orders by training them in the knowledge and virtues required by the dignity of the Priesthood and the Sacred Ministry." The seminarians participated in the activities of parish life in that early parochial setting in addition to their academic theological studies. Olier is credited with writing a manual, *Catéchisme chrétien pour la vie intérieure et journée chrétienne*, annotated by François Amat (Paris: Le Rameau, 1954). See also Pierre Pourrat, *Father Olier, Founder of St. Sulpice*, trans. W. S. Reilly (Baltimore: Voice Publishing Co., 1932), 150.

64. Baltimore: Fielding Lucas, n.d. Lucas made a practice of not dating many of his publications, maintaining that by doing so they were "always current" and not "dated." Wilfrid Parsons dates the catechism 1826; see Parsons, *Early Catholic Americana* (New York: Macmillan Co., 1939), #888, p. 209.

65. The copy examined by the present writer is in the Special Collection, Lauinger Library, Georgetown University, Washington, D.C.

66. No publisher named. Two copies of the Hogan catechism are among the holdings of the American Philosophical Society Library, Philadelphia; the Library Company (formerly the Benjamin Franklin Library) in Philadelphia also has a copy. A photostatic copy is in the Rare Book Collection, Mullen Library, Catholic University of America, Washington, D.C.

67. Philadelphia: Mifflin and Parry, 1827. A copy of this manual is among the holdings of the Rare Book Collection, Mullen Library, Catholic University of America, Washington, D.C.

68. ACHS, (1913) 24, p. 21. See also Francis E. Tourscher, OSA, *The Hogan Schism and Trustee Troubles in St. Mary's Church, Philadelphia, 1820-1829* (Philadelphia: Peter Reilly, 1930).

69. John Gilmary Shea, *History of the Catholic Church in the United States* (New York: D. H. McBride & Co., 1890), 3:229.

70. ACHS, 25 (1914), 164.

71. Hogan maintained that perfect contrition was the *only* remedy for actual, mortal sin. See Hugh J. Nolan, *The Most Reverend Francis Patrick Kenrick, Third Bishop of Philadelphia, 1830-1851* (Washington, D.C.: Catholic University

of America Press, 1948). See also Nolan's chapter in *The History of the Arch-diocese of Philadelphia*, ed. James F. Connelly (Philadelphia: Archdiocese of Philadelphia, 1976).
72. AAB, Conwell to Maréchal, 14-2-10.
73. ACHS, 18 (1907), 378.
74. ACHS, 25 (1914), 321.
75. Ibid., 330.
76. See Martin I. J. Griffin, "Life of Bishop Conwell of Philadelphia," *American Catholic Historical Society Records*, 24 (1913), 16-42, 162-178, 217-250, 348-361; 25 (1914) 52-67, 146-178, 217-248, 296-341; Shea, *History*, 3:228.
77. Conwell Catechism, p. 5.
78. AAB, England to Maréchal, 16-J-5.
79. "List of Sovereign Pontiffs of the Apostolic See of Rome," pp. 37-40. The popes are listed by the centuries in which they lived. Leo XII is the last and only pope cited in the nineteenth century.
80. APF, Scritture riferite nei Congressi America Centrale vol. 9, fols. 3574-3614, Maréchal to Propaganda, October 1, 1827.
81. Ibid., vol. 6, fol. 640^r, F. Rese to H. Conwell, May 15, 1827, written in Genoa as Rese was en route to Rome (in French).
82. APF, Scritture riferite nei Congressi, America Centrale, vol. 6, fols. 641^{rv} and 642^{rv}, F. Rese to H. Conwell, Feb. 6, 1828.
83. Shea, *History*, 3:260.
84. *Catéchisme de la Louisiane* Ré-Imprimé par ordre de Msgr. Joseph Rosati, Evêque de St. Louis et Administrateur Apostolique du Diocèse de Nouvelle Orléans (New Orleans: Buisson et Boinmaire, 1829), second edition. A copy of this manual is among the holdings of Tulane University. Neither the date nor the whereabouts of the first edition is known to this writer. See F. J. Easterly, *The Life of Rt. Rev. Joseph Rosati*, American Church History Series, 33 (Washington, D.C.: Catholic University of America Press, 1942).
85. Maksimilijan Jezernik, *Frederic Baraga* (New York-Washington, D.C.: Studia Slovenica, 1968), 31.
86. Ibid., 41 n. 24; 55.
87. Maccatebinessi and another young tribesman, Augustine Henehun, were sent to Rome the following year. Three months after they arrived Maccatebinessi became seriously ill and died on June 25, 1833. A year later Augustine's health began to fail drastically and he returned to his native land. See Jezernik, *Frederic Baraga*, 36, 39; see also Joseph Gregorich, *The Apostle of the Chippewas* (Chicago: Bishop Baraga Association, 1932), 24-27, and Robert Frederick Trisco, *The Holy See and the Nascent Church in the Middle Western United States, 1826-1850*, Analecta Gregoriana, 125 (Rome: Gregorian University Press, 1962), 212-214.
88. Gregorich, *Apostle*, 95; P. Chrysostom Verwyst, OFM, *Life and Labors of Rt. Reverend Frederic Baraga* (Milwaukee: M. H. Siltzins & Co., 1900), 371.
89. *Dictionary of the Ojibway Language*, 2nd ed. (Montreal: Beauchemin & Valois, 1880). Baraga had worked on the original dictionary for ten years; see Verwyst, *Frederic Baraga*, 225-226.
90. *Anamie-Misinaigan* (Ottawa) (Wawiyatamong: Geo. L. Whitney, 1832); see Gregorich, *Apostle*, 73, 74. See also Baraga's *Theoretical and Practical Grammar*

---

for the Otchipwe Language (Detroit: Jabez Fox, 1850). A copy of the latter is among the rare book holdings, Library of Congress.

91. This 215-page book was approved by Bishop Frederick Rese, and published in Paris (Paris: E. J. Bailey, 1837). A copy is among the rare book holdings, Library of Congress.

92. Jezernik, *Frederic Baraga*, 67 n. 43.

93. Ibid., 68.

94. Ibid.

95. Ibid., 69.

96. Jezernik, *Frederic Baraga*, 69 n. 50. Baraga wrote to the Holy Father from Paris following his visit in Rome. He assured His Holiness that he would make every correction recommended, thus displaying his desire to improve his work. A copy of his letter, dated May 12, 1837, is found in Jezernik, op. cit., 152.

97. Jezernik, *Frederic Baraga*, 69.

98. This pastoral letter was written shortly after his episcopal consecration. The "encyclical," entitled "One Thing is Necessary," may be found in its entirety in both Chippewa and English (on opposing pages) in Verwyst, *Frederic Baraga*, appendix, 430–446 (no date provided).

99. Jezernik, *Frederic Baraga*, 75.

100. Mary Letitia Lyons, *Francis Norbert Blanchet and the Founding of the Oregon Missions* (Washington, D.C. Catholic University of America Press, 1940); M. Leona Nichols, *The Mantle of Elias, The Story of Fathers Blanchet and Demers in Early Oregon* (Portland, Oreg.: Binfords and Mort, 1941).

101. *Chinook Dictionary, Catechism, Prayers and Hymns*. Composed in 1838 by Rt. Rev. Modeste Demers, Bp. of Vancouver's Island; revised, corrected and completed in 1867 by Most Rev. Francis Norbert Blanchet; with modifications and additions by Rev. L. N. St. Onge, Montreal, 1871. A copy of the seventh edition of this manual is among the rare book holdings, Library of Congress. See also *Dictionary of the Chinook Jargon* (Portland, Ore.: F. L. McCormick, 1879).

102. Charles Henry Carey, *History of Oregon* (Chicago: Pioneer Historical Publishing Co. 1922), 51.

103. *Catechism of the Christian Doctrine*, Published with the Approbation of the Most Rev. Archbishop Eccleston (Baltimore: John Murphy & Co., 1839). *An Abridgement of the Catechism of the Christian Doctrine* . . . (Baltimore: John Murphy & Co., 1839). A second printing of both catechisms appeared in 1850.

104. *A Short Abridgement of the Christian Doctrine: Newly Revised and Augmented* for the use of the Catholic Church in the Diocese of Boston. Published with the Approbation of the Rt. Rev. B. Fenwick (Boston: Thomas J. Flynn & Co., 1843). See O'Brien, "Catechism," 594.

105. See Guilday, *John England*, 1:337; see also Richard K. MacMaster, "Benedict Fenwick, Bishop of Boston, American Apprenticeship, 1782–1817," *Historical Records and Studies*, 47 (1959), 78–139.

106. See Robert H. Lord, John E. Sexton, and Edward T. Harrington, *History of the Archdiocese of Boston* . . . *1604–1943* (New York: Sheed and Ward, 1944), 2:52–109.

107. Ibid., 71, 156; see Shea, *History*, 3:140–155.

108. England's influence is acknowledged by historians. See Lord, et al., *Archdiocese of Boston*, 2:96, 332. *The Jesuit*'s first issue appeared on September 5, 1829. See Lord, et al., 198, 332.

109. Ibid.
110. Fenwick, *Catechism*, p. 2.
111. Pages 13–68.
112. Cited in Nolan, *Kenrick*, 139.
113. Ibid.
114. *"In Synodo Diocesana Philadelphiensi Prima,"* Statute No. 9, in *Constitutiones Diocesanae in Synodis Philadelphiensibus* (Philadelphia: McLaughlin Brothers, 1873), 5.
115. *Kleiner Katechismus* (Baltimore: J. T. Ganzsche, 1834).
116. *Katechismus, Oder Kurzer Inbegriff Christokatholischer Lehre*; no publisher credited in the copy available to this writer. The 64-page catechism bears the stated approval of Kenrick, Bishop of Philadelphia, and Purcell, Bishop of Cincinnati.
117. Cited in Nolan, *Kenrick*, 247. See also AAB 32–A–7, Kenrick to Eccleston, Feb. 19, 1839,
118. "Constitutiones Latae et Promulgatae a Reverendissimo D. Francisco Patricio Kenrick Episcopo Philadelphiensi," in *Constitutiones*, op. cit., 17, dated May 22, 1842.
119. It may be noted that Butler's catechism had been the model for John England, William Hogan, and others.
120. Michael J. Curley, *Venerable John Neumann, C.SS.R.* (Washington, D.C.: Catholic University of America Press, 1952), 55.
121. A second printing of the latter appeared in 1846. A copy of this catechism is in the Rare Book Collection, Mullen Library, Catholic University of America, Washington, D.C.
122. *Katholischer Katechismus*, verfasst von Johann Nep. Neumann, Bischof von Philadelphia. Zehnte Auflage. Mit Genehmigung des National Conciliums von Baltimore (Baltimore: John Murphy, 1853). Bernard Beck wrote that by 1889 the smaller catechism had gone through thirty-eight editions and the larger, twenty-one. See Beck, *Goldenes Jubiläum des Wirkens der Redemptoristevater an der St. Philomena Kirche in Pittsburg und Umgebung* (Ilchester, Md.: Collegium zu Ilchester, 1889), 154.
123. See the present writer's study, "An Accomplished Catechist: John Nepomucene Neumann," in *Living Light*, 14 (1977), 327–338.
124. John A. Berger, *Life of Right Rev. John N. Neumann, D.D.,* trans. Eugene Grimm (New York: Benziger Bros., 1884), 166.
125. Ibid., 68.
126. Curley, *John Neumann*, 163.
127. See ibid., 163, 431 n. 45.
128. Ibid., 162. In 1555 Peter Canisius published the first major catechism promulgated for Roman Catholics. In 1556 he published an abridged volume and in 1558 a smaller catechism for children. All three enjoyed enthusiastic popularity, and became models for catechisms in the next three centuries.
129. According to Curley, this book appeared in Pittsburgh. The *National Union Catalog*, vol. 444, indicates that the St. Vincent Archabbey library, Latrobe, Pennsylvania, has a copy of this Bible history.
130. See Berger, *John Neumann*, 41.
131. *The Autobiography of John Neumann*, trans. Alfred C. Rush, CSSR, (Boston: Daughters of St. Paul, 1976), 27.
132. Richard Gilmour, *Bible History* (New York: Benziger, 1869). For a review of Gilmour's work, see below, Chap. 3.

133. According to *SLF*, the four major tasks of catechesis are: (1) to proclaim Christ's message; (2) to participate in efforts to develop and maintain the Christian community; (3) to lead people to worship and prayer; and (4) to motivate them to serve others. See *SLF*, #39, 181, 213, 224, 227, 228, 243.

134. *Katholischer Katechismus oder Lehrbegriff* (Regensburg, 1847); an English translation by Rev. John Fauder, titled *A Full Catechism of the Catholic Religion*, bearing the imprimatur of John Cardinal McCloskey, archbishop of New York, was published in 1876 by Schwartz, Kirwin, and Fauss, publishers. This edition also carried the July 29, 1862, imprimatur of Cardinal Wiseman of Westminster, England. In 1868 a Polish translation of DeHarbe's manual was published in Chicago. The Rare Book Collection, Mullen Library, Catholic University of America, includes a number of DeHarbe manuals, including the English and Polish ones referred to.

135. Anthony N. Fuerst, *The Systematic Teaching of Religion* (New York: Benziger Brothers, 1946), 1:82. (Fuerst published a two-volume study of the history of catechetics.)

136. At least two catechisms were published which relied on or were derivations of DeHarbe's. One was a Thomas Linden (bibliography unknown); the other, edited by Th. Monnichs, SJ, entitled *Einheitskatechismus*, was adopted provisionally by the bishops of Germany in 1925.

137. Thomas Spalding, *Martin John Spalding* (Washington, D.C.: Catholic University of America Press, 1973), 2.

138. Ibid., 89–90, 103–104. Spalding was the editor, and Benedict J. Webb, a professional journalist, was the "proprietor." The *Advocate* succeeded the monthly, *St. Joseph's College Minerva* (Bardstown, 1834–1836), also founded and edited by Spalding. See Thomas F. Meehan, "Early Catholic Weeklies," in *Historical Records and Studies*, 28 (1937), 237–255; idem, "First Catholic Monthlies," ibid., 31 (1940), 140; and Joseph R. Frese; "Pioneer Catholic Weeklies," ibid., 30 (1939), 140–144.

139. See Meehan, "Weeklies," 238; Frese, "Weeklies," 140.

140. A copy of this catechism published in Louisville is in the Propaganda Fide Archives, Rome. See APF Scritture riferite nei Congressi, America Centrale, vol. 16, fol. 231–264.

141. *A General Catechism of the Christian Doctrine*. Prepared by order of the First Plenary Council of Baltimore for the use of Catholics in the United States of America. Approved by the Most Rev. M. J. Spalding, DD, Archbishop of Baltimore. (Baltimore: John B. Piet & Co., n.d.). A copy of the catechism is among the holdings of the American Catholic Historical Society of Philadelphia, St. Charles Seminary, Overbrook.

142. O'Brien, "Catechism," 595.

143. See Ralph Bayard, *Lone-Star Vanguard* (St. Louis: Vincentian Press, 1945); Charles Deuther, *Life and Times of the Right Reverend John Timon* (Buffalo: Charles Deuther, 1870).

144. John Timon, *Missions in Western New York and Church History of the Diocese of Buffalo* (Buffalo: Catholic Sentinel Print, 1862).

145. Ibid., 84.

146. Ibid., 39–46.

147. Ibid., 112–146.

148. Ibid., 244, 246, 250.

149. *A Short Abridgement of the Christian Doctrine; Newly Revised and Augmented.* Published with the Approbation of the Rt. Rev. John [Timon], Bishop of Buffalo (New York: John Kennedy, 1851), 3. A copy of Timon's catechism may be found in the Propaganda Fide Archives, Rome; APF, Scritture riferite nei Congressi, America Centrale, vol. 16, fols. 185–225. A photostatic copy is in the Rare Book Collection, Mullen Library, Catholic University of America, Washington, D.C.
150. Cited in Shea, *History*, 4:143.
151. Timon's *Catechism*, 30–31.
152. See above, Chap. 1, notes 72–73.
153. Spalding's letter (Sept. 20, 1852) to Kenrick in which he critiqued Timon's catechism appears in the Propaganda Fide Archives, Rome (APF, Scritture riferite nei Congressi, America Centrale, vol. 16, fols. 265^{rv}–266^{rv}). The present writer has a photostatic copy of this correspondence.
154. Cited by O'Brien, "Catechism," 596.

Chapter 3

1. In his brief, *Pastoralis Officii*, written July 15, 1598, Clement VIII ordered that the catechism to be published by Robert Bellarmine be "henceforth . . . [the] one method in teaching and learning the catechism"; cited in James Broderick, *The Life and Work of Blessed Robert Francis Cardinal Bellarmine, S.J.* (London: Burns, Oates and Washbourne, Ltd., 1928), 395. The text is taken from the *Summarium* in the cause for Bellarmine's beatification. Benedict XIII prescribed the same catechism for all of Italy in the Council of Rome, 1725. See Mansi, vol. 34, cols. 1845–1908. Benedict XIV urged all bishops of the Catholic world to use the Bellarmine catechism in his work *Etsi Minime*, Feb. 7, 1742, #17; see *Magnum Bullarium Romanum*, vol. 16 (Luxembourg, 1752), 64–66. Clement XIII lamented the multiplicity of catechisms, an evil, he maintained, that should be avoided; see *In Dominico Agro*, June 14, 1761, in *Bullarii Romani Continuatio*, Tome II, 134–136.
2. APF, Scritture riferite nei Congressi, America Centrale, vol. 9, fols. 357^{r}–361^{r}, October 1, 1827. See also Shea, *History*, 3:96.
3. AAB, 16–K–23, England to Maréchal, March 5, 1827.
4. AAB, 16–J–5, England to Maréchal, March 1, 1821.
5. AAB, 16–J–25, England to Maréchal, June 25, 1827. Previous letters pertaining to a proposed council or synod were written on July 6, 1821 (AAB, 16–J–14), March 15, 1827 (AAB, 16–K–23), April 26, 1827 (AAB, 16–K–24).
6. Murtha, Ronin John, OSB, *The Life of the Most Reverend Ambrose Maréchal, Third Archbishop of Baltimore, 1768–1828* (Washington, D.C.: Catholic University of America Press, 1965), 135. See ASMS Maréchal Files, Flaget to Maréchal, Bardstown, April 29, 1820.
7. Conwell to Maréchal, February 5, 1821; cited in ACHS Records, 25 (1914), 172.
8. UND, MC, 8725, Maréchal to England, Baltimore, July 28, 1821; cited in Murtha, *Maréchal* 168–169. The first synod was held in 1791, not 1790, as Maréchal indicated.
9. *Non sine magno*; cited in Shea, *History*, 3:408 n. 2.
10. Peter Guilday, *History of the Councils of Baltimore* (New York: Macmillan, 1932), 63.

11. Ibid.
12. *Concilia Provincialia Baltimori habita* (Baltimori: Joannes Murphy et Socium, 1858), #XXIII, p. 83. Related to this are the 34th and 35th decrees. The thirty-fourth contains the first legislation on Catholic schools. The Fathers decreed: "We judge it absolutely necessary that schools be established in which the young may be taught the principles of faith and morality, while being instructed in letters." In the thirty-fifth, they legislated for the publication of textbooks which would not contain prejudicial and false statements about the Church and Catholic doctrine and history. See Guilday, *Councils*, 95–98.
13. The years of successive provincial councils were 1833, 1837, 1840, 1843, 1846, and 1849.
14. Guilday, *Councils*, 128.
15. Hugh J. Nolan, *Pastoral Letters of the American Hierarchy, 1792–1970* (Huntington, Ind: Our Sunday Visitor Press, 1971), 24.
16. Nolan, *Pastoral Letters*, 25.
17. Ibid., 56. See also the present writer's study, "Religious Education in the Pastoral Letters and National Meetings of the U.S. Hierarchy," *Living Light*, 10 (1973), 249–263. Meanwhile new catechisms were published. A *Kleiner Katechismus*, bearing the approbation of Francis P. Kenrick, coadjutor to Bishop Henry Conwell in Philadelphia, addressed to German-speaking children and published in Baltimore, appeared in 1834. Two copies of this 36-page catechism are among the holdings in the Rare Book Collection, Mullen Library, Catholic University of America.
18. See Guilday, *Councils*, 168.
19. Ibid., 172.
20. Guilday, *Councils*, 176.
21. The catechism issue was not among the formal decrees promulgated by the council. It was, however, one of the pastoral recommendations emerging from the "Catechism Committee." See *"Congregatione Quinta Privata,"* in *Concilium Plenarium Totius Americae Septentrionalis Foederatae, Baltimori Habitum Anno 1852* (Baltimore: Joannes Murphy et Socios, 1853), 29. See also Guilday, *Councils*, 176.
22. Guilday, *Councils*, 176.
23. *Decreta Conciliorum Baltimorensis* (Baltimore: Joannes Murphy et Socios, 1853), #32, p. 14.
24. See Spalding's letter to Kenrick re: Timon Catechism, Sept. 20, 1852, APF, Scritture riferite nei Congressi, American Centrale, vol. 16, fols. 265–266^{rv}.
25. Cited by John K. Sharp, "How the Baltimore Catechism Originated," *Ecclesiastical Review*, 81 (1929), 585–586.
26. Cited by O'Brien, "Catechism," 594.
27. Baltimore: John B. Piet & Co. (no date printed). A copy of this catechism may be found in the American Catholic Historical Society holdings, St. Charles Seminary, Overbrook (Philadelphia).
28. *Concilium Plenarium Baltimorense*, XII, 1852, pp. 46–47.
29. *Concilii Plenarii Baltimorensis, II, Decreta* (Baltimore: Joannes Murphy, 1868), #387, p. 201; #502, #503, pp. 254–255.
30. O'Brien, "Catechism," 595–596.
31. *Concilii Plenarii*, II, #260, p. 140.
32. Ibid., #427–435, pp. 220–222.
33. Ibid., Title IX, #437–438, p. 223.

34. Nolan, *Pastoral Letters*, #25, pp. 152–153.
35. Ibid., #27, p. 153.
36. *Catéchisme du diocèse de La Nouvelle-Orléans* (Nouvelle-Orléans: Librairie J. Schweitzer, 1875). A copy of the catechism is in the Rare Book Collection, Mullen Library, Catholic University of America, Washington, D.C.
37. The volume's name was changed and its contents expanded in 1869. In that year it became *Bible History, Containing the Most Remarkable Events of the Old and New Testaments to which is added a compendium of Church History* (New York: Benziger, 1869).
38. The commendation appeared in each edition of Gilmour's *Bible History* from this date until the last volume rolled off of Benziger's presses in 1936. See Michael J. Hynes, *History of the Diocese of Cleveland — Origin and Growth (1847–1952)* (Cleveland: Diocese of Cleveland and World Publishing Co., 1952), 115.
39. See Hynes, 116–117.
40. See Verot's letter to M. Jaillon, March 3, 1857; cited in Michael Gannon, *Rebel Bishop* (Milwaukee: Bruce, 1964), 17. The letter is in the archives of the Society of St. Sulpice, Paris.
41. *General Catechism of Christian Doctrine* (Baltimore: John Murphy & Co., 1869). A copy of the 108-page manual is among the catechisms in the Rare Book Collection, Mullen Library, Catholic University of America, Washington, D.C.
42. Chapter 5, pp. 28–31. This section includes a treatment of the nature of prayer, the "Our Father," "Hail Mary," and the acts of faith, hope, love, and contrition.
43. The address was made on May 28, 1870; cited in Gannon, *Rebel Bishop*, 215–216. See John Tracy Ellis's "Foreword" to Gannon's biography, p. xiv.
44. A copy of the 1873 edition, *Short Catechism*, is among the holdings of St. Leo's Abbey, St. Leo, Florida.
45. In the section, "Short Catechism — for Converts from Protestantism," 57–58.
46. See W. J. Onahan, "Catholic Colonization of the West," *American Catholic Quarterly Review*, 6 (1881), 442.
47. Peter Beckman, *Kansas Monks* (Atchison, Kan.: Abbey-Student Press, 1957), 87.
48. Leavenworth: Rev. Martin Huhn, Publisher, 1880. A copy of this small manual is among the holdings of the American Catholic Historical Society, St. Charles Seminary, Overbrook (Philadelphia). An earlier volume is also important to cite here: *Pastoral Instructions* by Louis Maria Fink, OSB, Vicar Apostolic of Kansas. "Issued March 21, 1876." No publisher is credited. This 100-page volume appears to address adult Catholics. It is in the Rare Book Collection, Mullen Library, Catholic University of America, Washington, D.C.
49. See "Preface," *A Catechism of the Catholic Religion* (Atchison, Kan.: Abbey-Student Press, 1915). This 1915 edition carries the following statement on the cover page: "Revised and reprinted by order of Rt. Rev. John Ward, 1915." Ward became the fourth bishop of Leavenworth in 1910. He died in 1929. The see was moved from Leavenworth to Kansas City, Kansas, in 1947.
50. Paris: Nyon, 1806; published by order of Emperor Napoleon I (May 1, 1806).
51. See André Latreille, *Le catéchisme impérial de 1806* (Paris: Soc. d'Édition Les Belles Lettres, 1935). See also *Dictionnaire de Théologie Catholique*, 2, 2, (1932) cols. 1951–1952.
52. Mansi, vol. 49, col. 220. See also Michael T. Donnellan, *Rationale for a Uniform Catechism* (Ann Arbor, Mich.: University Microfilms, 1972), 17.

53. The schema was distributed on January 14, 1870. Pope Pius IX had formally opened the council on December 8, 1869.
54. Mansi, vol. 50, cols. 699–702.
55. Ibid., col. 826; translated by Donnellan, *Rationale*, 17.
56. Mansi, vol. 50, col. 765. Jean Mabile, bishop of Versailles: "Romanus sumus, sit igitur catechismus noster romanus."
57. Mansi, vol. 50, col. 793; Donnellan, *Rationale*, 68.
58. Mansi, vol. 50, cols. 819–823. Antonio Monesillo, bishop of Jaen, Spain, made the observation.
59. Donnellan, *Rationale*, 61; Mansi, vol. 50, cols. 749–752.
60. Donnellan, *Rationale*, 62; Mansi, vol. 50, cols. 751–760.
61. Mansi, vol. 50, cols. 706–709.
62. See Pius IX, *Pontificis Maximi Acta*, Pars Prima, 2:485–491.
63. Mansi, vol. 50, cols. 718–724.
64. Paris: Charles Dunoil, 1862. *Méthode* was a two-volume work. An English translation appeared in a single volume under the title *The Ministry of Catechising* (London: Griffith, Farran and Welsh, 1890).
65. According to one critic, Dupanloup "sums up the highest development in pedagogy and catechetics of the nineteenth century." See Joseph B. Collins, *Teaching Religion: An Introduction to Catechetics* (Milwaukee: Bruce, 1953), 33.
66. Mansi, vol. 50, cols. 719–721.
67. Ibid., cols. 739–745.
68. Mansi, vol. 51, cols. 481–482.
69. Mansi, vol. 50, cols. 726–728; 745–748.
70. Ibid., col. 166.
71. *Chicago Tribune* (Feb. 6, 1870); cited in Gannon, *Rebel Bishop*, 207.
72. Mansi, vol. 50, col. 736.
73. "Equidem desidero, et ex intimo meo corde"; Mansi, vol. 51, col. 469.
74. See Harry H. Browne "The Letters of Bishop McQuaid from the Vatican Council," *Catholic Historical Review*, 41 (1956), 425.
75. Mansi, vol. 51, cols. 501–512.
76. Mansi, vol. 50, col. 735.
77. See Paul J. Hallinan, "The American Bishops at the Vatican Councils," *Catholic Historical Review*, 51 (1965), 381. Hallinan was archbishop of Atlanta when he wrote this article.
78. Mansi, vol. 50, col. 51.
79. New York: P. J. Kenedy, 1872.
80. Chicago: Graham & Sons, n.d.
81. A copy of the England/Lynch catechism is in ADC.
82. *A Catechism of the Catholic Religion.* Translated from the German of the Rev. Joseph DeHarbe, S.J. (New York: Schwartz, Kirwin and Fauss, 1878). A photostatic copy of this 177-page manual is in the Rare Book Collection, Mullen Library, Catholic University of America, Washington, D.C. DeHarbe's catechism was originally published in Germany in 1849. The first English translation intended for use in this country was in 1869.
83. Rev. M. Muller, *Catechism of Christian Doctrine for Beginners* (Baltimore: Kreuzer Bros., 1875), 121 pages. This was the first of a two-catechism series. Of particular interest is the fact that Bayley (1814–1872), the eighth archbishop of Baltimore, was the nephew of Elizabeth Bayley Seton.

84. Corrigan Catechism; a copy is in the Rare Book Collection, Mullen Library, Catholic University of America, Washington, D.C.
85. *The Faith of Our Fathers* (Baltimore: J. Murphy & Co., 1876).
86. John Tracy Ellis, *The Life of James Cardinal Gibbons, Vol. I, 1834-1921* (Milwaukee: Bruce Publishing Co., 1952), 145ff, 153, 177.
87. Gibbons was consecrated with the title of bishop of Adramyttium *in partibus infidelium* by Archbishop Martin J. Spalding on August 16, 1868. He was bishop of Richmond from 1872 to 1877 and also administrator of the Vicariate Apostolic of North Carolina. In May 1877 he was named coadjutor to James R. Bayley, archbishop of Baltimore, and succeeded Bayley as archbishop on October 19. In May 1886 he was named a cardinal by Pope Leo XIII and the "red hat" was conferred on him in the Baltimore Cathedral on June 30 of the same year.
88. Ellis, *Gibbons*, 1:146.
89. AAB, 78-J-11, Kain to Gibbons, August 11, 1884; AAB, 78-K-7, Janssens to Gibbons, August 15, 1884.
90. *Acta et Decreta Concilii Plenarii Baltimorensis Tertii* (Baltimore: Joannes Murphy et Sociorum, 1886), xxv-xxvi.
91. AAB, 78-L-12, Gibbons to members of the catechism committee, August 25, 1884.
92. See Sharp, "Baltimore Catechism," 575. In this article Sharp published Messmer's correspondence and recollections, "hitherto unpublished information."
93. Cited in Sharp, "Baltimore Catechism," 575.
94. For more comprehensive and complete details, see the present author's study, *The Influence of the Catechism of the Third Plenary Council of Baltimore* (Ann Arbor, Mich.: University Microfilms, 1971).
95. Decree #219, in *Acta et Decreta*, 118-120.
96. Sharp, "Baltimore Catechism," 575; Sloyan, in *Modern Catechetics*, 88.
97. Januarius de Concilio was the pastor of St. Michael's Church in Jersey City, N.J., who had written Gibbons before the council requesting his own attendance at the council and offering to be a theologian for any bishop who might accept him. Gibbons assigned him to Bishop James O'Connor of Nebraska. Cf. AAB, 77-T-13, de Concilio to Gibbons, October 8, 1884; Sharp, "Baltimore Catechism," 576; C. D. Hinrichsen, "De Concilio, Januarius Vincent," *NCE*, 4, 704.
98. Cited from Mark Moesslein, "Origin of the Baltimore Catechism," *Ecclesiastical Review*, 93 (1935), 613.
99. Cf. *Catechismo della Dottrina Cristiana di Monsignor G. De Concilio* (New York: Società delle Pubblicazioni Cattoliche, 1886). This small volume carried the imprimatur of Michele Agostino, Arcivescovo di New York, March 20, 1886, and the approval of Giacomo Gibbons, Arcivescovo di Baltimore, March 20, 1886.
100. AAB, 79-A-1, Spalding to Gibbons, January 2, 1885. David Sweeney explained that a Lawrence Kehoe (1832-1890) was at the time editor of the Catholic Publication Society founded by Issac Hecker in 1866. Cf. David E. Sweeney, *The Life of John Lancaster Spalding* (New York: Herder & Herder, 1965), 175.
101. AAB, 79-E-15, Spalding to Gibbons, February 23, 1885.
102. Gibbons's statement was included on the title page: "The Catechism ordered by the Third Plenary Council of Baltimore, having been diligently compiled and examined, is hereby approved." The copyright was issued to J. L. Spalding; *A Catechism of Christian Doctrine Prepared and Enjoined by order of the Third Plenary Council of Baltimore* (New York: The Catholic Publication Co., 1885).

The Library of Congress copyright records show that two copies of the manual were received there on April 20, 1885.

103. *A Catechism of Christian Doctrine, Abridged from the Catechism Prepared and Enjoined by order of the Third Plenary Council of Baltimore* (New York: Catholic Publication Society, 1885).

104. Spalding combined selected questions from chapters four and five in the larger catechism into chapter four in the smaller. In the same way, condensed forms of chapters eleven and twelve became chapter ten; chapters nineteen and twenty became chapter sixteen. He lifted question #110 out of chapter 10 in the original manual and put into chapter 13 of the abridged edition.

105. Library of Congress records show that the Boston City Public Library has a copy of this abridged catechism.

106. Sloyan, in *Modern Catechetics*, 89.

107. *The Catechism Ordered by the National Synod of Maynooth and Approved by the Cardinal, the Archbishops and the Bishops of Ireland* (Dublin: M. H. Gill & Son, 1882).

108. John M. McCaffrey, *Catechism of Christian Doctrine for General Use* (New York: P. O'Shea; Baltimore: John Murphy & Co., 1866).

109. Cited in Sharp, "Baltimore Catechism," 583.

110. O'Brien, "Catechism," 596.

111. AAB, 78-L-11, Gibbons to Allemary, August 25, 1884.

112. David E. Sweeney, *The Life of John Lancaster Spalding* (New York: Herder and Herder, 1965).

113. Sloyan, *Modern Catechetics*, 90.

114. Sweeney, *Spalding*, 34.

115. Cf. *Synodus Diocesana Cincinnatensis Secunda* (no publication data given, 1886), "De Catechismo," 6.

116. *Fasciculus Constitutionum Synodalium* (Harrisburg) (Baltimore: Typis Foley Fratrum, 1893), 31. Sections XVI and XVII advocated a German translation of the Baltimore Catechism.

117. *Synodus Diocesana Chicagiensis Prima* (Chicago: Amberg et Sociorum, 1887), 28, and *Synodus Diocesana Chicagiensis Tertia* (Chicago: Amberg Sociique, 1906), 10–11.

118. *Synodus Diocesana Davenportensis Secunda* (Davenport, Iowa: Henry Chosgrove, 1904), 126.

119. AAB, 80-S-3, Gilmour to Gibbons, April 11, 1886.

120. The writer signed his critiques with a simple "X." See "Zur Kritik des Neuen Concils-Katechismus," in *Pastoral Blatt*, 19 (September 1885, 97–102, and subsequent issues).

121. W. Faerber, *Catechism for the Catholic Parochial Schools of the United States* (St. Louis: B. Herder, 1897). A copy of this volume is in the Rare Book Collection of Mullen Library, Catholic University of America, Washington, D.C.

122. Cited by Sharp, "Baltimore Catechism," 574–575.

123. AAB, 94-A-1, Hewitt to Gibbons, September 2, 1895.

124. AAB, 94-B-1, Minutes of the Annual Meeting of the Most Rev. Archbishops, October 2, 1895.

125. AAB, 94-S-3, Minutes of the Annual Meeting of the Most Rev. Archbishops, October 21, 22, 1896.

126. "It having been remarked in the discussion of the question, that it was rumored that the Holy See thought of ordering the preparation of a catechism for

universal use, it was voted that further action on our part should be postponed, the Secretary being instructed to ascertain the intention of the Holy See in the matter" (AAB, 100-D-4, Minutes of the Annual Meeting of the Archbishops of the United States, November 13, 1902).

127. *Compendio della dottrina cristiana* (Roma: Tipografia Vaticana, 1905). American editions appeared in 1906: *Short Catechism — Abridgement of Christian Doctrine*, trans. Sebastian Byrne, Bishop of Nashville; New York: Fr. Pustet & Co., 1906). Pius X wrote thirty-five works on catechetics between 1903 and 1913. Besides *Acerbo Nimis* (*ASS*, 37 [1904-1905], 613-625), the following works are of special importance: *Opus a Catechismis*, commending the work of catechizing, *ASS*, 38 (1905-1906), 378-379; *Inter Multa et Gravia Munera*, on the religious instruction of first communicants, *ASS*, 37 (1904-1905); *Quod Hierarchia Catholica* a letter addressed to the cardinal archbishops and bishops of Brazil on the value of teaching Christian doctrine, *AAS*, 3 (1911), 263-264.

128. Peter C. Yorke, *Text-Books of Religion* (San Francisco: The Text-Book Publishing Co., 1898). The first volume (*Grade One*) appeared in 1898; the volume for the second grade, in 1900; grade three, 1900, and the volume for grade four in 1901. The plates of the series were destroyed in the San Francisco earthquake in 1906. The complete set was edited and published a second time in 1907. Yorke engaged the assistance and guidance of sisters in the diocese who were teaching in parochial schools to critique the texts and advise him in the composition of the original and second series. See Joseph S. Brusher, SJ, *Consecrated Thunderbolt: Father Yorke of San Francisco* (Hawthorne, N.J.: Joseph F. Wagner, 1973).

129. *Catechetical Instructions of St. Cyril of Jerusalem* — From the Italian of Canon D. Fanucchi (New York: The Catholic Publication Society Co., 1893). The thirty-eight-page copy available to this writer was a second edition in the Sulpician archives, Baltimore, under the file LPB File-A 5. Chatard had been rector of North American College in Rome prior to being named bishop of Vincennes in 1878.

130. See Lesson IX, pp. 11-12.

131. Among Galura's works were *Katechisiermethode* (Freiburg, 1793) and *Freiburger Katechesen* (1804). Overburg wrote *Christkatholisches Religions-Handbuch* (Münster: Anton B. Uschendorf, 1804); a second edition appeared in 1827. Another work, *Katechismus der Christkatholischen Lehre zum Gebrauche der Kleinen Schüler*, was also published in 1804 (Münster) with a second edition published in 1852. This 96-page manual is among the holdings of the Rare Book Collection, Mullen Library, Catholic University of America, and once belonged to Ambrose Maréchal, Baltimore's third archbishop, whose name is inscribed on the title page. Hirscher published a 240-page catechism entitled *Katechismus der Christkatholischen Religion* (Freiburg: Herder, 1852). A copy of the Hirscher *Katechismus* is also is Catholic University's Rare Book Collection. For more expanded studies of Overburg and Hirscher, see Walter Braun, *Geschlectliche Erziehung im Katholischen Religionsunterricht* (Trier: Spee-Verlag, 1970), 14-20, 204-205.

132. *Katechetische Blätter* was published in Munich. The 1982 volume is numbered 107. *Christlich-pädagogische Blätter* was published in Vienna. Volume 95 is the current edition as of this writing.

Chapter 4

1. *ASS*, 36 (1903-1904), 129-139, October 4, 1903. Pius X was canonized on May 29, 1954. See the English translation in Sr. Claudia Carlen, IHM, *The*

Papal Encyclicals, 1903-1939 (Wilmington, N.C.: McGrath Publishing Company, 1981).
2. *ASS*, op. cit., 131.
3. Cited and translated by Joseph B. Collins in *Catechetical Documents of Pope Pius X* (Paterson, N.J.: St. Anthony Guild Press, 1946), liii.
4. Ibid.
5. *ASS*, 37 (1904-1905), 613-625. See Collins, *Documents*, 13-27; see also Carlen, op. cit.
6. Collins, *Documents*, xxvi.
7. Ibid., xix-xx. See also Merry Del Val, *Memories of Pope Pius X* (Westminster, Md.: Newman Press, 1951).
8. Collins, *Documents*, xxvi.
9. Roma: Typografia Vaticana, 1905.
10. Collins, *Documents*, xxvi.
11. *Short Catechism—Abridgement of Christian Doctrine*, trans. Sebastian Byrne, Bishop of Nashville (New York: Fr. Pustet & Co., 1906); *Large Catechism—Abridgement of Christian Doctrine*, trans. Sebastian Byrne, Bishop of Nashville (New York: Fr. Pustet & Co., 1906).
12. *ASS*, 37 (1904-1905), 617; see Collins, *Documents*, 18.
13. See Mary Charles Bryce, "The Confraternity of Christian Doctrine," in Robert Trisco, ed., *Catholics in America, 1776-1976* (Washington, D.C.: National Conference of Catholic Bishops, 1976), 149-153.
14. See Miriam Marks, "Teaching Christ in America," in Leo R. Ward, ed., *The American Apostolate* (Westminster, Md.: Newman Press, 1952), 187.
15. Canevin was Pittsburgh's fifth ordinary. See Francis F. Coakley, "Archbishop Canevin," in *Catholic Pittsburgh's One Hundred Years, 1843-1943* (Chicago: Loyola University Press, 1943), 68-72; see also Leo Lanham, *The Missionary Confraternity of Christian Doctrine in the Diocese of Pittsburgh* (Washington, D.C.: Catholic University of America Press, 1945), 2-4. When Canevin resigned as bishop of Pittsburgh in 1921 he was promoted to the titular archiepiscopal see of Pelusium.
16. They described themselves as "Workers for God and Country." The membership consisted largely of Catholic teachers and/or principals in the public school system who provided religious instruction for Catholic children attending public school. See Raymond J. G. Prindiville, *The Confraternity of Christian Doctrine* (Philadelphia: American Ecclesiastical Review, 1932), 14-17.
17. See James Gerard Shaw, *Edwin Vincent O'Hara, American Prelate* (New York: Farrar, Straus, and Cudahy, 1957), 98-123. Edwin V. O'Hara, *The Church and the Country* (New York: Macmillan Co., 1927), 83. See also Mary Charles Bryce, "Pioneers of Religious Education in the 20th Century," *Religious Education*, 73 (1978—Special Edition), 51-57.
18. Shaw, *O'Hara*, 65.
19. O'Hara, *Church and Country*, 83-84.
20. Ibid., 83; see Bryce, "Confraternity," 151.
21. O'Hara, *Church and Country*, 83
22. Edwin V. O'Hara, "The Rural Problem and Catholic Education," *Catholic Educational Association Bulletin*, 17 (1920), 235.
23. Report of Executive Secretary of the NCRLC, 1943, Bruce Files, Milwaukee. See Raymond Philip Witte, *Twenty-Five Years of Crusading* (Des Moines, Iowa: The National Catholic Rural Life Conference, 1948), 58.

24. Witte, *Crusading*, 183.
25. Ibid., 58.
26. Shaw, *O'Hara*, 7; Witte, *Crusading*, 182; *The Confraternity Comes of Age—A Historical Symposium* (Paterson, N.J.: Confraternity Publications, 1956), 28.
27. O'Hara, "Rural Problem," 242.
28. *Confraternity Comes of Age*, 42; Witte, *Crusading*, 181–186.
29. Shaw, *O'Hara*, 77–79, 80. See Joseph P. Donovan, "Solving the Rural Problem in Missouri," *Ecclesiastical Review*, 71 (1924), 590–598.
30. Reported in Witte, *Crusading*, 182.
31. See Edward W. O'Rourke, "The Catholic Church in the Rural Midwest," in Louis J. Putz, ed., *The Catholic Church, USA* (Chicago: Fides, 1956), 202–210.
32. O'Hara, "Rural Problem," 243.
33. Ibid. The principle of adaptation is emphasized in several places in the documents of Vatican II: *Ad Gentes*, "Decree on the Missionary Activity of the Church," # 22; *Sacrosanctum Concilium*, "Constitution on the Sacred Liturgy," #37, 40, 44, 107, 128. The *GCD* refers to it eight times: #2a, 2b, 5, 6, 13, 34, 36, 46. #34 is quite explicit: "Catechesis . . . cannot be restricted to repetition of traditional formulas; in fact, it demands that these formulas be understood, and be faithfully expressed in language adapted to the intelligence of hearers, using even new methods when necessary."
34. See Witte, *Crusading*, 74–75; "Archbishop Edwin V. O'Hara: A Biographical Survey," in *Confraternity Comes of Age*, 12.
35. See "Religious Discussion Clubs," in *Confraternity Comes of Age*, 82.
36. *Proceedings of the National Catechetical Congress of the CCD, 1935* (Paterson, N.J.: St. Anthony Guild Press, 1936), 47.
37. See Witte, *Crusading*, 94–96.
38. Ibid., 96.
39. See "The National Center of the CCD," in *Confraternity Comes of Age*, 149.
40. Ibid.
41. At this writing that location houses the offices of the National Conference of Catholic Bishops (NCCB) and the United States Catholic Conference.
42. See Bertrand J. Gulnerich, "Catechetical Congresses," in *Confraternity Comes of Age*, 221–234.
43. Shaw, *O'Hara*, 272. This was part of Burke's welcoming address at the Buffalo congress, September 26, 1956.
44. Undoubtedly the appearance of the decree *Provido Sane Consilio*, "On the Better Care and Promotion of Catechetical Instruction," by the Sacred Congregation of the Council played a persuasive role in this decision. The decree included a series of pertinent questions regarding the catechizing of children and youth. See *AAS*, vol. 27 (1935), 145–154. For an English translation, see *Ecclesiastical Review*, 93 (1935), 45–57.
45. Cicognani (1883–1973) was apostolic delegate to the United States from 1933 to 1958.
46. Cited in Shaw, *O'Hara*, 157.
47. Connell (1888–1967) had earned an STD degree from the Angelicum in Rome in 1923. He was Dean of the School of Sacred Theology, Catholic University of America, from 1958 to 1967. See also Shaw, *O'Hara*, 170; *Confraternity Comes of Age*, 113–114; 189–193.
48. *Confraternity Comes of Age*, 189–201; Shaw, *O'Hara*, 160–172.
49. *A Catechism of Christian Doctrine*, revised edition of the Baltimore Catechism (Paterson, N.J.: St. Anthony Guild Press, 1941).

50. John Timothy McNicholas, OP (1877–1950), was the fourth archbishop of Cincinnati (Ohio), where he served as episcopal leader for twenty-five years (1925–1950). In 1904 he had earned a doctorate in sacred theology from Minerva University (Dominican) in Rome.

51. *Confraternity Comes of Age*, 194.

52. Ibid., 194–195.

53. Ibid., 195.

54. *Catechism*, 99–101.

55. *Confraternity Comes of Age*, 194.

56. Sacra Congregatio pro Clericis, *Directorium Catechisticum Generale* (Città del Vaticano: Libreria Editrice Vaticana, 1971); *General Catechetical Directory* (English translation) (Washington, D.C.: United States Catholic Conference, 1971).

57. See Una O'Neill, "Perspectives on the Hierarchy of Truths," *Living Light*, 14 (1977), 377–391.

58. *Catechetics in Context* (Huntington, Ind.: Our Sunday Visitor Press, 1973), 69–70.

59. O'Neill, "Perspectives," 391.

60. "Trinity and Theology," *Sacramentum Mundi*, 6 (Montreal: Palm Publishers, 1970), 5.

61. *De Catechizandis Rudibus*, popularly known, according to Augustine's own description, as "The First Catechetical Instruction" (*Retractationes*, 2:14) See *The First Catechetical Instruction*, trans. Joseph P. Christopher, Ancient Christian Writers (Westminster, Md.: Newman Press, 1946).

62. Gatterer (1862–1942) was a professor of catechetics at Innsbruck from 1897 until the late 1930s. He wrote *Katechetik* (1909), *Die Erstkommunion der Kinder* (1911), *Elementarkatechesen* (1923), and a four-volume work *Das Religions buch der Kirche* (1928–1930). See W. Croce in *Lexikon für Theologie und Kirche*, 4, 529–530. On Jungmann, see J. Hofinger, "J. A. Jungmann (1889–1975): In Memoriam," *Living Light*, 13 (1976), 350–359. Jungmann's doctoral dissertation was on the catechetical kerygmatic formulations of the doctrine of grace in the first three centuries (Innsbruck, 1926). Regarded primarily as a scholar and authority in the field of liturgy, Jungmann was also renowned for his research and insights in catechesis. In 1936 he published *Die Frohbotschaft und unsere Glaubensverkundigung*, which was translated into English in 1962 as *The Good News Yesterday and Today*. In 1953 his *Katechetik* (Wien: Verlag Herder, 1953) appeared and was translated into English as *Handing on the Faith* (New York: Herder & Herder, 1962). Both works continue to be read by scholars today.

63. Paul Marx, *Virgil Michel and the Liturgical Movement* (Collegeville, Minn.: Liturgical Press, 1957), 152–154.

64. Published by Macmillan Co., New York, 1935–1941.

65. Yorke's four volumes were published in San Francisco by Text Book Publishing Co. between 1898 and 1904. See above, Chap. 3, n. 128.

66. See Wolfgang Beinert, "Do Short Formulas Dilute the Faith?" *Theology Digest*, 22 (1974), 257–260.

67. Pope John Paul II has pointed out that the "ecclesial community at all levels has a twofold responsibility with regard to catechesis: it has the responsibility of providing for the training of its members, but it also has the responsibility of welcoming them into an environment where they can live as fully as possible what they have learned" (CT, #24). The *GCD* has specified that "not only priests and catechists but the entire Christian community . . . is engaged in this work"; *GCD*, #130; see also, #101, #107.

68. This version is named for Richard Challoner (1691–1781), titular bishop (*in partibus infidelium*) and vicar apostolic of the London District, and the two cities in which the Bible had been translated into English from the Latin Vulgate. Rheims, in northern France, had seen the publication of the New Testament in 1582; Douai, a city then in Belgium (now in France) witnessed the production of the two-volume Old Testament in 1609–1690. In 1749 Challoner "provided English Catholics with a more readable Bible by revising the Douai-Rheims" version. See "Richard Challoner" by J. Cartmell, in *Clergy Review*, 44 (1959), 577–587.
69. The Latin Vulgate is associated with St. Jerome (d. 420) who served as translator, reviser, and editor of existent manuscripts. The term "vulgate" indicates that the version was for the poorly educated and not for the cultural elite. In 1593 a two-man team under the direction of Pope Clement VIII (1592–1605) edited, revised, and made mechanical improvements on the Jerome translation. Considered "official," the work appeared in 1593 and 1598. It is referred to as the "Clementine text" and/or the "Latin vulgate." It was from the Clementine text that the U.S. translators worked in preparing the Confraternity edition of 1941.
70. See *Confraternity Comes of Age*, 202–203, and Edward P. Arbez, "New Catholic Translation of the Old Testament," *Catholic Biblical Quarterly*, 14 (1952), 237–254.
71. *The New Testament*, Sponsored by the Episcopal Committee of the Confraternity of Christian Doctrine (Paterson, N.J.: St. Anthony Guild Press, 1941).
72. *AAS*, 35 (1943), 297–325, September 30, 1943. See Carlen, vol. 2, *Encyclicals, 1939–1958* (1982).
73. Arbez, "New Catholic Translation," 237–254.
74. Ibid., 237–238; see also *Confraternity Comes of Age*, 217–218.
75. Shaw, *O'Hara*, 195.
76. See John E. Steinmueller, "Catholic Biblical Association of America," *Commonweal*, 28 (October 14, 1938), 629–630; William H. McClellan, "American Bible Scholars Organize for New Advances," *America*, 58 (November 27, 1937), 176–177; William L. Newton, "A Catholic Biblical Quarterly," *Journal of Religious Instruction*, 9 (1938), 266–269.
77. Cited in Shaw, *O'Hara*, 196.
78. See *The Assisi Papers; Proceedings of the First International Congress of Pastoral Liturgy* (Collegeville, Minn.: Liturgical Press, 1957), 167–175.
79. Gibson Winter analyzed some of the enterprises associated with O'Hara in sociological terms as "hierarchy-agency structures." "The hierarchic principle represents the cultic, doctrinal and juridical line of development; thus the line of authority from Holy See to diocese, explicitly formulated in Canon Law, preserves the integrity of the Catholic Faith as a sacramental system. . . . The agency line develops in terms of functional problems in an increasingly complex national society; this functional principle produces the diocesan-territorial structures and yet depends on the authority of the bishops." Winter identifies the forum or clearinghouse (my term) as "the National Catholic Welfare Conference of O'Hara's day and the present United States Catholic Conference of today." See Gibson Winter, *Religious Identity* (New York: Macmillan Co., 1968), 61–62.
80. As chairman of the Episcopal Committee of the CCD O'Hara was called upon in the fall of 1951 to present a request to Rome for the optional use of English in connection with the rites of Baptism, Marriage, the Sacrament of Anointing, and Burial. He, in turn, called upon the expertise of at least two scholars dedicated to the promotion of the liturgical movement in this country.

He asked Gerald Ellard, SJ (1894–1963), and Godfrey Diekmann, OSB (1908–), to undertake the preparation and presentation of the *Collectio Rituum*. He further sought their advice and direction in preparing congresses and programs. See Michael Mathis, "*Collectio Rituum*," in *Confraternity Comes of Age*, 301–310.
81. See *Confraternity Comes of Age*, 265.
82. See Saul E. Bronder, *Social Justice and Church Authority. The Public Life of Archbishop Robert E. Lucey* (Philadelphia: Temple University Press, 1982). Chapter 5 is entitled "The Confraternity of Christian Doctrine and Operation Latin America." See also "Archbishop Lucey . . . Champion of Social Justice," *Our Sunday Visitor*, 66 (August 14, 1977), 1; "Justice for the Mexicans," *Commonweal*, 49 (November 12, 1948), 117.
83. See "Interest in Latin America," in Matthew F. Brady, "The Episcopal Committee of the Confraternity of Christian Doctrine," in *Confraternity Comes of Age*, 121–122, and Monseñor Alberto Deane, "Conferencia sobre la mente de la iglesia sobre la CDC," *Proceedings of the Confraternity of Christian Doctrine Congress, 1961* (Paterson, N.J.: St. Anthony Guild Press, 1962), 333–340 (Monseñor Deane was bishop of Villa María in Argentina). See also Pe. Dr. Lemidas Maximiliano Didonet, "Necessidade e efficia de mesa directora paróquial, ibid., 349–359 (Dr. Didonet was from the diocese of Santa Maria, Rio Grande do Sul, Brazil).
84. The meeting dates were June 22–27. See Virgil Elizondo and Alan Oddie, "San Antonio International Study Week of Mass Media and Catechetics: A Report," *Living Light*, 6 (Winter 1969), 67–74.
85. Alfonso Nebreda, "Mass Media and Catechetics," *America*, 121 (1969), 29.
86. See *International Catechetical Congress* (Rome), edited by William J. Tobin (Washington, D.C.: United States Catholic Conference, 1971), 109.
87. *AAS*, 58 (1966), 680–681; translation from Walter M. Abbott, ed., *The Documents of Vatican II* (New York: Herder and Herder, 1966), 407–408.
88. See one-page letter in San Antonio Chancery Archives, on Archdiocese of San Antonio stationery, June 15, 1967.
89. See "Statement of His Excellency, Most Rev. Robert E. Lucey, Archbishop of San Antonio." No date; one-page, preregistration flyer.
90. "Catechetical Living," Remarks of His Excellency, Most Rev. Robert E. Lucey, Archbishop of San Antonio, Assumption Seminary, San Antonio, Friday, July 14, 1967; 8:00 PM. See San Antonio Chancery Archives.
91. Ibid., 5.
92. Information obtained in personal interviews, July 26, 1981, and August 6, 1981.
93. See Francis C. Kelley, "Only an Incident," *Commonweal*, 31 (November 3, 1939), 31–32, which describes his visit to Louvain.
94. Maisie Ward, "The Catholic Evidence Guild," in *Unfinished Business* (New York: Sheed and Ward, 1964), 78–95. One of the best-known of the Hyde Park street preachers was a Dominican priest, Vincent McNabb. One of his most "persistent hecklers" later wrote a small volume in tribute and admiration of him. See E. A. Siderman, *A Saint in Hyde Park* (Westminster, Md.: Newman Press, 1950).
95. See Ward, *Guild*, 81–82.
96. Leven was named auxiliary bishop to Archbishop Lucey, San Antonio, in December 1955. He was installed Bishop of San Angelo, October 22, 1969. Leven resigned in 1979.

97. Letter from Leven to the present writer, July 29, 1981. Buswell's concern for the apostolate took a distinct direction as he became intent on implementing the principles and ideas of Vatican II during his episcopacy. See, for example, "Active Participation in the Sacraments," in *North American Liturgical Week, 1963* (Washington, D.C.: Liturgical Conference, 1964), 24–30.

98. See the description in Dorothy F. Golden, "'Catholic Revivals' in the Bible Belt," *Journal of Religious Instruction*, 9 (April 1939), 660–663; Leven, "Curb Service in Christian Doctrine," *Extension*, 37 (August 1942), 11–12.

99. Personal interview, July 26, 1981.

100. Cited by Maye Korioth, "The Apostolate of Good Will," in *Confraternity Comes of Age*, 261. See Leven, "Street Preaching," *Proceedings, Confraternity Congress, 1938* (Paterson, N.J.: St. Anthony Guild Press, 1939), 375–382.

101. Cited in James Gaffey, *Francis Clement Kelley and the American Dream* (Bensenville, Ill.: The Heritage Foundation, Inc., 1980), 2:233.

102. Information given in personal interview with Stephen A. Leven and confirmed by him in writing, August 1981.

103. See *Treasure in Clay* (Garden City, N.Y.: Doubleday & Co., 1980), 59. See also D. P. Noonan, "The Microphone of God," in *The Passion of Fulton Sheen* (New York: Dodd, Mead & Co., 1972), 51–65.

104. See Gaffey, *American Dream*, 1:xii.

105. Ibid., 2:310.

106. Ibid., 311.

107. This writer counts her few months as Kelley's secretary pro tempore as a valuable formative influence in her own life as a young nun. She was introduced to the works and insights of such writers as Mencken and to the poetry of Eileen Duggan. That time afforded her access, too, to Kelley's immense library and stimulating conversation while working on his manuscripts, as well as many hours of reading and serious reflection. She came to know the bishop as a wise, dedicated, generous, and witty individual. Of his writings she typed *Tales from the Rectory* (1943) and "Conversations with an Electric Fan," a baccalaureate address he gave at Oklahoma University (Norman, Oklahoma) in the summer of 1942. For references to these works, see Gaffey, *American Dream*, 2:306–307; 312.

108. *Letters to Jack—Written by a Priest to His Nephew* (Chicago: Extension Press, 1917); *The Epistles of Father Timothy to His Parishioners* (Chicago: Extension Press, 1924). According to Gaffey, *Letters to Jack* was Kelley's greatest success; see Gaffey, *American Dream*, 2:328.

109. *Confraternity of Christian Doctrine Proceedings, October 9–12, 1937* (Paterson, N.J.: St. Anthony Guild Press, 1938), 236–244. See also Gaffey, *American Dream*, 2:24–41.

110. *Confraternity . . . Proceedings, 1937* (Paterson, N.J.: St. Anthony Guild Press, 1938), 242.

111. See above, n. 62.

112. Ibid.

113. Kelley could and did use fantasy well. He wrote short works such as "Soliloquy of a Raindrop," "Lament of a Penny," "Autobiography of a Dollar," "Reflections of a Dog," and "Monologue with Judas." Longer stories include *Pack Rat* (Milwaukee: Bruce, 1942) and *Problem Island* (Paterson, N.J.: St. Anthony Guild Press, 1937). Kelley explained his objective in writing: "I don't write to entertain; I write to teach." See Gaffey, *American Dream*, 2:312.

114. Ibid., 1:93–94.

115. This observation was made in a letter from Noll's nephew, John J. Fink, president of Our Sunday Visitor, Inc., to the present writer, August 10, 1981.

116. See Noll's biography in Richard Ginder, *With Ink and Crozier—A Biography of John Francis Noll* (Huntington, Ind.: Our Sunday Visitor Press, 1953).

117. See the foreword in Vincent A. Yzermans, ed., *Days of Hope and Promise—the Writings and Speeches of Paul J. Hallinan* (Collegeville, Minn. Liturgical Press, 1973). No paginaton. Bernardin is currently the cardinal archbishop of Chicago. While archbishop of Cincinnati, prior to his going to Chicago, Bernardin had delivered the keynote address at a Religious Education Institute, June 18, 1973. The address was published in *L'Osservatore Romano* (Eng. ed.), September 13, 1973, and subsequently in the Australian journal, *Our Apostolate*, 21 (November 1973), 197-203.

118. Ibid.

119. Paul J. Hallinan, "Catholic Adult Education," in Yzermans, *Days of Hope*, 6.

120. "The Common Goal," *America*, 116 (1967), 14.

121. Ibid., 15.

122. Bernardin, op. cit., note 117.

123. "Catechetical Ladder to the Liturgical Summit," in *Vatican II and Renewal Through the CCD—Proceedings, 1966* (Paterson, N.J.: St. Anthony Guild Press, 1967), 172.

124. Ibid., 170. In this passage Hallinan paraphrased and linked certain passages from the Vatican II Decree on the Pastoral Office of Bishops, *Christus Dominus*; see paragraphs 13-15; *AAS*, 58 (1966), 678-680.

125. "Catechetical Ladder," 171-172.

126. Ibid.

127. "Common Goal," 14.

128. "Catechetical Ladder," 173.

129. Rome: Catholic Book Agency, 1966.

130. Ann Arbor, Mich.: University Microfilms, 1969.

131. "Catechesis and the Media of Social Communication," in William J. Tobin, ed., *International Catechetical Congress* (Rome, 1951) (Washington, D.C.: United States Catholic Conference, 1971), 84.

132. *GCD*, #20, 92, 96.

133. *GCD*, #91, 101, 107, 130.

134. "Apostolic Value of Religious Discussion Clubs," in Joseph B. Collins, ed., *Religious Education through CCD* (Washington, D.C.; Catholic University of America Press, 1961), 84.

135. See "The Lay Apostolate" (October 5, 1957), in *The Pope Speaks*, 14 (1957-1958), 123.

136. "Encyclical Letter to the American Hierarchy (*Sertum Laetitiae*), in *The Pope Speaks* (New York: Harcourt, Brace and Co., 1940), 198-215. See also Carlen, vol. 2, *Encyclicals, 1939-1958*.

137. See Lucker, "Apostolic Value," 87.

138. Matthew F. Brady, Bishop of Manchester, "The Episcopal Committee of the Confraternity of Christian Doctrine," in *Confraternity Comes of Age*, 110.

139. "The National Center of the CCD," ibid., 151-152.

Chapter 5

1. See Theodore Filthaut, "Katechetische Erneuerung," *Lexikon für Theologie und Kirche*, 6, cols. 37-39 (1961).

2. Michael Gatterer is credited with naming the method for the city in which it began. Gatterer was a Jesuit pastoral theologian, a leader in the catechetical movement, who taught at Innsbruck. He "insisted that catechesis should begin with the actual concerns of the child about his soul and should teach him to live devoutly." See Gatterer, *Die Erstkommunion der Kinder* (1911), p. 120. See Chap. 4, n. 62.

3. G. Fischer, "Katechetische Methoden," *Lexikon für Theologie und Kirche*, 6, cols. 42–46 (1961); Anthony N. Fuerst, *The Systematic Teaching of Religion* (New York: Benziger Brothers, 1946), 2:465; 608–609; Josef A. Jungmann, *Handing on the Faith* (New York: Herder & Herder, 1959), 33–34, 47. Fuerst (vol. 2:614) outlined the Munich Method succinctly: "The Munich Method in its present form has three main steps: presentation, explanation and application with two secondary steps; preparation together with the declaration of the objective and the recapitulation. The instruction embodying those steps is usually concluded, if possible, with practice, that is, with the application of the teaching to a life-situation. In some form or other all, or practically all, modern methods, even the so-called formlessness of the 'progressive school,' incorporates these steps, if not in name, at least in idea, into the learning process for the children and the teaching process for the teacher." Fuerst, 2:614.

4. Fuerst, *Systematic Teaching*, 1:96–97.

5. *Orbem Catholicum*, June 29, 1923; *AAS*, 15 (1923), 327–329.

6. *De Catechetica Disciplina in Sacris Seminariis*, *AAS*, 18 (1926), 453–455.

7. See Fuerst, *Systematic Teaching*, 1:97–98; K. Schrems, "Zweiter Katechetischer Kongress," *Katechetische Blätter*, 29 (new series, 1928), 369–384.

8. See "Der Kinderpredigt," *Katechetische Blätter*, op. cit., 482–483. Luis Erdozain, "The Evolution of Catechetics," *Lumen Vitae*, 25 (1975), 9.

9. For Barbera's address, see K. Schrems, ed., *Zweiter Katechetischer Kongress München, 1928* (Donauworth: L. Auer, 1928), 28.

10. See George Delcuve, "Report of the International Catechistic Congress . . . Rome," *Lumen Vitae*, 5 (1950), 639–644.

11. Ibid., 643.

12. Ibid., 644. See *Perquam Laeto . . .*, *AAS*, 42 (1950), 816–820.

13. J. Jungmann, *Die Frohbotschaft und unsere Glaubensverkundigung* (Regensburg: Verlag Friedrich Pustet, 1936); English translation, *The Good News Yesterday and Today*, trans. and ed. William A. Heusman (New York: William H. Sadlier Co., 1962), 56.

14. J. Jungmann, "Theology and Kerygmatic Teaching," *Lumen Vitae*, 5 (1950), 258–259.

15. Idem, *Good News*, 4–5.

16. J. Hofinger, "The Place of the Good News in Modern Catechetics," an appraisal in Jungmann's *Good News*, 173.

17. "Die Lehre von der Gnade in den Katechetischen und kerygmatischen Texten der ersten drei Jahrhunderte"; defended October 27, 1923.

18. See Domenico Grasso's appraisal of Jungmann's *Good News*, "The Good News and the Renewal of Theology," in *Good News*, 204.

19. Karl Barth (1886–1968) was a Swiss theologian who constructed a theology from the historical perspective of God's self-revelation to humankind in Christ.

20. Jungmann, "Theology and Kerygmatic Teaching," 262–263.

21. *Decretum, De Norma Servanda . . .*, *AAS*, 16 (1924), 431.

22. Jules Gerard-Libois, "The International Summer Session at Antwerp: Catechesis for Our Time," *Lumen Vitae*, 2 (1956), 498–500.

23. George Delcuve, "International Session: Mission and Liturgy," *Lumen Vitae*, 15 (1960), 153–159. See Erdozain, "Evolution of Catechetics," 7–31.

24. George Delcuve, "Mission and Catechesis," *Lumen Vitae*, 15 (1960), 723–737. The major address, conclusions, and basic principles agreed upon may be found in Johannes Hofinger and Clifford Howell, eds., *Teaching All Nations* (New York: Herder and Herder, 1961). See also Gerard S. Sloyan, "The International Study Week on Mission Catechetics," *Worship*, 35 (1960–1961), 48–57.

25. See Sloyan, "International Study Week," 51.

26. Ibid., 55–56.

27. J. Jungmann, *Handing on the Faith*, 397.

28. Cited by Erdozain, "Evolution of Catechetics," 17. See D. Grasso, "Il Kerygma e la Predicazione," *Gregorianum*, 41 (1960), 427. See also Alfonso Nebreda, "East Asian Study Week on Mission Catechetics" (Bangkok), *Lumen Vitae*, 17 (1962), 717–730.

29. Theodore Stone, "The Bangkok Study Week," *Worship*, 37 (1962), 184–190.

30. George Delcuve, "Pan-African Week of Catechetical Studies . . .," *Lumen Vitae*, 20 (1965), 127–130; see "Conclusions," ibid., 130–137. See also Robert J. Ledogar, *Katigondo* (London: Geoffrey Chapman, 1965).

31. *Teaching All Nations* (periodical sponsored by East Asian Pastoral Institute), 4 (July 1967), 268; author not identified.

32. See Alfonso Nebreda, "Special Commission on International Cooperation," in *The Medellin Papers*, eds. Johannes Hofinger and Terrence J. Sheridan (Manila: East Asian Pastoral Institute, 1969), 206.

33. Joseph Bournique, "Present Realities in Catechesis as a Basis for Reform in Latin America," *Medellin Papers*, 112.

34. Ibid., 115–116.

35. Ibid., 131.

36. François Houtart, "Reflection on the New Thinking in Latin America," *Medellin Papers*, 72–74.

37. *Medellin Papers*, 215.

38. Ibid., 217.

39. Ibid., #17, p. 219.

40. Villot had been the archbishop of Lyon, France.

41. *Medellin Papers*, 12, 209.

42. Vatican II solemnly opened on October 11, 1962, and closed on December 8, 1965.

43. *Directorium Catechisticum Generale* (Città del Vaticana: Libreria Editrice Vaticana, 1971).

44. See Mary Charles Bryce, "Evolution of Catechesis from the Catholic Reformation to the Present," in John H. Westerhoff and O. C. Edwards, eds., *A Faithful Church* (Wilton, Conn.: Morehouse-Barlow, 1981), 204–235.

45. See *GCD*, #21, 23, 38, 101, 107, 130.

46. Voting on the proposal of a universal catechism was taken on May 4, 1870, with the following results: 491 *placet* (in favor), 56 *non placet* (against), and 44 *placet juxta modum* (qualified approval). See Mansi, vol. 51, cols. 501–512.

47. This proposal is cited among other pre-Vatican II suggestions summarized in *Acta et Documenta Concilio Oecumenico Vaticano II Apparendo. Series I, Appendix Voluminis II Analyticus conspectus consiliorum et votorum quae ab episcopis et praelatis data sunt*, Par. 2 (Vatican: Typis Polyglottis Vaticanis, 1960), 482. Of pertinent interest is the fact that in a plenary assembly in 1960 the bishops

of France requested and commissioned the publication of a *Directoire de la Caté-chétique à l'usage des Diocèses de France*. The text of this directory appeared in its entirety in *Catéchèse*, 4 (January 1964), 1-81. See also Berard L. Marthaler, *Catechetics in Context* (Huntington, Ind.: Our Sunday Visitor Press, 1973), xxvi, n. 29. In 1966 the conference of Italian bishops (*Conferenza Episcopale Italiana* [CEI]) decided to commission and sponsor the renewal of catechesis throughout Italy through a three-step process which would include (1) the formulation of a foundational document, *Documento di Base*—comparable to a source book or directory, (2) the compiling of four catechisms, and (3) the development of working procedures. Three years later *Documento di Base: Il Rinnovamento della Catechesi* (Torino-Leumann: Elle Di Ci, 1970) appeared. See Berard L. Marthaler, "The Renewal of Catechesis in Italy," *Religious Education*, 66 (1971), 357-363.

48. See *Schema Decreti de Catechistica Populi Christiana Institutione* (Vatican: Typis Polyglottis Vaticanis, 1962), 6-8. See also Berard L. Marthaler, "The Origin, Context and Purpose of the Directory," *Living Light*, 9 (1972), 9.

49. *AAS*, 58 (1966), 695-696.

50. See *L'Osservatore Romano* (Eng. ed.), July 1, 1971, 5, 8.

51. This writer was invited to act as consultant to the committee assigned to compile the "new" catechism. Subsequently she was likewise invited to serve on the Advisory Committee for the proposed source book by a letter from Bishop Charles P. Greco, August 11, 1966. Hence, in her files can be found copies of the "Questionnaire on New American Catechism" (January 30, 1965), correspondence from Archbishop Joseph T. McGucken, additional correspondence related to these proposals, and other pertinent material from Bishop Greco, bishop of Alexandria and chairman of the bishops' committee of the Confraternity of Christian Doctrine.

52. *The Living Light* devoted the entire Fall 1971 issue to the directory, calling on theologians, religious educators, developmentalists, and Protestant and Catholic educationalists for their evaluations (*Living Light*, 9 [1971], 4-157). See also: "God Does More Than Keep Score," *Liguorian*, 60 (Summer 1972), 50-52; "Symposium," *Sisters Today*, 43 (Fall 1972), 317-339; V. Mallon, "The General Catechetical Directory," *The Priest*, 28 (March 1972), 11-19; M. C. Bryce, "Toward an Open Catechetics," *America*, 126 (April 15, 1972), 394-396; R. Duckworth, "Catechetics: The New Directory," *Tablet* 225 (July 3, 1971), 213-219.

53. John Cardinal Wright, "The New Catechetical Directory and Initiation to the Sacraments of Penance and Eucharist," *Homiletic and Pastoral Review*, 72 (December 1971), 7-24.

54. "Wright Says Catechetical Directory Meant Only as Guideline, not as Law," *National Catholic Reporter*, 7 (October 8, 1971), 19.

55. See *Medellin Papers*, 12, 209.

56. *Quam Singulari, AAS*, 2 (1910), 583, promulgated by the Sacred Congregation of the Sacraments, August 15, 1910.

57. Thomas F. Sullivan, "The General Catechetical Directory: Some Implications for Teachers," *Momentum*, 3 (February 1972), 46.

58. Cited above, n. 47. The first edition was "sold out" within a year; a second edition appeared in 1974.

59. *Catechetics in Context*, xiii.

60. Frequently referred to here as *GCD*.

61. See also *GCD*, #101, 130.

62. William J. Tobin, ed., *International Catechetical Congress* (Washington, D.C.: United States Catholic Conference, 1971), 11.

63. Ibid., 14.

64. Ibid., 15.

65. Archbishop Robert E. Lucey, Bishops Raymond A. Lucker and William E. McManus, Mary Charles Bryce, OSB, Francis J. Buckley, SJ, Mrs. Dolores Curran, Maria de la Cruz, HHS, Mark Dinardo, Virgilio Elizondo, Mark Heath, Susan Hofweber, OP, Carol Frances Jegen, BVM, Elise Kranz, SND, Berard L. Marthaler, OFM, Conv., Charles McDonald, Janann Manternach, Russell R. Novello, Carl Pfeifer, William R. Reedy, William J. Tobin, and Michael Warren.

66. Tobin, *Congress*, 80–85.

67. See above, Chap. 4, nn. 129–130.

68. Tobin, *Congress*, 109.

69. Ibid., 113.

70. Ibid., 91–102; 105–117.

71. Ibid., 121–128.

72. Ibid., 132–133.

73. Ibid., 145–148.

74. Ibid., 137–141. See also "Report on International Catechetical Congress," *Living Light*, 8 (1971), 80–99; "The Rome International Congress on Catechetics," Lumen Vitae, 27 (1972), 103–115.

75. "8000 Flock to CCD Meet," *National Catholic Reporter*, 8 (November 5, 1971), 3.

76. Unlike previous CCD congresses, the addresses of the Miami meeting were not published in a single volume.

77. *To Teach As Jesus Did* (Washington, D.C.: United States Catholic Conference, 1972).

78. McManus chaired the committee from November 1969 through November 1972. See William E. McManus, "To Teach as Jesus Did: A Chronicle," *Living Light*, 10 (1973), 278–283.

79. Completed October 28, 1965; see *AAS*, 58 (1966), 728–739.

80. Mark Heath, "To Teach as Jesus Did: A Critique," *Living Light*, 10 (1973), 286–287.

81. Reported by Charles C. McDonald, "The Background and Development of 'The Basic Teachings' Document," *Living Light*, 10 (1973), 265.

82. The periodical *The Catholic Mind* included the entire text of the document in its May 1973 issue. See *The Catholic Mind*, 71 (May 1973), 44–64.

83. See Berard L. Marthaler, *An Official Commentary on Sharing the Light of Faith* (Washington, D.C.: United States Catholic Conference, 1981), 4.

84. Ibid. "National Catechetical Directory . . ." is the subtitle for *Sharing the Light of Faith*.

85. "Foreword," *GCD*, 2.

86. Marthaler, *Official Commentary*, 5.

87. Ibid., 5.

88. See letter, October 30, 1978, p. 1, National Catechetical Directory Files. Most Rev. Maximino Romero de Lema was the secretary of the Sacred Congregation of the Clergy.

89. A more detailed history of the work may be found in Marthaler, *Official Commentary*, 4–7.

90. Consultation of the faithful has always been an ideal and practice in the Church but not always easily accomplished. The German catechism, *Der Katechismus der Bistümer Deutschlands* (1955) appeared in final form after review copies had been widely disseminated to the faithful, clergy, and bishops in that country. Subjected to "public criticism," it received an astonishing 12,000 recommendations and as many changes. See Josef-Andre Jungmann, "The New German Catechism," *Lumen Vitae*, 10 (1956), 573–586. See also *Lexikon der Pastoral Theologie*, 5, 242–243.

91. See "Dimensions of Catechesis," *Origins* (March 15, 1979), 611. See also *Official Commentary*, 7.

92. See M. C. Bryce, "Sharing the Light of Faith: Catechetical Threshold for the U.S. Church," *Lumen Vitae*, 34 (1979), 407.

93. See Catherine Dooley, OP, "Catechesis in Our Time," *Louvain Studies*, 7 (1979), 195–204.

94. University Microfilms, Ann Arbor, Michigan, 1981.

95. Titular Bishop of Maggiori.

96. Bryce, "Sharing," 407. Of significance here, particularly for its emphasis on the formation of adults,which the *SLF* emphasizes, is the work of Jay P. Dolan, *Catholic Revivalism: The American Experience, 1830–1900* (Notre Dame, Ind.,: University of Notre Dame Press, 1978).

97. See "The Synod on Catechetics," *Luman Vitae*, 33 (1978), 7–53.

98. Papers and critiques of this preparatory symposium were published under the title *Catechesis: Realities and Visions*, edited by Berard L. Marthaler and Marianne Sawicki (Washington, D.C.: United States Catholic Conference, 1977).

99. See Wilfrid H. Paradis, "Excerpts from a Personal Journal," *Living Light*, 15 (1978), 107–108.

100. Recorded by Paradis, "Journal," 108.

101. Cited by Marianne Sawicki in "Purpose, Papers and Proceedings of the Synod," *Living Light*, 15 (1978), 10.

102. See "Second General Assembly," *L'Osservatore Romano* (Eng. ed.), October 13, 1977, 7–8.

103. The complete text may be found in *Living Light*, 15 (1978), 33–36. See also *L'Osservatore Romano* (Eng. ed.), October 6, 1977, 11–12.

104. Ibid., 34.

105. "Archbishop Urges Dialogue of Bishops, Theologians," *Origins*, 7 (October 20, 1977), 284–286.

106. Ibid., 286.

107. Whealon, "Catechesis that Relates to Human Problems," *Origins*, 7 (October 20, 1977), 275.

108. Lucker, "Needed: Adult Catechesis," *Origins*, 7 (October 20, 1977), 276–277. See M. C. Bryce, "Hopes for the Coming Synod," *America*, 137 (October 8, 1977), 215–217.

109. Paradis, "Journal," 109.

110. Manning, "Catechesis for Special Groups," a synopsis in *Living Light*, 15 (1978), 60.

111. Reported by Paradis, "Journal," 119.

112. "Cardinal Wright: The Key to Catechetical Renewal," *Origins*, 7 (October 20, 1977), 283–284.

113. Ibid., 284.

114. "Catechesis in a World of Religious Pluralism," *Origins*, 7 (1977–1978), 288.
115. Ibid.
116. Cited by Paradis, "Journal," 111.
117. Ibid.
118. Ibid., 118.
119. Ibid., 111.
120. Ibid., 114.
121. Ibid. See "The Family's Role in Catechesis", *Origins*, 7 (1977–1978), 334–335.
122. Ibid., 112.
123. Ibid., 118. See "Recognizing the Role of Women in Catechesis," *Origins*, 7 (1977–1978), 332–333.
124. Paradis, "Journal," 118. See also "The Qualities of Catechists," *Origins*, 7 (1977–1978), 319–320.
125. Ibid., 119.
126. "Message to the People of God," *Origins*, 7 (November 10, 1977), 321–328. See also *L'Osservatore Romano* (English edition), 7, November 17, 1977, 6–10.
127. Campion wrote a two-part study of the synod in 1977. See "The Slumbering Synod," *America,* 137 (1977), 328–330; 355–358.
128. See Paradis, "Journal," 117.
129. Ibid., 118.
130. Campion, op. cit., 358.
131. Ibid., 330.
132. See "Voices from the Synod of Bishops," *Our Sunday Visitor*, 66 (October 23, 1977), 1ff.

Chapter 6

1. Note especially the works of J. P. Migne (1800–1875), *Patrologia Graeca* and *Patrologia Latina*.
2. See the works of Matthias Scheeben (1835–1888), especially his *Mysterien des Christentums* (Freiburg: Herder 1865), which was translated and edited by Cyril Vollert in 1951, *Mysteries of Christianity* (St. Louis: B. Herder, 1952).
3. *GCD*, "Foreword." See also *GCD*, #7, 10.
4. Hunthausen, "Catechetics: Into an Era of Action," *Origins*, 11 (1981), 309.
5. "Conversion" has become an area of intense exploration for theologians in recent years. According to Bernard Lonergan, "When conversion is viewed as an ongoing process, at once personal, communal, and historical, it coincides with living religion"; *A Second Collection* (Philadelphia: Westminster Press, 1975), 65–66; 79, 217, 237. See also Lonergan's *Method in Theology* (New York: Herder & Herder, 1972), 188, 298–299; Walter E. Conn, ed., *Conversion: Perspectives on Personal and Social Transformation* (New York: Alba House, 1979); Francis H. Hegel, "'Conversion' and 'Repentance' in Lucan Theology," *The Bible Today*, 37 (1968), 2598.
6. François Coudreau, "Open Air Christian Faith and Children's Education," *Lumen Vitae*, 17 (March 1962), 175–188.
7. Povish, "What a Catechism Should Do," *Liguorian*, 60 (July 1972), 11.
8. See "Faith" and "Faith and Knowledge" in *Sacramentum Mundi*, 2:314. See also pp. 318; 329–334.
9. Marthaler, *Catechetics in Context*, #25, p. 59; see also #21, p. 53.

10. See Ann Marie Mongoven, *The Relationship between Revelation and Catechesis in* Sharing the Light of Faith (Ann Arbor, Mich.: University Microfilms, 1983); William P. Loewe, "Revelation: Dimensions and Issues," *Living Light*, 16 (Summer 1979), 155–167; Karl Rahner, "Revelation: Theological Interpretation," *Sacramentum Mundi* (New York: Herder & Herder, 1970), 5:348–353.

11. *Catechesi Tradendae, AAS*, 71 (1979) 1277–1340, #12.

12. See Peter's Second Letter, the *Didache*, Augustine's *First Catechetical Instruction*, Cyril of Jerusalem's pre- and postbaptismal catecheses.

13. *SLF*, #213, 227, 228.

14. See also *GCD*, #75, 79, 97.

15. See James I. H. McDonald, *Kerygma and Didache: The Articulation and Structure of the Earliest Christian Message* (Cambridge: Cambridge University Press, 1980), 7, 11, 99–100.

16. *ASS*, 37 (1905), 613–625.

17. Cited by Edwin V. O'Hara, "The Parish Confraternity of Christian Doctrine in the United States," *Lumen Vitae*, 6 (1951), 363. O'Hara referred to the citation, "In a letter to the American Hierarchy." This writer is unable to locate the full text of that letter.

18. "Catholic Adult Education: Necessity and Challenge," in *Days of Hope*, 6, 10, 11.

19. "U.S. Bishops Call for Full Use of Women in Catechesis," *Our Sunday Visitor*, 66 (November 6, 1977), 3.

20. "Sisters Work in the Confraternity," *Catechetical Congress of the Confraternity of Christian Doctrine* (Paterson, N.J.: St. Anthony Guild Press, 1937), 86–92.

21. "The Sisterhood in the Spirit of the Council," *Sisters Today*, 39 (1967–1968), 137–145.

22. See Hallinan, "Wanted: Valiant Women," in *Days of Hope*, 138–139.

23. Tobin, *Congress*, 128.

24. Hunthausen, "Catechetics: Into an Era of Action," *Origins*, 11 (October 29, 1981), 309–311. A number of such centers are in operation around the world under episcopal auspices. Belgium, Canada, and Germany, for example, have catechetical centers functioning under bishops' directions.

25. Hunthausen, *ibid.*, 311.

Bibliography

Official Documents

Acta et Documenta Concilio Oecumenico Vaticano II Apparendo. Vatican: Typis Polyglottis Vaticanis, 1960.

Acta Synodi Diocesana Philadelphensis Primae, Philadelphiae. Philadelphia: Eugenius Commiskey, 1832.

Benedict XIV. *Etsi Minime.* In *Magnum Bullarium Romanum*, vol. 16, pp. 64–69. Luxembourg: n.p., 1752.

Clement XIII. *In Dominico Agro.* In *Bullarii Romani Continuatio*, 2 (1761), 134–139.

Concilia Provincialia Baltimori. Baltimore: J. Murphy, 1851.

Conférence Épiscopal Française. *Directoire de la Catéchétique a l'usage des Diocèses de France.* In *Catéchèse*, 4 (January 1964), 1–81.

Conferenza Episcopale Italiana. *Documento di Base: Il Rinnovamento della Catechesi.* Torino-Leumann: Elle Di Ci, 1970.

Constitution of the Roman Catholic Churches of the States of North Carolina, South Carolina and Georgia. Charleston, S.C.: Burges and James, 1840.

Constitutiones Diocesanae in Synodis Philadelphiensibus. Philadelphia: McLaughlin Bros., 1873.

Decreta Conciliorum Baltimorensis. Baltimore: Joannes Murphy, 1853.

Fasciculus Constitutionum Synodalium. Baltimore: Typis Foley Fratrum, 1893.

John Paul II. *Catechesi Tradendae.* AAS, 71 (1979), 1277–1340. Trnaslated: *On Catechesis in Our Time.* Boston: Daughters of St. Paul, 1979.

National Conference of Catholic Bishops. *Basic Teachings.* Washington, D.C.: United States Catholic Conference, 1973.

_____. "Catechesis in a World of Religious Pluralism." *Origins*, 7 (1977–78).

_____. *Sharing the Light of Faith.* Washington, D.C.: United States Catholic Conference, 1979.

_____. *To Teach as Jesus Did.* Washington, D.C.: United States Catholic Conference, 1972.

Pius X. *Acerbo Nimis.* ASS, 37 (1904–1905), 613–625.

_____. *Inter Multa et Gravia Munera.* ASS, 37 (1904–1905).

_____. *Opus a Catechismis.* ASS, 38 (1905–1906), 378–379.

_____. *Quod Hierarchia Catholica. AAS*, 3 (1911), 263-264.

Pius XI. *De Catechetica Disciplina in Sacris Seminariis. AAS*, 18 (1926), 453-455.

_____. *Orbem Catholicum. AAS*, 15 (1923), 327-329.

Sacra Congregatio pro Clericis. *Directorium Catechisticum Generale.* Città del Vaticano: Libreria Editrice Vaticana, 1971. Eng. translation: *General Catechetical Directory.* Washington: United States Catholic Conference, 1971.

Sacred Congregation of the Council. *Provido Sane Consilio. AAS*, 27 (1935), 145-154. English translation: "On the Better Care and Promotion of Catechetical Instruction." *The Ecclesiastical Review*, 93 (1935), 45-57.

Schema Decreti de Catechistica Populi Christiana Institutione. Vatican: Typis Polyglottis Vaticanis, 1962.

Second Vatican Council. *Christus Dominus. AAS*, 58 (1966), 678-690.

Synodus Diocesana Chicagiensis Prima. Chicago: Amberg, 1887.

Synodus Diocesana Chicagiensis Tertia. Chicago: Amberg, 1906.

Synodus Diocesana Cincinnatensis Secunda. N.p.: 1886.

Synodus Diocesana Davenportensis Secunda. Davenport, Iowa: Henry Chosgrove, 1904.

Catechisms

Ambrose of Milan. *The Mysteries.* Fathers of the Church, vol. 44. Tr. by Roy J. Deferrari. Washington, D.C.: Catholic University of America Press, 1963.

Augustine of Hippo. *De Catechizandis Rudibus. The First Catechetical Instruction.* Tr. by Joseph P. Christopher. *Ancient Christian Writers*, vol. 2. Westminster, Md: Newman Press, 1962.

Baraga, Frederic. *Anamie-Misinaigan* (catechism in Ottawa language.) Wawiyatamong: Geo. L. Whitney, 1832.

Bellarmine, Robert. *Opera Omnia.* 12 vols. Ed. by Justinus Fevre. Paris: L. Vives, 1870-1874.

Butler, James. *A Catechism for the Instruction of Children*, 20th ed. Dublin: R. Conolly, 1807.

Canisius, Peter. *Catechismi Latini et Germanici.* 2 vols. Ed. by Fridericus Streicher. Rome: Pontificia Universitas Gregoriana, 1936.

Catechism of the Council of Trent for Parish Priests. Tr. by John A. McHugh and Charles J. Callan. New York: Joseph F. Wagner, 1923.

Catechism on Foundations of the Christian Faith. Approved by John Carroll. New York: L'École Économique, 1811.

Catechism Ordered by the National Synod of Maynooth and Approved by the Cardinal, the Archbishops and the Bishops of Ireland. Dublin: M. H. Gill & Son, 1882.

Catéchisme de la Louisiane. By Order of Joseph Rosati, Bishop of New Orleans. 2nd. ed. New Orleans: Buisson et Boinmaire, 1829.

Catéchisme du diocèse de La Nouvelle-Orléans. New Orleans: J. Schweitzer, 1875.

Chrysostom, John. *Baptismal Instructions.* Tr. and annotated by Paul W. Harkins. Westminster, Md.: Newman Press, 1963.

Compendia della dottrina cristiana. Rome: Tipografia Vaticana, 1905. American edition: *Short Catechism—Abridgement of Christian Doctrine.* Tr. by Sebastian Byrne. New York: Fr. Pustet, 1906.

Connell, Francis J., CSSR, ed. *A Catechism of Christian Doctrine*. Revised edition of the Baltimore Catechism. Paterson, N.J.: St. Anthony Guild Press, 1941.

Conwell, Henry. *A Catechism of Christian Doctrine Wherein the Principles of the Roman Catholic Religion are Briefly Explained, with Morning and Evening Prayers*. Philadelphia: Mifflin and Parry, 1827.

Cyril of Jerusalem. *Catechetical Instructions*. New York: Catholic Publication Society, 1893.

_____. *Lectures (Catecheses) on the Christian Sacraments*. Ed. and tr. by F. L. Cross. London: SPCK, 1966.

David, John Baptist. *Catechism of the Diocess [sic] of Bardstown*. Bardstown, Ky.: N. Wickliff & S. Bailey, 1825.

De Concilio, G. *Catechismo della Dottrina Christiana, di Monsignor G. De Concilio*. New York: Società delle Pubblicazioni Cattoliche, 1886.

DeHarbe, Joseph, SJ. *Katholische Katechismus oder Lehrbegriff*. Regensburg: n.p, 1847. Tr. by John Fauder: *A Full Catechism of the Catholic Religion*. New York: Schwartz, Kirwin and Fauss, 1876.

Demers, Modeste. *Chinook Dictionary, Catechism, Prayers and Hymns*. Revised by F. N. Blanchet and L. N. St. Onge. Montreal: n.p, 1871.

Eccleston, Samuel. *Catechism of the Christian Doctrine*. Baltimore: John Murphy, 1839.

England, John. *Catechism of the Roman Catholic Faith, Published for the Use of His Flock*. Charleston, S.C. Hoff, 1821.

Faerber, W. *Catechism for the Catholic Parochial Schools of the United States*. St. Louis: B. Herder, 1897.

Fleury, Claude. *Catéchisme historique contenant en abrégé l'histoire sainte et la doctrine chrétienne*. Lyon: Jean Marie Bruyset, 1767. Translated: *An Historical Catechism . . . by Monsieur Claude Fleury*. Dublin: Ignatius Kelly, 1753.

Galura, Bernhard. *Freiburger Katechesen*. Freiburg: n.p., 1804.

_____. *Katechisiermethode*. Freiburg: n.p., 1793.

Gatterer, Michael. *Elementarkatechesen*. Ed. by Augustin Gruber. Innsbruck: F. Rauch, 1923.

_____. *Kinderseelosorge*. Innsbruck: F. Rauch, 1923.

General Catechism of the Christian Doctrine. Baltimore: John B. Piet, n.d.

Gregory of Nyssa. *Oratio Catechetica Magna. The Catechetical Oration of Gregory of Nyssa*. Ed. by James H. Srawley. Cambridge: Cambridge University Press, 1903.

Hay, George. *An Abridgement of Christian Doctrine*. Philadelphia: Matthew Carey, 1800.

_____. *The Sincere Christian Instructed in the Faith of Christ*. Edinburgh: n.p, ca. 1780.

Hirscher, Johannes. *Katechismus der Christkatholischen Religion*. Freiburg: Herder, 1852.

Hogan, William, ed. *The Most Rev. Dr. James Butler's Catechism*. Philadelphia, Pa.: n.p., 1821.

Katechismus, Oder Kurzer Inbegriff Christokatholischer Lehre. Approved by Francis P. Kenrick, bishop of Philadelphia, and John B. Purcell, bishop of Cincinnati. N.p., 1865.

Katholischer Katechismus der Bistumer Deutschlands. Freiburg: Herder, 1955. Translation: *A Catholic Catechism.* New York: Herder and Herder, 1957.

Kleiner Katechismus. Baltimore: J. T. Ganzsche, 1834.

Latreille, André. *Le catéchisme impérial de 1806.* Paris: Société d'Édition Les Belles Lettres, 1935.

Lingard, John. *Catechistical Instructions on the Doctrines and Worship of the Catholic Church.* 2nd. ed. New York: P. S. Casserly and Sons, 1841.

McCaffrey, John M. *Catechism of Christian Doctrine for General Use.* New York: P. O'Shea; Baltimore: John Murphy, 1866.

Muller, M. *Catechism of Christian Doctrine for Beginners.* Baltimore: Kreuzer Bros., 1875.

Neumann, John N. *Katholischer Katechismus.* Baltimore: John Murphy, 1853.

Olier, Jean-Jacques. *Catéchisme chrétien pour la vie intérieure et journée chrétienne.* Annotated by François Amat. Paris: Le Rameau, 1954.

Overburg, Bernard. *Christkatholisches Religions-Handbuch.* Münster: Anton B. Uschendorf, 1804.

_____. *Katechismus der Christkatholischen Lehre zum Gebrauche der Kleinen Schüler.* Münster: n.p., 1804.

Reuter, Fridericus Caesarius. *Katechetischer Unterricht für die Christl. Katholische Jugend.* Baltimore: Gedruckt ben Samuel Saur, 1797.

Short Abridgement of the Christian Doctrine; Newly Revised and Augmented. Approved by B. Fenwick, bishop of Boston. Boston: Thomas J. Flynn, 1853.

Short Catechism for the Use of the Catholics in the United States of America. Approved by Ambrose Maréchal. Baltimore: Fielding Lucas, n.d.

Spalding, J. L. *A Catechism of Christian Doctrine Prepared and Enjoined by Order of the Third Plenary Council of Baltimore.* New York: Catholic Publication Co., 1885.

Timon, John. *A Short Abridgment of the Christian Doctrine; Newly Revised and Augmented.* New York: John Kennedy, 1851.

Vaux, Laurence. *A Catechism of Christian Doctrine by Laurence Vaux, D.D.* Manchester: Chetham Society, 1885.

Yorke, Peter C. *Text-Books of Religion.* San Francisco: Text-Book Publishing Co., 1898.

Books

Abbott, Walter, M., ed. *The Documents of Vatican II.* New York: Herder and Herder, 1966.

Augustine of Hippo. *De Catechizandis Rudibus. The First Catechetical Instruction.* Tr. by Joseph P. Christopher. Ancient Christian Writers, vol. 2. Westminster, Md.: Newman Press, 1962.

Baraga, Frederic. *Dictionary of the Ojibway Language.* 2nd ed. Montreal: Beauchemin and Valois, 1880.

_____. *Theoretical and Practical Grammar for the Otchipwe Language.* Detroit: Jabez Fox, 1850.

Bayard, Ralph. *Lone-Star Vanguard.* St. Louis: Vincentian Press, 1945.

Beck, Bernard. *Goldenes Jubiläum des Wirkens der Redemptoristevater an der St. Philomena Kirche in Pittsburg und Umgebung.* Ilchester, Md.: Collegium zu Ilchester, 1889.

Beckman, Peter. *Kansas Monks.* Atchison, Kan.: Abbey-Student Press, 1957.

Berger, John A. *Life of Right Rev. John N. Neumann, D.D.* Tr. by Eugene Grimm, New York: Benziger Bros., 1884.

Billington, Allen. *The Protestant Crusade, 1800–1860. A Study of the Origins of American Nativism.* New York: Rinehart and Co., 1952.

Braun, Walter. *Geschlectliche Erziehung im Katholischen Religionsunterricht.* Trier: Spee-Verlag, 1970.

Broderick, James. *The Life and Work of Blessed Robert Francis Cardinal Bellarmine, S.J.* London: Burns, Oates and Washbourne, 1928.

Bronder, Saul E. *Social Justice and Church Authority. The Public Life of Archbishop Robert E. Lucey.* Philadelphia: Temple University Press, 1982.

Bryce, Mary Charles, OSB. *The Influence of the Catechism of the Third Plenary Council of Baltimore.* Ann Arbor, Mich.: University Microfilms, 1971.

Buetow, Harold A. *Of Singular Benefit.* New York: Macmillan, 1970.

Burns, James A. CSC, Kohlbrenner, Bernard J., Peterson, John B. *A History of Catholic Education in the United States.* New York: Benziger Bros., 1937.

Burns, James A., CSC. *The Principles, Origin and Establishment of the Catholic School System in the United States.* New York: Benziger Bros., 1912.

Burton, Edwin H. *The Life and Times of Bishop Challoner.* London: Longmans Green and Co., 1909.

Carey, Patrick. *An Immigrant Bishop: John England's Adaptation of Irish Catholicism to American Republicanism.* Yonkers, N.Y.: U.S. Catholic Historical Society, 1982.

Carlen, Claudia, IHM. *The Papal Encyclicals, 1903–1939.* Wilmington, N.C.: McGrath, 1981.

Collins, Joseph B. *Teaching Religion: An Introduction to Catechetics.* Milwaukee: Bruce, 1953.

————, ed. *Catechetical Documents of Pope Pius X.* Paterson, N.J.: St. Anthony Guild Press, 1946.

————, ed. *Religious Education through CCD.* Washington, D.C.: Catholic University of America Press, 1961.

Colomb, Joseph. *La doctrine de vie au catéchisme.* Paris: Société de Saint Jean l'Évangéliste, 1955.

Confraternity of Christian Doctrine. *The Confraternity Comes of Age—A Historical Symposium.* Paterson, N.J.: Confraternity Publications, 1956.

————. *Vatican II and Renewal through the CCD—Proceedings, 1966.* Paterson, N.J.: St. Anthony Guild Press, 1967.

Congress of Pastoral Liturgy. *The Assisi Papers—Proceedings of the First International Congress of Pastoral Liturgy.* Collegeville, Minn.: Liturgical Press, 1957.

Conn, Walter E., ed. *Conversion: Perspectives on Personal and Social Transformation.* New York: Alba House, 1979.

Curley, Michael J. *Venerable John Neumann, C.SS.R.* Washington, D.C.: Catholic University of America Press, 1952.

Del Val, Merry. *Memories of Pope Pius X.* Westminster, Md.: Newman Press, 1951.

Deuther, Charles. *Life and Times of the Right Reverend John Timon.* Buffalo: Charles Deuther, 1870.

D'Hotel, Jean Claude. *Les origines du catéchisme moderne.* Paris: Aubier, 1966.

Dolan, Jay P. *Catholic Revivalism: The American Experience, 1830–1900.* Notre Dame, Ind.: University of Notre Dame Press, 1978.

Donnellan, Michael T. *Rationale for a Uniform Catechism.* Ann Arbor, Mich.: University Microfilms, 1972.

Dummler, Ernst L., ed. *Poetae Latine Aevi Carolini,* vol. I. Berlin: Verlag Weidmann, 1881.

Dupanloup, Félix A. *The Ministry of Catechising.* London: Griffith Farran, 1890.

Easterly, F. J. *The Life of Rt. Rev. Joseph Rosati.* American Church History Series, vol. 33. Washington, D.C.: Catholic University of America Press, 1942.

Ellis, John Tracy. *American Catholicism.* 2nd. rev. ed. Chicago: University of Chicago Press, 1972.

————. *The Life of James Cardinal Gibbons.* Milwaukee: Bruce, 1952.

England, John. *The Roman Missal.* New York: William H. Creagh, 1822.

Fecher, V. J., SVD. *A Study of the Movement for German National Parishes in Philadelphia and Baltimore (1787–1802).* Analecta Gregoriana, vol. 77. Rome: Gregorian University Press, 1955.

Fink, Louis Maria, OSB. *Pastoral Instructions.* N.p., 1876.

Finotti, Joseph. *Bibliographia Catholica Americana.* New York: Catholic Publishing House, 1872.

Flannery, Austin. *Vatican Council II — The Conciliar and Post-Conciliar Documents.* Collegeville, Minn.: Liturgical Press, 1975.

Fox, Columba. *The Life of the Right Reverend John Baptist David.* New York: U.S. Catholic Historical Society, 1925.

Fuerst, Anthony N. *The Systematic Teaching of Religion.* 2 vols. New York: Benziger Bros., 1946.

Gaffey, James P. *Francis Clement Kelley and the American Dream.* 2 vols. Bensenville, Ill.: The Heritage Foundation, 1980.

Gannon, Michael. *Rebel Bishop.* Milwaukee: Bruce, 1964.

Gatterer, Michael. *Katechetik.* Innsbruck: Rauch, 1909. (Translated by J. B. Culemans. *Theory and Practice of the Catechism.* New York: F. Pustet, 1914).

————. *Die Erstkommunion der Kinder.* Innsbruck: Rauch, 1911.

————. *Das Religionsbuch der Kirche.* 4 vols. Innsbruck: Rauch, 1928–1930.

Gibbons, James. *The Faith of Our Fathers.* Baltimore: J. Murphy, 1876.

Gilmour, Richard. *Bible History.* New York: Benziger, 1869.

Ginder, Richard. *With Ink and Crozier — A Biography of John Francis Noll.* Huntington, Ind.: Our Sunday Visitor Press, 1953.

Grant, Dorothy Fremont. *John England, American Christopher.* Milwaukee: Bruce, 1949.

Gregorich, Joseph. *Apostle of the Chippewas.* Chicago: Bishop Baraga Association, 1932.

Guilday, Peter. *A History of the Councils of Baltimore*. New York: Macmillan, 1932.

_____. *The Life and Times of John Carroll*. Westminster, Md.: Newman Press, 1954.

_____. *Life and Times of John England*. 2 vols. New York: Arno Press and New York Times, 1969.

_____, ed. *The National Pastorals of the American Hierarchy, 1792-*1919. Washington, D.C.: National Catholic Welfare Conference, 1923.

Hanley, Thomas O'Brien, ed. *The John Carroll Papers*. Notre Dame, Ind.: University of Notre Dame Press, 1976.

Herbermann, Charles G. *The Sulpicians in the United States*. New York: Encyclopedia Press, 1916.

Hofinger, Johannes, and Howell, Clifford, eds. *Teaching All Nations*. New York: Herder and Herder, 1961.

Hofinger, Johannes, and Sheridan, Terrence J., eds. *The Medellin Papers*. Manila: East Asian Pastoral Institute, 1969.

Hynes, Michael J. *History of the Diocese of Cleveland—Origin and Growth (1847-1952)*. Cleveland: Diocese of Cleveland and World Publishing Co., 1952.

Jansen, Raymond J. *Canonical Provisions for Catechetical Instructions*. Washington, D.C.: Catholic University of America Press, 1937.

Jezernik, Maksimilijan. *Frederic Baraga*. New York-Washington: Studia Slovenica, 1968.

Jungmann, Josef A. *Die Frohbotschaft und unsere Glaubensverkundigung*. Regensburg: Verlag Friedrich Pustet, 1936. Translated and edited by William A. Heusman, *The Good News Yesterday and Today*. New York: William H. Sadlier, 1962.

_____. *Katechetik*. Wien: Herder, 1953. English translation: *Handing on the Faith*. New York: Herder and Herder, 1962.

Kelley, Francis Clement. *The Epistles of Father Timothy to His Parishioners*. Chicago: Extension Press, 1924.

_____. *Letters to Jack—Written by a Priest to His Nephew*. Chicago: Extension Press, 1917.

Koob, Albert C. *What's Happening to Catholic Education?* Washington, D.C.: National Catholic Education Association, 1966.

Lanham, Leo. *The Missionary Confraternity of Christian Doctrine in the Diocese of Pittsburgh*. Washington, D.C.: Catholic University of America Press, 1945.

Latreille, André. *L'église catholique et la révolution française*. Paris: Éditions du Cerf, 1970.

LeBuffe, Leon. *Tensions in American Catholicism, 1820-1870; An Intellectual History*. Ann Arbor, Mich.: University Microfilms, 1973.

Ledogar, Robert J. *Katigondo*. London: Geoffrey Chapman, 1965.

Lemarié, Charles. *Les origines religieuses du Kentucky. Mgr. J.-B. David, 1761-1841. Études sur les missionnaires bretons dans le Middle West Américain*, vol. I. Angers: C. Lemarié, 1973.

Liégé, André. *Consider Christian Maturity.* Chicago: Priory Press, 1966.

Lonergan, Bernard. *Method in Theology.* New York: Herder and Herder, 1972.

_____. *A Second Collection.* Philadelphia: Westminster Press, 1975.

Lord, Robert H., Sexton, John E., Harrington, Edward T. *History of the Archdiocese of Boston, 1604-1943.* New York: Sheed & Ward, 1944.

Lucker, Raymond A. *The Aims of Religious Education in the Early Church and in the American Catechetical Movement.* Rome: Catholic Book Agency, 1966.

Lyke, James P. *The Black Perspective on the National Catechetical Directory.* Ann Arbor, Mich.: University Microfilms, 1981.

Lyons, Mary Letitia. *Francis Norbert Blanchet and the Founding of the Oregon Missions.* Washington, D.C.: Catholic University of America Press, 1940.

Marthaler, Berard L. *Catechetics in Context.* Huntington, Ind.: Our Sunday Visitor Press, 1973.

_____. *An Official Commentary on Sharing the Light of Faith.* Washington, D.C.: United States Catholic Conference, 1981.

Marthaler, Berard L., and Sawicki, Marianne, eds. *Catechesis: Realities and Visions.* Washington, D.C.: United States Catholic Conference, 1977.

Marx, Paul. *Virgil Michel and the Liturgical Movement.* Collegeville, Minn.: Liturgical Press, 1957.

McAvoy, Thomas T., ed. *Roman Catholicism and the American Way of Life.* Notre Dame, Ind.: University of Notre Dame Press, 1960.

McCluskey, Neil G., SJ. *Catholic Education in America—A Documentary History.* New York: Columbia University, 1964.

McDonald, James I. H. *Kerygma and Didache—The Articulation and Structure of the Earliest Christian Message.* Cambridge: Cambridge University Press, 1980.

McGucken, William J., SJ. *The Catholic Way in Education.* Chicago: Loyola University Press, 1962.

McLoughlin, Emmet. *American Culture and Catholic Schools.* New York: Lyle Stuart/Polyglot Press, 1960.

Melville, Annabelle M. *Elizabeth Bayley Seton, 1774-1821.* New York: Charles Scribner's Sons, 1960.

_____. *Jean Lefebvre de Cheverus, 1768-1836.* Milwaukee: Bruce, 1958.

_____. *John Carroll of Baltimore.* New York: Charles Scribner's Sons, 1955.

Messmer, Sebastian G., ed. *John England's Works.* Cleveland: Arthur H. Clark, 1908.

Mongoven, Ann Marie, OP. *The Relationship between Revelation and Catechesis in* Sharing the Light of Faith. Ann Arbor, Mich. University Microfilms, 1983.

Moran, Gabriel. *Catechesis of Revelation.* New York: Herder & Herder, 1966.

Murtha, Ronin John, OSB. *The Life of the Most Reverend Ambrose Maréchal, Third Archbishop of Baltimore, 1768-1828.* Washington, D.C.: Catholic University of America Press, 1965.

Nichols, M. Leona. *The Mantle of Elias: The Story of Fathers Blanchet and Demers in Early Oregon.* Portland, Oreg.: Binfords and Mort, 1941.

Nolan, Hugh J. *The Most Reverend Francis Patrick Kenrick, Third Bishop of Philadelphia, 1830-1851.* Washington, D.C.: Catholic University of America Press, 1948.

_____, ed. *The Pastoral Letters of the American Hierarchy, 1792-1970.* Huntington, Ind.: Our Sunday Visitor Press, 1971.

Neumann, John N. *The Autobiography of John Neumann.* Tr. by Alfred C. Rush, CSSR. Boston: Daughters of St. Paul, 1976.

Noonan, D P. *The Passion of Fulton Sheen.* New York: Dodd, Mead & Co., 1972.

O'Hara, Edwin V. *The Church and the Country.* New York: Macmillan, 1927.

O'Hare, Padraic, ed. *Foundations of Religious Education.* New York: Paulist Press, 1978.

Olmstead, Clifford. *History of Religion in the United States.* Englewood Cliffs, N.J.: Prentice-Hall, 1960.

_____. *Religion in America: Past and Present.* Englewood Cliffs, N.J.: Prentice-Hall, 1961.

Prindiville, Raymond J. G. *The Confraternity of Christian Doctrine.* Philadelphia: American Ecclesiastical Review, 1932.

Putz, Louis J., ed. *The Catholic Church, USA.* Chicago: Fides, 1956.

Reynolds, Ignatius A., ed. *The Works of the Right Rev. John England.* 5 vols. Baltimore: John Murphy, 1849.

Rousseau, Olivier. *The Progress of the Liturgy.* Westminster, Md.: Newman Press, 1951.

Ruane, Joseph W. *The Beginnings of the Society of St. Sulpice in the United States (1791-1829).* Washington, D.C.: Catholic University of America Press, 1935.

Scheeben, Matthias. *Mysterien des Christentums.* Freiburg: Herder, 1865. Translated by Cyril Vollert, *Mysteries of Christianity.* St. Louis: B. Herder, 1952.

Shaughnessy, Gerald. *Has the Immigrant Kept the Faith?* New York: Macmillan, 1925.

Shaw, James Gerard. *Edwin Vincent O'Hara, American Prelate.* New York: Farrar, Straus, and Cudahy, 1957.

Shea, John Gilmary. *History of the Catholic Church in the United States.* New York: D. H. McBride, 1890.

_____. *History of the Catholic Missions among the Indian Tribes of the United States, 1529-1854.* New York: P. J. Kenedy, 1883.

_____. *Life and Times of the Most Reverend John Carroll.* 2 vols. New York: John G. Shea, 1888.

_____. *Memorial of the First Centenary of Georgetown College.* Washington, D.C./New York: P. F. Collier, 1891.

Sheen, Fulton J. *Treasure in Clay.* Garden City, N.Y.: Doubleday, 1980.

Shields, Currin V. *Democracy and Catholicism in America.* New York: McGraw-Hill, 1958.

Siderman, E. A. *A Saint in Hyde Park.* Westminster, Md.: Newman Press, 1950.

Sloyan, Gerard S. *Modern Catechetics.* New York: Macmillan, 1962.

_____, ed. *Shaping the Christian Message.* New York: Macmillan, 1958.

Sommervogel, Carlos. *Bibliothèque de la Compagnie de Jésus.* 12 vols. Brussels: O. Schepens; Paris: A. Picard, 1890–1960.

Spalding, Thomas, *Martin John Spalding.* Washington, D.C.: Catholic University of America Press, 1973.

Sweeney, David E. *The Life of John Lancaster Spalding.* New York: Herder and Herder, 1965.

Timon, John. *Missions in Western New York and Church History of the Diocese of Buffalo.* Buffalo: Catholic Sentinel, 1862.

Tobin, William J., ed. *International Catechetical Congress.* Washington, D.C.: United States Catholic Conference, 1971.

Trisco, Robert Frederick. *The Holy See and the Nascent Church in the Middle Western United States, 1826–1850.* Analecta Gregoriana, vol. 125. Rome: Gregorian University Press, 1962.

———, ed. *Catholics in America, 1776–1976.* Washington, D.C.: National Conference of Catholic Bishops, 1976

Trouscher, Francis E., OSA. *The Hogan Schism and Trustee Troubles in St. Mary's Church, Philadelphia, 1820–1829.* Philadelphia: Peter Reilly, 1930.

Van Doren, Carl. *Benjamin Franklin.* New York: Viking Press, 1938.

Verwyst, P. Chrysostom, OFM. *Life and Labors of Rt. Reverend Frederic Baraga.* Milwaukee: M. H. Siltzins, 1900.

Wakin, Edward, and Scheuer, Joseph F. *The De-Romanization of the American Catholic Church.* New York: Macmillan, 1966.

Walace, Patrick. *Irish Catechesis — The Heritage from James Butler II, Archbishop of Cashel, 1774–1791.* Ann Arbor, Mich.: University Microfilms, 1975.

Ward, Leo R., ed. *The American Apostolate.* Westminster, Md.: Newman Press, 1952.

Ward, Maisie. *Unfinished Business.* New York: Sheed and Ward, 1964.

Westerhoff, John H., and Edwards, O. C., eds. *A Faithful Church.* Wilton, Conn.: Morehouse-Barlow, 1981.

White, Andrew. *Relatio Itineris in Marylandiam.* Baltimore: John Murphy, 1874.

Winter, M. Gibson. *Religious Identity.* New York: Macmillan, 1968.

Witte, Raymond Philip. *Twenty-Five Years of Crusading.* Des Moines, Iowa: The National Catholic Rural Life Conference, 1948.

Woodford, F., and Hyma, A. *Gabriel Richard: Frontier Ambassador.* Detroit: Wayne State University Press, 1958.

Yzermans, Vincent A., ed. *Days of Hope and Promise — The Writings and Speeches of Paul J. Hallinan.* Collegeville, Minn.: Liturgical Press, 1973.

Articles

Arnold, Franz. "The Act of Faith, A Personal Commitment." *Lumen Vitae,* 5 (1950), 251–255.

Audinet, Jacques. "Catechesis: The Church Building the Church within a Given Culture." *Our Apostolate,* 24 (1976), 132–156.

Beinert, Wolfgang. "Do Short Formulas Dilute the Faith?" *Theology Digest,* 22 (1974), 257–260.

Bournique, Joseph. "Present Realities in Catechesis as a Basis for Reform in Latin America." In Hofinger and Sheridan, eds., *The Medellin Papers*.

Brady, Matthew F. "The Episcopal Committee on the Confraternity of Christian Doctrine.' In *The Confraternity Comes of Age*.

Browne, Harry H. "The Letters of Bishop McQuaid from the Vatican Council." *Catholic Historical Review*, 41 (1956), 425.

Bryce, Mary Charles, OSB. "An Accomplished Catechist: John Nepomucene Neumann." *Living Light*, 14 (1977), 327-338.

_____. "The Confraternity of Christian Doctrine." In Trisco, ed., *Catholics in America, 1776-1976*, 149-153.

_____. "Evolution of Catechesis from the Catholic Reformation to the Present." In Westerhoff and Edwards, eds., *A Faithful Church*, 204-235.

_____. "Hopes for the Coming Synod." *America*, 137 (October 8, 1977), 215-217.

_____. "The Interrelationship of Liturgy and Catechesis." *American Benedictine Review*, 28 (1977), 1-29.

_____. "Pioneers of Religious Education in the 20th Century." *Religious Education*, 73 (1978 – Special Edition), 51-57.

_____. "Religious Education in the Pastoral Letters and National Meetings of the United States Hierarchy." *Living Light*, 10 (1973), 249-263.

_____. "Sharing the Light of Faith: Catechetical Threshold for the U.S. Church." *Lumen Vitae*, 34 (1979), 406-410.

_____. "Toward an Open Catechetics." *America*, 126 (April 15, 1972), 394-396.

Buswell, Charles A. "Active Participation in the Sacraments." In *North American Liturgical Week, 1963*. Washington, D.C.: The Liturgical Conference, 1964, pp. 24-30.

_____. "The Sisterhood in the Spirit of the Council." *Sisters Today*, 39 (1967-1968), 137-145.

Carmody, Charles J. "The 'Carroll Catechism' – A Primary Component of the American Catechetical Tradition." *Notre Dame Journal of Education*, 7 (Spring 1976), 76-95.

Cartmell, J. "Richard Challoner." *Clergy Review*, 44 (1959), 577-587.

Colomb, Joseph. "The Catechetical Method of Saint Sulpice." In Sloyan, ed., *Shaping the Christian Message*, 91-111.

_____. "Quelques réflexions sur la méthode catéchistique." in idem, *La doctrine de vie au catéchisme, vol. 1*.

Coudreau, François. "Open-Air Christian Faith and Children's Education." *Lumen Vitae*, 17 (1962), 175-188.

Crichton, J. D. "Challoner's Catechism", *The Clergy Review*, 63 (1978) 140-146.

_____. "Bishop Challoner and Teaching the Faith." *Clergy Review*, 65 (1980), 6-15.

_____. "Religious Education in England in the Penal Days (1559-1778)." In Sloyan, ed., *Shaping the Christian Message*.

_____. "Richard Challoner: Catechist and Spiritual Writer." *Living Light*, 18 (Summer 1981), 103-111.

Deane, Alberto. "Conferencia sobre la mente de la iglesia sobre la CDC." In *Proceedings of the Confraternity of Christian Doctrine Congress, 1961*, 333-340.

De Bretagne, Guy. "History of the Textbook." *Lumen Vitae*, 5 (1950), 470–476.

Delcuve, George. "International Session: Mission and Liturgy." *Lumen Vitae*, 15 (1960), 153–159.

————. "Mission and Catechesis." *Lumen Vitae*, 15 (1960), 723–737.

————. "Pan-African Week of Catechetical Studies." *Lumen Vitae*, 20 (1965), 127–130.

————. "Report of the International Catechetic Congress . . . Rome." *Lumen Vitae*, 5 (1950), 639–644.

————. "What the Catechisms Say of the Holy Spirit." *Lumen Vitae*, 17 (1962), 240–255.

Donohue, Francis J. "Textbooks for Catholic Schools Prior to 1840." *The Catho-School Journal*, 40 (1940), 64–68.

Donovan, Joseph P. "Solving the Rural Problem in Missouri." *Ecclesiastical Review*, 71 (1924), 590–598.

Dooley, Catherine. "Catechesis in Our Time." *Louvain Studies*, 7 (1979), 195–204.

Duckworth, R. "Catechetics: The New Directory." *Tablet*, 225 (July 3, 1971), 213–219.

Elizondo, Virgil, and Oddie, Alan. "San Antonio International Study Week of Mass Media and Catechetics: A Report." *Living Light*, 6 (Winter 1969), 67–74.

Erdozain, Luis. "The Evolution of Catechetics." *Lumen Vitae*, 25 (1970) 7–31.

Fossion, André, SJ. "La catéchèse scolaire d'hier à demain." *Nouvelle Revue Théologique*, 112 (1980), 3–21.

Frye, Mariella. "The Family's Role in Catechesis." *Origins*, 7 (1977–1978), 334–335.

————. "Recognizing the Role of Women in Catechesis." *Origins*, 7 (1977–1978), 332–333.

Gerard-Libois, Jules. "The International Summer Session at Antwerp: Catechesis for Our Time." *Lumen Vitae*, 2 (1956), 498–500.

Golden, Dorothy F. "'Catholic Revivals' in the Bible Belt." *Journal of Religious Instruction*, 9 (April 1939), 660–663.

Grasso, D. "The Good News and the Renewal of Theology." In Jungmann, *The Good News Yesterday and Today*, 201–210.

————. "Il Kerygma e la Predicazione." *Gregorianum*, 41 (1960).

Griffin, Martin I. J. "Life of Bishop Conwell of Philadelphia." *American Catholic Historical Society Records*, 24 (1913), 16–42, 162–178, 217–250, 348–361; 25 (1914), 52–67, 146–178, 217–248, 296–341.

Gulnerich, Bertrand J. "Catechetical Congresses." In *The Confraternity Comes of Age*, 221–234.

Hallinan, Paul J. "The American Bishops at the Vatican Councils." *Catholic Historical Review*, 51 (1965), 381.

————. "Catechetical Ladder to the Liturgical Summit." In *Vatican II and Renewal through the CCD—Proceedings, 1966*.

————. "Catholic Adult Education: Necessity and Challenge." In Yzermans, ed., *Days of Hope and Promise*.

Heath, Mark. "To Teach as Jesus Did: A Critique." *Living Light*, 10 (1973), 286–287.

Hofinger, Johannes. "J. A. Jungmann (1889–1975): In Memoriam." *Living Light*, 13 (1976), 350–359.

_____. "The Place of the Good News in Modern Catechetics." In Jungmann, *The Good News Yesterday and Today*.

Houtart, François. "Reflections on the New Thinking in Latin America." In Hofinger and Sheridan, eds., *The Medellin Papers*.

Hunthausen, Raymond G. "Catechetics: Into an Era of Action." *Origins*, 11 (1981), 309.

Jadot, Jean. "Dimensions of Catechesis." *Origins*, 9 (1979), 611.

Jungmann, Josef A. "The New German Catechism. *Lumen Vitae*, 10 (1956), 573–586.

_____. "Theology and Kerygmatic Teaching." *Lumen Vitae*, 5 (1950), 258–259.

Kelley, Francis C. "Only an Incident." *Commonweal*, 31 (November 3, 1939), 31–32.

Korioth, Maye. "The Apostolate of Good Will." In *The Confraternity Comes of Age*.

Leven, Stephen A. "Curb Service in Christian Doctrine." *Extension*, 37 (August 1942), 11–12.

_____. "Street Preaching." *Proceedings, Confraternity Congress, 1938*, 375–382.

Living Light. "Special Issue: The General Catechetical Directory." *Living Light*, 9 (1971), 4–157.

Loewe, William P. "Revelation: Dimensions and Issues." *Living Light*, 16 (Summer 1979), 155–167.

Lucey, Robert E. "Catechetical Living." Address given Friday, July 14, 1967. San Antonio: Chancery Archives, 1967.

Lucker, Raymond A. "Catechesis and the Media of Social Communication." In Tobin, ed., *International Catechetical Congress*.

_____. "Needed: Adult Catechesis." *Origins*, 7 (October 20, 1977), 276–277.

MacEachen, Roderick. "The Catechism: Its Origin and Development." *The Catholic University Bulletin*, 27 (1921), 3–21.

MacMaster, Richard K. "Benedict Fenwick, Bishop of Boston, American Apprenticeship, 1782–1817." *Historical Records and Studies*, 47 (1959), 78–139.

Mallon, V. "The General Catechetical Directory." *The Priest*, 28 (March 1972), 11–19.

Manning, Timothy. "Catechesis for Special Groups." *Living Light*, 15 (1978), 58–62.

Marks, Miriam. "Teaching Christ in America." In L. R. Ward, ed., *The American Apostolate*.

Marthaler, Berard L., OFM Conv. "The Origin, Context and Purpose of the Directory." *Living Light*, 9 (1972).

_____. "The Renewal of Catechesis in Italy." *Religious Education*, 66 (1971), 357–363.

_____. "Socialization as a Model for Catechetics." In O'Hare, ed., *Foundations of Religious Education*, 64–92.

McAvoy, Thomas T. "The Formation of the Catholic Minority in the United States, 1820–1860." *Review of Politics*, 10 (1948), 13–34.

McDonald, Charles C. "The Background and Development of 'The Basic Teachings' Document." *Living Light*, 10 (1973), 263–267.

McManus, William E. "To Teach as Jesus Did: A Chronicle." *Living Light*, 10 (1973), 278–283.

McSweeney, Edward. "Ecclesiastical Charleston." *American Ecclesiastical Review*, 32 (1905).

Moesslein, Mark. "Origin of the Baltimore Catechism." *Ecclesiastical Review*, 93 (1935).

Nebreda, Alfonso. "East Asian Study Week on Mission Catechetics." *Lumen Vitae*, 17 (1962), 717–730.

_____. "Mass Media and Catechetics." *America*, 121 (1969), 28–30.

_____. "Special Commission on International Cooperation." In Hofinger and Sheridan, eds., *The Medellin Papers*.

O'Brien, Raymond J. "History of Our English Catechism." *Ecclesiastical Review*, 91 (1934), 591–596.

O'Hara, Edwin V. "The Parish Confraternity of Christian Doctrine in the United States." *Lumen Vitae*, 6 (1951), 190–194.

_____. "The Rural Problem and Catholic Education." *Catholic Educational Association Bulletin*, 17 (1920), 233–241.

Onahan, W. J. "Catholic Colonization of the West." *American Catholic Quarterly Review*, 6 (1881), 68–75.

O'Neill, Una. "Perspectives on the Hierarchy of Truths." *Living Light*, 14 (1977), 377–391.

O'Rourke, Edward W. "The Catholic Church in the Rural Midwest." In Putz, ed., *The Catholic Church, USA*, 202–210.

Paradis, Wilfrid H. "Excerpts from a Personal Journal." *Living Light*, 15 (1978), 107–115.

Pickering, Bernard. ""Bishop Challoner and Teaching the Faith," *The Clergy Review*, 65 (1980), 6–15.

Povish, Kenneth. "What a Catechism Should Do." *Liguorian*, 60 (July 1972), 128–132.

"Report on International Catechetical Congress." *Living Light*, 8 (1971), 80–99.

"Rome International Congress on Catechetics." *Lumen Vitae*, 27 (1972), 103–115.

Sawicki, Marianne. "Purpose, Papers and Proceedings of the Synod." *Living Light*, 15 (1978), 8–12.

Schrems, K. "Zweiter Katechetischer Kongress." *Katechetische Blätter*, 29 (new series, 1928), 369–384.

Sharp, John K. "How the Baltimore Catechism Originated." *Ecclesiastical Review*, 81 (1929), 585–586.

Sloyan, Gerard S. "The International Study Week on Mission Catechetics." *Worship*, 35 (1960–1961), 48–57.

Stone, Theodore. "The Bangkok Study Week." *Worship*, 37 (1962), 184–190.

Sullivan, Thomas F. "The General Catechetical Directory: Some Implications for Teachers." *Momentum*, 3 (February 1972), 45–52.

Theodore of Mopsuestia. "Commentary of Theodore of Mopsuestia on the Lord's Prayer and on the Sacraments of Baptism and Eucharist." *Woodbrooke Studies*, 6 (1933).

Whealon, John F. "Catechesis that Relates to Human Problems." *Origins*, 7 (October 20, 1977), 275–278.

Wright, John Cardinal. "The Key to Catechetical Renewal." *Origins*, 7 (October 20, 1977), 283–284.

_____. "The New Catechetical Directory and Initiation to the Sacraments of Penance and Eucharist." *Homiletic and Pastoral Review*, 72 (December 1971), 7–24.

Subject Index

Index of Names